The Social Psychology of Interpersonal Discrimination

Edited by
BERNICE LOTT
University of Rhode Island

DIANE MALUSO
University of Hawaii at Manoa

Foreword by STUART OSKAMP

The Guilford Press
New York London

©1995 The Guilford Press
A Division of Guilford Publications
72 Spring Street, New York, NY 10012

Printed in the United States of America

This book is printed on acid-free paper.

Last digit is print number: 9 8 7 6 5 4 3 2 1

Library of Congress Cataloging-in-Publication-Data

The social psychology of interpersonal discrimination
  / edited by Bernice Lott, Diane Maluso
     p.   cm.
   Included bibliographical references and index.
   ISBN 1-57230-021-3
   1. Prejudices. 2. Discrimination.   3. Racism.
  4. Stereotype (Psychology) I. Lott, Bernice
  II. Maluso, Diane.
  BF575.P9S64   1995
  303.3'85—dc20   95-2851
                                        CIP

*This book is dedicated to
Samone and Rachel*

*We hope their adult world will be truly one in
which human diversity is a source of enrichment
and pleasure.*

Contributors

Roxanna Alcaraz earned her MA in experimental psychology from California State University–San Bernardino in 1991. She is currently project coordinator and research associate on grants from the University of California Tobacco-Related Disease Research Program and the Tobacco Control Section of the California Department of Health Services to Hope Landrine and Elizabeth A. Klonoff.

Heather E. Bullock is an assistant professor at Nebraska Wesleyan University. She earned a PhD from the experimental/social psychology program at the University of Rhode Island where she was also assistant to the director of the Women's Studies Program. She received her BA in psychology at Allegheny College in 1988. She is pursuing research on the social psychology of poverty and classism.

Laura L. Carstensen is an associate professor at Stanford University in the Department of Psychology. She obtained her BS at the University of Rochester in 1978, and her PhD in clinical psychology from West Virginia University in 1983. She is interested in lifespan development, particularly in socioemotional development in old age.

J. L. Fernald is a doctoral student in the experimental/ social psychology program at the University of Rhode Island. Fernald received a BA in psychology at Roger Williams College in 1984, an MA from the University of Rhode Island in 1990, has taught courses in psychology and women's studies at the University of Rhode Island and Rhode Island College, and is currently investigating sexist and heterosexist discrimination.

Elizabeth A. Klonoff earned her PhD in clinical psychology from the University of Oregon in 1977, and is currently professor of psychology at California State University–San Bernardino and executive director of the university's Behavioral Health Institute. She is principal investigator on a grant from the Tobacco Control Section of the California Department of Health Services and coinvestigator on a grant from the University of California Tobacco-Related Disease Research Program. She is coauthor (with Hope Landrine) of *African-American Acculturation: Deconstructing Race and Reviving Culture* (Sage Publications, 1995) and *Preventing Psychiatric Misdiagnosis in Women* (Sage Publications, 1995).

Hope Landrine received her PhD in clinical psychology from the Universtiy of Rhode Island in 1983, and postdoctoral training in social psychology at Stanford University and in preventive medicine from the University of Southern California Medical School. She is a research scientist at the Public Health Foundation in California, where she is the principal investigator on a grant from the Univeristy of California Tobacco-Related Disease Program. She is the editor of *Bringing Cultural Diversity to Feminist Psychology: Theory, Research, and Practice* (American Psychological Association, 1995) and is coauthor (with Elizabeth A. Klonoff) of *African-American Acculturation: Deconstructing Race and Reviving Culture* (Sage Publications, 1995) and *Preventing Psychiatric Misdiagnosis in Women* (Sage Publications, 1995).

Bernice Lott received her PhD from the University of California at Los Angeles. She is a professor of psychology and women's studies at the University of Rhode Island where she teaches social psychology. She has published in the areas of interpersonal attraction, sexist discrimination, sexual harassment, and the social construction of gender. In 1988 she received her university's Award for Scholarly Excellence, and she served as president of the American Psychological Association's Division on the Psychology of Women in 1990–1991. Her book *Women's Lives: Themes and Variations in Women's Lives*, originally published in 1984, is now in its second edition (Brooks/Cole, 1994), and she is coeditor (with Mary Ellen Reilly) of *Combatting Sexual Harassment in Higher Education* (NCA, 1995).

Diane Maluso, an assistant professor of psychology and women's studies at the University of Hawaii at Manoa, earned her PhD in experimental/social psychology from the University of Rhode Island. Her research interests include the intersection of racism and sexism, unobtrusive measures of interpersonal distancing, and social behaviors in virtual environments.

Stuart Oskamp received his doctorate from Stanford University and is a professor of psychology at Claremont Graduate School. He has served as president of the American Psychological Association's Division of Population and Environmental Psychology and of the Society for the Psychological Study of Social Issues. His books include *Attitudes and Opinions* and *Applied Social Psychology*, as well as coedited volumes of *The Claremont Symposium on Applied Social Psychology*. His research interests focus on attitudes and attitude change, environmentally responsible behavior, and social issues and public policy.

Monisha Pasupathi is a doctoral student in the Department of Psychology at Stanford University. She received a BA in psychology and English from Case Western Reserve University in 1991. She is interested in lifespan approaches to motivation, particularly in the domain of emotion regulation.

Judyth Scott received her BA in sociology from California State University– San Bernardino in 1993. She is currently project associate and research assistant on grants directed by Elizabeth A. Klonoff and Hope Landrine for the University of California Tobacco-Related Disease Research Program.

Jeanne L. Tsai is a doctoral student in clinical psychology at the University of California at Berkeley. She received her BA in psychology at Stanford University and her MA at the University of California at Berkeley. Her research focuses on the influences of culture/ethnicity and old age on the physiological, subjective, and behavioral aspects of emotional responding.

Phyllis Wilkins earned an MS in counseling psychology from California State University–San Bernardino in 1994, and was a research assistant on grants to Hope Landrine and Elizabeth A. Klonoff for the University of California Tobacco-Related Disease Research Program. She is currently a consumer services coordinator at the Inland Regional Center in Colton, CA.

Foreword

Prejudice against outgroup members is one of the oldest of human characteristics—and one of the earliest topics of social-psychological research. Over the years, many social scientists have studied it, and much has been learned. The names of LaPiere, Allport, Adorno et al., the Clarks, and Cook, as well as many later contributors, remind us of how much effort social scientists have put into understanding and eradicating intergroup antagonism. Yet still prejudice and discrimination continue as common phenomena in our world.

In some ways and some places during this century, humanity seems to have made great strides in lessening prejudice, reducing discrimination, and increasing egalitarianism. In the United States, opportunities for women, minorities, and disabled individuals have expanded markedly. In many countries, laws and customs have increasingly prescribed norms of fair and equal treatment of all individuals. Yet despite these advances, when we find ourselves faced with ethnic genocide in Russia, Rwanda, or Bosnia, or intergroup conflict in Los Angeles, Miami, or Montreal, we realize how much more we need to learn in order to eliminate interpersonal aversion and inequity.

This book will make an important contribution to that goal. In several ways, it broadens the horizons of past study of prejudice and discrimination. First, it focuses most heavily on *behavior*—on people's discriminatory actions, not just on their aversive feelings or individious beliefs about other groups. The behaviors involved may range from passive avoidance through active exclusion, derogatory stories and comments, unfair treatment and evaluation, to physical attacks and even murder. This focus on observing and measuring behavioral responses adds a vital component to our science's recent heavy concentration on cognitive aspects such as attitudes, stereotypes, and beliefs.

Second, this volume expands the dimensions of intergroup discrimination studied, going well beyond the typical bounds of most past research. In addition to chapters on the frequently investigated topics of racism and sexism, it also focuses attention on the much less studied dimensions of heterosexism, classism, and ageism as bases of discrimination. Moreover, the book examines similar themes and patterns that cut across these areas, revealing commonalities in the ways that we tend to treat outgroup members—not just in extreme, destructive actions, but also in everyday, unnoticed patterns of distancing and avoidance. It is both provocative and distressing to realize that similar patterns of exclusion and avoidance can be seen in typical treatment of women, of ethnic minorities, of poor people, of gays and lesbians, and of the elderly.

A third special strength of this volume is its focus on the ways in which discrimination occurs in one-to-one interpersonal relationships (or nonrelationships). While recognizing the many institutionalized, structural patterns of exclusion and inequity in our society, it concentrates mainly on how these structural patterns combine with private feelings and beliefs to produce discriminatory actions in individual interpersonal contacts with people from low-status categories. Interpersonal discrimination and institutional discriminiation are inevitably interrelated and may act in ways that strengthen each other, but it is valuable to have this analysis that distinguishes between the two and focuses primarily on the interpersonal level.

Fourth, and particularly important, the authors in this volume go beyond scientific analysis to discuss social implications of discriminatory patterns and to recommend ameliorative actions and policies that can contribute to a more equitable and humane society. For instance, they analyze the merits of interventions designed to reduce discriminatory behaviors, and they recommend both individual actions and public policies directed at egalitarian treatment of all individuals.

For all these reasons I heartily welcome this book, and I expect that many psychologists, like myself, will find it an essential resource in their teaching and research.

STUART OSKAMP
Claremont Graduate School

Acknowledgments

We would like to say thank you first of all to Barbara Watkins, our editor at Guilford, who encouraged us to proceed with this project, provided us with incisive and constructive criticism, asked just the right questions, and made marvelous suggestions. Whatever is still lacking in this book must be attributed to us.

The authors who contributed chapters to this volume also merit recognition for their cooperation with deadlines and editorial suggestions, as well as for their willingness to be bold and to point to new directions for theory and research.

Al Lott and Jill Briggs stood by us through late hours and many months of distracted attention while this book took shape and came to fruition. Jodi Creditor did the painstaking production work at The Guilford Press that made the final publication possible and deserves heartfelt thanks. And enabling us to work together face to face, without needing to bridge distances by FAX or telephone, was the invitation to Bernice by the University of Hawaii's Department of Psychology and its chair, Karl Minke, to be a visiting professor during the first summer session of 1994. We hope the book reflects the "aloha" spirit that is so irresistible in Hawaii, as well as the deep appreciation for multiculturalism that is the essence of the Hawaiian experience.

BERNICE LOTT
DIANE MALUSO

Contents

1

Introduction
Framing the Questions

BERNICE LOTT
DIANE MALUSO

Our hope is that this book will be informative and also disruptive, in the most positive sense of that word. We agree with Fine (1992) "that researchers always take positions within politics, if typically unacknowledged and conservative, and that the only way to do activist research is to be positioned with questions but not answers; as mobile and multiple, . . . within spaces of rich surprise" (p. 230). The various "isms" that constitute the subject matter of this book are rarely considered together within contemporary social psychology, and some, like interpersonal classism, are almost invisible concerns. In our journals, one is far more likely to find research on gender differences than research on sexism, and studies of racism have become more and more narrowly focused on stereotypes. Yet, as U.S. Bureau of Labor Statistics disclose, whereas 47% of the current work force is comprised of nonimmigrant White[1] males, by the year 2000 85% of new entrants to the work force will be women, men of color, and new immigrants (see Betters-Reed & Moore, 1992).

In this book we refocus attention on the behavior directed to people in socially devalued categories—in other words, on the stuff that makes up so much of the daily experiences of older people, women, people of color, poor people, and lesbians and gay men. Such "stuff" is found in examining the ways in which persons in low-status categories are treated in a variety of situations. For example, in writing about women in management, Betters-Reed and Moore (1992) note that women of color occupy a disproportionate share of "dead-end" jobs, and that they "are more frequently placed in positions without appropriate budgets, without upward mobility, without line authority, and without sufficient training" (p. 85). Moreover, reports from the National Institute against Prejudice (see Root, 1993) indicate that on college campuses across the United States, incidents of ethnic violence are on the rise. Finally, observations of personal interactions in "daily life" inform us that privilege deriving from one social category may be associated with the learning of distancing responses toward the less privileged even by those who occupy a low-status position in another social category. Thus White women may avoid or exclude women of color on the job, and heterosexual Black women may distance themselves from Black lesbians. A recent example of this phenomenon can be drawn from a review by Susan Cheever (in the July 3, 1994, issue of the *New York Times Book Review*) of Norma McCorvey's autobiography, *I Am Roe: My Life, Roe v. Wade, and Freedom of Choice*, and reactions to that review. Susan Cheever, an educated, middle-class European-American woman, wrote that Norma McCorvey was not the symbol that feminists would have chosen for their fight for reproductive choice. Among those who responded with concern and dismay to this opinion was Susan Weisser (1994), who asked, "What is it about Ms. McCorvey that makes her unfit to be a feminist heroine in the reviewer's eyes? Is it her lesbianism, her unwanted pregnancies, her job as a cleaning woman or her unhappy childhood?" (p. 31).

"Cross-ism" research, we suggest, will reveal that interpersonal discrimination in all areas is defined by behaviors that limit and control the lives of those toward whom it is directed. The various social discriminations supported by our institutions and acquired by individuals as interpersonal behavior cannot be arranged hierarchically, and their elimination requires an understanding of their commonalities—how they function both independently and in combination. That this is a matter of great social urgency is a belief we share with others. As noted by Snyder and Milne (1994), "Prejudice and discrimination are not restricted to matters of race . . . [and their costs]—the psychological pain, the physical suffering, the economic costs, the lost opportunities . . . —are beyond calculation" (p. 34).

The chapters in this book focus on theory and empirical research relevant to interpersonal discrimination. Of central concern are the responses made by individuals in the actual or symbolic presence of other individuals that demean, avoid, and/or exclude them under conditions in which this behavior is primarily a response to a social category rather than to personal characteristics. We use the term "discrimination," whether active or passive, to refer to the distancing from and avoidance and exclusion of persons in low-status social categories by persons with greater power. This is in the tradition of its use within social psychology. Bourhis (1994), for example, has demonstrated empirically that "without power, social categorization is not sufficient to trigger discriminatory behavior" (p. 200). The consequences of discrimination are well known to include interference with access to resources, and restriction of movement and opportunities—the defining characterisics of low power.

In presenting the discussions of discrimination that comprise this book, we assume commonalities among racism, classism, heterosexism, ageism, and sexism that stem from the association of all with inequities in social status and power. From this sociocultural standpoint, these various forms of negative bias (in attitudes, beliefs, and overt actions) are situated in relationships embedded in institutions; our emphasis, however, is on individual behavior exhibited in the context of interpersonal interaction. Whereas the literature on institutional discrimination is extensive, particularly with respect to race/ethnicity and gender, psychologists have paid far less attention to the documentation, description, explanation, and prediction of discrimination in face-to-face interpersonal situations. Bourhis (1994) refers to the latter as the "interindividual" level of analysis (in contrast to the more typical intergroup analysis).

Institutional discrimination refers to the normative practice of exclusion within social institutions (e.g., in religion, employment, and politics). Such discrimination, which exists in various forms as an everyday phenomenon in our society, provides a cultural context for interpersonal face-to-face discriminatory behavior. Although inevitably interrelated, the phenomena of institutional and interpersonal discrimination are nevertheless theoretically and empirically distinguishable from each other and require separate study. For example, from an analysis of the oral histories of 52 elderly African-American women who had made significant contributions to the progress of their communities, Lykes (1983) concluded that "evidence from this study . . . suggests the importance of a distinction between personal and institutional discrimination" (p. 98). The women's remembered histories included multiple examples of both—discrimination resulting from institutional barriers to resources (jobs, promotions, etc.), as well as from the slights and exclusions imposed by persons with whom they were in direct interpersonal contact. Exclusion of persons from full participation in social institutions, communities, families, and groups is not just the result of impersonal forces, but also of interpersonal avoidance and distancing in face-to-face interactions. We certainly agree with theorists like Smith (1987), who argues, for example, that "the exclusion of women . . . is in this day largely organized by the ordinary processes of socialization, education, work, and communication" (p. 26). We must remember, however, that the "everyday world" to which Smith refers includes the actions of people who exclude, deride, and avoid others in interpersonal situations. In each of the chapters in this book, the authors move beyond what is already known about institutional discrimination to focus on, and critique, the current state of research on interpersonal discrimination in actual or simulated face-to-face situations. The reader will find separate discussions of interpersonal discrimination based on gender, race/ethnicity, sexual orientation, social class, and age, followed by a chapter concerned with the intersections among these social/constructed categories. The contributors to this volume bring their own theoretical perspectives and organization to bear on the partcular domains they are considering and the issues they are addressing, but a unifying theme is a focus on behavior. Attention is directed by all contributors to this book to the actions and reactions of individuals in real or simulated situations in the presence of persons from less valued social categories.

Allport's (1954) description of discrimination as a continuum of behaviors is still useful and relevant. This continuum, he proposed, ranges from anti-locution to extermination and includes avoidance, active exclusion, and physical attack. The assumption of such a continuum provides a link among such widely disparate behaviors as sexual harassment; more severe sentencing of African-American than of European-American criminal offenders; middle-class persons' distancing themselves from the poor by abandoning public parks and public schools; lesbian baiting and gay bashing; and medical practitioners' frequent failure to pay serious attention to older patients. Not all of these examples of interpersonal discrimination are discussed in this book, but our focus is on what peoople do in the presence of other people socially defined as members of low-status groups. The relationships between what people do (behavior) and their relevant attitudes and beliefs are also explored, with some contributors devoting considerable attention to this literature.

The reader will note the wide variety of measures that have been used to assess interpersonal discrimination, varying with the area of study, type of behavior, theoretical framework, and/or investigator preference. Violent responses, for example, are sometimes directly operationalized as acts of physical assault and sometimes indirectly measured as willingness to subject another person to some noxious stimulus (e.g., electric shock). Avoidance, a less extreme form of interpersonal discrimination, has been operationalized by direct observations of, for example, clerks responsiveness to customers differing in ethnicity or gender, or in the seating distance chosen and time spent by White interviewers of Black confederates (Word, Zanna, & Cooper, 1974). It has also been operationalized by simulated measures, beginning with Bogardus's (1925) Social Distance Scale and illustrated by the Photo Choice Task (Lott, Lott, & Fernald, 1990), developed as a measure of sexist discrimination. Unobtrusive and nonreactive measures have been suggested by investigators of racism for more than two decades, but are still largely absent from both that literature and the literature on sexism. Such measures would add much to our understanding of interpersonal discrimination.

This book is distinguishable from other books in social psychology by its clear and direct focus on behavior. The question addressed by the contributors is what people *do* in the presence of persons from low-status/low-power social categories, as distinct from what they say they feel or believe. This emphasis challenges the trend that has prevailed in social psychology for about two decades—a preoccupation with cognition. The relative absence of attention to behavior among contemporary social psychologists in the United States is apparent from an examination of the contents of our journals. A review of articles published early in 1994 in seven journals (*Journal of Applied Social Psychology* [three issues], *Journal of Experimental Psychology* [two issues], *Journal of Personality and Social Psychology* [two issues], *Journal of Social Psychology* [two issues], *Personality and Social Psychology Bulletin* [one issue], *Psychology of Women Quarterly* [two issues], and *Sex Roles* [one issue]) indicated that of the 114 articles in these issues, only 30 (26%) presented findings on overt behaviors—actions that were either directly observed or verbally reported in actual or simulated situations. This book is also distinguishable from others in its emphasis on individual acts of discrimination rather than on institutional discrimination, and in its broad coverage of such acts. We have brought together chapters that examine the interpersonal discrimination experienced by many in our society as a function of their gender, race/ethnicity, sexual orientation, social class, age, and membership in multiple low-status social categories.

In general, the reader can expect to find in each chapter a critical review of the relevant published literature, sometimes including empirical findings from the author's or authors' own program of research, and qualitative material from a variety of sources. In reviews of relationships between interpersonal discrimination and antecedent or correlated factors, attention is paid to situational sources of variation and to other mediators. Multiple sources of information in the contexts of both discovery and verification are acknowledged and respected, and no verifiable source of information or method of inquiry or study is considered more privileged or closer to the "truth" than others.

We have omitted consideration of interpersonal discrimination based on mental or physical handicaps or on such physical attributes as weight. Such omissions do not reflect a belief that these categories do not frequently function as cues for avoidance, or the absence of a body of relevant literature. The decisions as to what to include in this volume were based on considerations of space and time, as well as on assumpions about what areas have been the most studied. Important work has been done on discriminatory behavior directed toward handicapped persons, as illustrated by the classic study of Snyder, Kleck, Strenta, and Mentzer (1979) on avoidance of people in wheelchairs by persons making a choice between two movies. Social psychologists have more recently begun to pay specific attention to prejudice and stereotypes relevant to fat people and to issues of discrimination. Crandall (1994) has concluded that "in contrast to racism and sexism, the overt expression of antipathy toward fat people is currently affected only modestly by normative pressures and concerns about social desirability" (p. 892); the result is considerable untempered and overt interpersonal discrimination against people considered fat.

In Chapter 2, by Lott, sexism is conceptualized in terms of three independent but related components: prejudice (defined as negative attitudes toward women), stereotypes (defined as well-learned, widely shared beliefs about women), and discrimination (overt behaviors that achieve separation from women through exclusion, avoidance, or distancing). The problematic relationship among attitudes, beliefs, and behavior is discussed. The central focus of this chapter is on women's experiences of interpersonal discrimination by men who are said to acquire this behavior as part of their learning to "do gender" (i.e., to act like men). Discriminatory behavior toward women by men is predicted in relatively neutral situations in which men do not expect sexual pleasure, nurturance, or some situation-related reward. Lott presents empirical support for this proposition from her ongoing program of research.

In Chapter 3, on interpersonal racism, Maluso discusses recent theories and pays particular attention to the relationships that have been empirically examined among racist/ethnic prejudice, stereotyping, and discrimination. She notes the directional nature of discrimination, and suggests that "it is theoretically and methodologically unsound to equate the attitudes, beliefs, and behaviors *toward* the oppressed with those *of* the oppressed." Maluso describes her own work on the development of unobtrusive measures of discrimination, and presents the results of an investigation of the relative merits of different interventions designed to reduce racist behaviors.

Fernald's chapter on heterosexism (Chapter 4) discusses the history of definitions and research in this area, and devotes considerable attention to reviewing the literature on anti-lesbian and anti-gay attitudes and beliefs, their correlates, and relationships with overt behavior. Noting that interpersonal discrimination against lesbians and gay men has taken many forms ranging "from jokes and put-downs to murder," Fernald discusses what we know about the circumstances in which such discrimination occurs, devoting most attention to aggressive behavior. The evidence for differential patterns of victimization of gay men and lesbians is also discussed. Fernald concludes that attitudes and beliefs are not good predictors of the behavior of heterosexuals in face-to-face interactions with lesbians and gay men, and that we need to seriously examine the experience of the latter in order to discover new ways of operationalizing interpersonal heterosexist discrimination.

Bullock's focus in Chapter 5 is on middle-class responses to the poor (i.e., on classist discrimination). She discusses the ways we define social class and poverty, as well as what we know about classist attitudes and stereotyped beliefs—particularly with respect to recipients of welfare, who are "typically characterized as dishonest, dependent, lazy, uninterested in education, and promiscuous." She contrasts three dominant explanations for poverty (individualistic, structural, and fatalistic), and their consequences for or relationships with other beliefs and behaviors directed toward or relevant to poor people. Bullock notes that although instances of interpersonal discrimination abound in the anecdotal reports of poor people themselves, "research examining face-to-face discrimination in the everyday lives of poor people is virtually nonexistent." She surveys the scant empirical literature, and also lets us listen to the voices of a small sample of welfare women who shared their experiences with her. These experiences reflect being responded to by middle-class persons as "other"—being distanced from, avoided, and excluded.

In the chapter on ageism (Chapter 6), Pasupathi, Carstensen, and Tsai prefer to talk about "age-differentiated behavior" (i.e., behavior that differs when directed toward older and younger persons). They raise the question as to whether such behavior is always ageist or discriminatory, and present empirical data that are ambiguous with respect to how the question should be answered. One problem in interpreting the behavior of younger people toward older people, they note, is that unlike race and gender, "aging is associated with genuine changes that may require accommodation by social partners." They suggest that a useful strategy in studying responses made to the elderly is to examine the positive or negative impact of such responses from an elderly person's perspective.

In Chapter 7, Landrine, Klonoff, Alcaraz, Scott, and Wilkins have taken on the extremely difficult task of trying to come to grips with how, and under what circumstances, intersections and interactions among low-status social categories affect interpersonal discrimination. They explore possible answers to the problem described earlier by Smith and Stewart (1983), who noted that "Black women . . . are faced with the dilemma of trying to decide which of their characteristics (racial, sexual, both, or neither) led to any given experience" (p. 9). Landrine et al. make the dilemma even more complex by asking us to consider the situation of the Black woman who may also be poor and lesbian. The authors of this chapter focus on persons who are in "multiple jeopardy" within a social stratification system topped by upper-class heterosexual White men who maintain their privileged position by a variety of means. They argue that persons in similar social positions share common experiences, including that of being discriminated against (avoided, excluded, derided), and they ask what kind of discrimination is experienced by persons who are in more than one low-status position. Landrine et al. point out that there is a paucity of research directed to this question, and also that most studies of discrimination have involved primarily White respondents. They point to the need to examine how persons from low-status ethnic groups respond to persons in other status categories. It is clear from the theoretical and empirical material presented in this chapter that we are far from understanding the effects of the intersection of low-status categories (i.e., multiple jeopardy) on interpersonal discrimination.

Each chapter ends with comments on the social implications of the research findings relevant to interpersonal sexism, racism, heterosexism, classism, and ageism. What can we say from the accumulation of empirical information to those who set policy and make decisions in the areas of education, government, law, health, human relations, and so on that will put our findings to use in the direction of achieving a more equitable and humane society? In a discussion of the relationship between basic research and practical problems, Snyder (1993) has noted that the major problems in the contemporary world, including "prejudice and discrimination of all forms," are, of course, human problems. We agree with his conclusion that these "problems caused by the actions of humans . . . will require action by humans if solutions are to be found" (p. 251).

For example, the results of juror studies that show more punitive responses to ethnic minority defendants by nonminority jurors have clear implications for the law. One such study (Rector, Bagby, & Nicholson, 1993) had a largely European-American sample of college students assume the role of jurors in a hypothetical rape trial, and found that although the "positive appeal" of the defendant was the best predictor of his being judged not guilty, "overall positive appeal of the defendant was . . . rated lower when he was presented as Black" (p. 657). In a more ambitious and complex study (Perez, Hosch, Ponder, & Trejo, 1993), a large sample of people in either Anglo- or Hispanic-majority six-person simulated juries deliberated to reach a unanimous verdict after viewing a 75-minute videotaped trial of either an Anglo or a Hispanic defendant accused of robbery. Anglo-majority jury panels were found to be less lenient with a Hispanic defendant than with an Anglo defendant, whereas the ethnicity of the defendant made no difference in the decisions reached by Hispanic-majority juries.

To take another example, what implications can be drawn for those who work with the elderly in senior centers, nursing homes, community groups, political clubs, businesses, or other settings from a study such as that by Harris, Moniz, Sowards, and Krane (1994), which identified "ways in which people might act differently with the elderly" (pp. 47–48). Participants who were given the task of teaching a game to a hypothetical 61-year-old retired woman were more nervous and less friendly, and tended to teach fewer concepts and give fewer clues, than participants who were given the task of teaching the game to a 19-year-old female college student. And what message for families and schools is contained in the findings reported by Pleck, Sonenstein, Freya, and Ku (1993) from their analysis of data from a national survey of adolescent males? Among this sample of young men, those who were more traditional in their self-reported masculinity ideology reported less intimacy with sexual partners and were more likely to view relations between women and men as adversarial. These findings held across ethnicities and did not vary significantly among White, Black, and Hispanic adolescent males. The implications of such findings seem chillingly clear. Among the suggested remedies for reducing interpersonal discrimination in our schools is the simple and feasible program suggested by Thorne (1993), for example. Thorne calls for

> eliminating the gender typing of tasks and activities, [and] . . . allocating opportunities, resources, and teacher attention without regard to the social categories of students. . . . [S]chool staff should try to open, rather than diminish, opportunities for boys and girls, and students of different class, racial, and ethnic backgrounds, and physical abilities, to get to know one another as individuals and friends. (p. 159)

Research on interpersonal discrimination typically looks at persons who are responded to as members of a low-status social category in terms of their stimulus or cue functions. The focus of inquiry is generally on the behavior of those who interact with such persons. Certainly, and undeniably, the targets of interpersonal discrimination are not passive recipients of the actions of others and do exhibit varying interactive responses, some of which result in changes in the behavior of the discriminators. The focus of this book, however, is on the excluding, distancing, and avoiding behaviors of the latter. We leave examination of possible interactive scripts and the consequences of various action and reaction patterns for later projects and for other investigators. A fine example of what might be a second phase in the study of interpersonal discrimination—that is, the study of reactions to it—is the work of Lykes (1983), referred to earlier. Lykes's analysis of the lives of elderly African-American women leaders addressed not only their experiences of discrimination, but also how they coped with or dealt with them and how variations in their responses were related to situational or contextual factors.

NOTE

1. The terms "Black" and "White" are capitalized throughout this book because they do not really denote skin color, but rather are shorthand terms for "African-American" and "European-American," respectively.

REFERENCES

Allport, G. W. (1954). *The nature of prejudice.* Reading, MA: Addison-Wesley.
Betters-Reed, B. L., & Moore, L. L. (1992, November–December). The technicolor workplace. *Ms.*, pp. 84–85.
Bogardus, E. (1925). Measuring social distance. *Journal of Applied Sociology, 9,* 299–308.
Bourhis, R. Y. (1994). Power, gender, and intergroup discrimination: Some minimal group experiments. In M. P. Zanna & J. M. Olson (Eds.), *The Ontario Symposium: Vol. 7. The psychology of prejudice* (pp. 171–208). Hillsdale, NJ: Erlbaum.
Cheever, S. (1994, July 3). An accidental symbol. [Review of "I am Roe: My life, Roe v. Wade, and freedom of choice," by Norma McCorvey]. *New York Times Book Review*, p. 7.
Crandall, C. S. (1994). Prejudice against fat people: Ideology and self interest. *Journal of Personality and Social Psychology, 66,* 882–894.
Fine, M. (1992). *Disruptive voices: The possibilities of feminist research.* Ann Arbor: University of Michigan Press.
Harris, M. J., Moniz, A. J., Sowards, B. A., & Krane, K. (1994). Mediation of interpersonal expectancy effects: Expectancies about the elderly. *Social Psychology Quarterly, 57,* 36–48.
Lott, B., Lott, A. J., & Fernald, J. L. (1990). Individual differences in distancing responses to women on a photo choice task. *Sex Roles, 22,* 97–110.
Lykes, M. B. (1983). Discrimination and coping in the lives of Black women. *Journal of Social Issues, 39*(3), 79–100.
Perez, D. A., Hosch, H. M., Ponder, B., & Trejo, G. C. (1993). Ethnicity of defendants and jurors as influencers on jury decisions. *Journal of Applied Social Psychology, 23,* 1249–1262.
Pleck, J. H., Sonenstein, F. L., Freya, F. L., & Ku, L. C. (1993). Masculinity ideology: Its impact on adolescent males' heterosexual relationships. *Journal of Social Issues, 49*(3), 11–29.
Rector, N. A., Bagby, R. M., & Nicholson, R. (1993). The effect of prejudice and judicial ambiguity on defendant guilt ratings. *Journal of Social Psychology, 133,* 651–659.
Root, M. P. P. (1993, October). Prejudice polarizes college campuses. *APA Monitor,* p. 40.
Smith, A., & Stewart, A. J. (1983). Approaches to studying racism and sexism in Black women's lives. *Journal of Social Issues, 39*(3), 1–15.
Smith, D. E. (1987). *The everyday world as problematic.* Boston: Northeastern University Press.

Snyder, M. L. (1993). Basic research and practical problems: The promise of a "functional" personality and social psychology. *Personality and Social Psychology Bulletin, 19,* 251–264.

Snyder, M. L., Kleck, R. E., Strenta, A., & Mentzer, S. J. (1979). Avoidance of the handicapped: An attributional ambiguity analysis. *Journal of Personality and Social Psychology, 37,* 2297–2306.

Snyder, M. L., & Milne, P. (1994). On the functions of stereotypes and prejudice. In M. P. Zanna & J. M Olson (Eds.), *The Ontario Symposium: Vol. 7. The psychology of prejudice* (pp. 33–54). Hillsdale, NJ: Erlbaum.

Thorne, B. (1993). *Gender play: Girls and boys in school.* New Brunswick, NJ: Rutgers University Press.

Word, C. O., Zanna, M. P., & Cooper, J. (1974). Avoidance behaviors as measures of discrimination in interpersonal situations. *Journal of Experimental Social Psychology, 10,* 109–120.

Weisser, S. (1994, July 31). [Letter to the editor]. *New York Times Book Review,* p. 31.

2

Distancing from Women
Interpersonal Sexist Discrimination

BERNICE LOTT

*I*nterpersonal sexist discrimination is distinguishable from institutional sexist discrimination, but the latter provides a necessary cultural context for the former. Institutional discrimination refers to the normative practice of exclusion within social institutions (e.g., in religion, employment, and politics), and can be defined as "actions or practices carried out by members of dominant groups, or their representatives, which have a differential and negative impact on members of subordinate groups" (Feagin & Feagin, 1978, pp. 20–21). Institutional sexist discrimination describes the "everyday practices" of a sexist society (Young, 1992), in which man is the norm and woman is "the other." Viewing woman as "the other," Hare-Mustin and Marecek (1990) have pointed out, involves exaggerating her differences from man and represents a "distancing and alienating view of women by the dominant male culture [that] opens the way to treating women as objects" (p. 38).

Obvious examples of institutional sexist discrimination in current U.S. society include the fact that women are typically paid less than men for equal work, and that they are barred by custom or rule from certain positions, places, or practices in both private and public spheres. The existence of institutional discrimination and of general sexism is assumed as a background condition for my examination of interpersonal sexist discrimination—that is, the distancing behavior of individual men in the presence of individual women. It is further assumed that institutional discrimination and interpersonal face-to-face discrimination are the same in their general effects: Both are instrumental in achieving separation from women.

Serving as background for this chapter is the research and theoretical analysis of interpersonal attraction in which I was engaged for many years (e.g., A. J. Lott & Lott, 1968, 1972, 1974; B. Lott & Lott, 1985). In that work, antecedents and consequences of liking and disliking were identified, defined in behavioral terms, and related to learning theory variables. The objective of my current research program, the subject of this chapter, is to go beyond the earlier work and to systematically investigate one piece of the reverse side of the attraction model—avoidance behavior, specifically as directed toward women by men. Such behavior, I propose, operationally defines sexist discrimination in face-to-face interpersonal situations.

SEXISM

"Sexism" can be defined generally, as suggested by Young (1992), as the oppression or "inhibition" of women "through a vast network of everyday practices, attitudes, assumptions, behaviors, and institutional rules" (p. 180). It is structural and systemic, and results in the privileging of men. The pervasiveness of sexism in a society, as MacKinnon (1989) has noted, results in its being "so much a part of the omnipresent background of life that a massive effort of collective concentration is required even to discern that it has edges" (p. 90). Sexism reflects, but also results in, the greater status and power of men relative to women. As Young (1992) argues, "The freedom, power, status, and self-realization of men [are] possible precisely because women work for them" (p. 183). Similarly, Graumann and Wintermantel (1989) note that "social discrimination" associated with sexism, racism, or negative behaviors directed against outgroups in general "is in the service of maintaining dominance" (p. 189). In the context of the perspective offered in this chapter, it is proposed that sexism has positive outcomes for men, and thus behavior that is instrumental in maintaining it will be strengthened.

To translate this into social-psychological language, and to place it within the theoretical framework that informs and guides my analysis and empirical work in this area, sexism is conceptualized in terms of three independent but related components: prejudice, stereotypes, and discrimination. These components can be distinguished conceptually as follows: (1) "Prejudice" is defined as negative attitudes toward women (i.e., feelings of hostility or dislike); (2) "stereotypes" are defined as well-learned, widely shared, socially validated general beliefs or cognitions about women, which reinforce, complement, or justify the prejudices and often involve an assumption of inferiority; and (3) "discrimination" denotes overt behaviors that achieve separation from women through exclusion, avoidance, or distancing.

Other social psychologists have presented similar definitions. Thus, for example, Stroebe and Insko (1989) have noted that "the distinction between stereotype and prejudice parallels the distinction commonly made between beliefs or opinion and attitudes . . . [with] prejudice [defined as] an attitutde toward members of some outgroup . . . in which the evaluative tendencies are predominantly negative" (p. 8). Like other social psychologists, they accept the classic definition of discrimination proposed over four decades ago by Gordon Allport (1954)—namely, any behavior that denies persons the equal treatment they desire. Although negative opinions and dislike "may be deplorable," Stroebe and Insko argue, it is primarily discriminatory behavior that consitutes "a social problem" (p. 10)—a position with which I strongly agree.

The focus of this chapter and of my current program of research is on sexist discrimination in actual or simulated interpersonal or face-to-face situations—that is, on what men *do* in the presence of women, not on what they say they feel or believe. As noted by MacKinnon (1989), "Women know that much if not most sexism is unconscious, heedless, patronizing, well-meant, or profit motivated. It is no less denigrating, damaging, or sex-specific for not being 'on purpose' " (p. 230). Thus, the present focus on behavior is definite and important. It is with what men do in the presence of women that I am concerned, specifically with acts of interpersonal discrimination, operationalized as distancing behavior. As argued by Skinner (1987), "There can scarcely be anything more familiar than human behavior. . . . Nor can there be anything more important. . . . Nevertheless it . . . has seldom been thought of as a subject matter in its own right, but rather has been viewed as the mere expression or symptom of more important happenings inside the behaving person" (p. 780). The general dismissal in recent years of behavior-focused research in social psychology has been noted and criticized by others. Graumann and Wintermantel (1989), for example, have pointed to the "neglect of (overt) behavior . . . [and its generation of] far less research interest than cognition and motivation" (p. 187).

Most investigations of sexism in the psychological literature have been concerned with attitudes or beliefs and not with overt acts. A sizable literature supports the generalization that stereotyped beliefs and prejudice against women (particularly in nontraditional or atypical situations) are common among men in our society (see B. Lott, 1994). Eagly and Mladinic (1994) are now arguing that women tend to be evaluated positively, at least by the college students who remain the primary respondents. On the other hand, a review of relevant work (Del Boca, Ashmore, & McManus, 1986) concluded that "with few exceptions, researchers report that the male stereotype comprises a larger number of elements—and a larger number of favorable attributes—than does that for the female" (p. 125). In a thorough review of the literature, Deaux and Kite (1993) note that "gender stereotypes have shown remarkable staying power. . . . [Although] there is some suggestion that the positive–negative evaluation of the sexes has shifted slightly, . . . the core beliefs in the instrumental and agentic qualities of men and the emotional and communal attributes of women persist" (p. 127). So powerful are the data on gender stereotypes that Judge Gerhard Gesell of the U.S. Court of Appeals referred to them in his landmark decision in 1990 in the case of *Price-Waterhouse v. Hopkins* in which he ruled that Ann Hopkins had been denied a partnership in Price-Waterhouse solely on the basis of her gender and its influence on perceptions about her (see Deaux & Kite, 1993). The issue that is more relevant to the present discussion, however, is that the overt behaviors of men that are instrumental in avoiding or distancing themselves from women in face-to-face situations have seldom been the focus of study. As noted by Geffner and Gross (1984), "there have been . . . very few experiments investigating discriminatory behavior in actual interactions between men and women" (p. 974).

Underlying my model of sexism and predictions about men's behavior in the presence of women are some important assumptions. The first assumption is that feelings (prejudice), beliefs (stereotypes), and overt acts (discrimination) may be learned independently and maintained by different sets of conditions—an issue to which I return later. Second, although avoidance behaviors by men toward women are typically learned in our society under a variety of differing circumstances, we know that approach behaviors are also learned. It is therefore expected that distancing responses to women will be manifested primarily in relatively neutral situations, where there is little expectation that such responses will meet with serious disapproval or other negative consequences, and in situations in which approach behaviors are not likely to be instrumental in obtaining nurturance, sexual pleasure, status enhancement, or some specific situation-related reward. I also return to a discussion of approach behaviors later in this chapter.

WOMEN'S EXPERIENCES OF INTERPERSONAL DISCRIMINATION

My objective in pursuing a systematic investigation of men's distancing behavior in face-to-face interactions with women is to empirically validate the personal experience reported anecdotally by many women—namely, that men tend to ignore and turn away from us (in situations in which there is minimal expectation of sexual or nurturant consequences). In taking women's experiences as its starting place, this research can be seen as an example of feminist scholarship. In particular, it can be regarded as part of a feminist agenda in social psychology that extends existing areas of research and opens new areas, presenting questions and hypotheses that come from the study of women's lives (B. Lott, 1985b, 1990, 1991). As noted by MacKinnon (1989), "plac[ing] women's experiences, and the perspective from within that experience, at the center of an inquiry into the lived-out reality of gender . . . pays close attention to women's everyday lives and gives priority to women's point of view" (p. 38). Feminist theorists who speak of "women's experience," emphasize, according to Ferguson (1993, p. 5), "what women *do* or what women *are*." Less often considered, but no less important, are the responses made *to* women.

In describing the experiences of women administrators in universities, Rowe (1973) spoke more than 20 years ago about the frequency with which a woman found her name "mysteriously missing" from lists. "Hers are the announcements and invitations which fail to come. . . . It is her work which by mistake was not properly acknowledged, . . . not responded to, . . . her opinion which is not asked for" (p. 4). Rowe referred to such behaviors as "the minutiae of sexism." Anecdotal reports of such "minutiae" in work and social situations continue to be shared by women almost everywhere, as illustrated in a *Sylvia* cartoon by Nicole Hollander (see Figure 2.1).

As in the cartoon, which makes some of us laugh and cry simultaneously, the head of a department of mechanical engineering in a Western university described the following experience: "Although she had looked

SYLVIA   **by Nicole Hollander**

FIGURE 2.1. *Sylvia* cartoon by Nicole Hollander (*Providence Journal-Bulletin*, June 28, 1993, p. D7). Copyright 1993 by Nicole Hollander. Reprinted by permission.

foward to serving on the dean's academic council, once there, she found that her suggestions were either ignored outright or politely received with no follow-up. In fact, she had never found mention in the council minutes of anything important that she had said" (cf. Bennett & Green, 1983, p. 58). Similar examples of "subtle, and often unconscious, sexist behavior" (p. 59) are talked about among women in a variety of other settings, and match the observations made by Wolman and Frank (1975) in their now classic field study of reactions of men coworkers to "solo women" in a professional setting. These investigators observed six small groups over an extended period of time and found that the women members tended to be isolated and ignored. A study reported almost 20 years later (MacCorquodale & Jensen, 1993) of 200 attorneys in Arizona found that 38% of the women and 6% of the men questioned believed that judges pay more attention to the opinions and arguments of male counselors in court than to female counselors. No one believed more attention was given to women, and "*no one* believed that a female attorney would command more respect" (p. 590).

Similar observations have been made of the behavior of boys toward girls, and it seems likely that men begin to learn to distance from women when they are young. Maccoby (1988) has noted that boys in the United States stop responding to suggestions, requests, and influence attempts by girls when they are somewhere between the ages of 3½ and 5½. Whether this is because they have begun to dislike girls at this age (i.e., to have negative attitudes toward girls) is not clear. Perhaps, as Tavris (1992) has suggested, it is simply that the boys "are mimicking the adult patterns of male dominance that they observe" (p. 291). They are behaving in ways, then, that are likely to be accepted and rewarded.

Thorne (1993), in describing the play behavior of children in school, presents it as a representation of the differential power of girls and boys. She notes:

> On school playgrounds boys control as much as ten times more space than girls. . . . In addition to taking up more space, boys more often see girls and their activities as interruptible; boys invade and disrupt all-female games and scenes of play much more often than vice versa. . . . In complex dialectics of power, boys treat girls' spaces, activities, and sheer physical presence as contaminating. (p. 83)

What the boys do in their play is to keep girls out and to manifest exclusionary, distancing behavior in a variety of ways. This theme is echoed in findings from a number of studies of the behavior of boys, from preschool on up the grades. Libby and Aries (1989), for example, asked a sample of 3- to 5-year-olds to complete six stories and found that whereas girls told an equal number of stories in which girls and boys were the central characters, "no boy ever told a story specifying a character to be female" (p. 302). In a study of 540 kindergarten children, Riley (1981), who asked the children to draw pictures of what they wanted to be when they grew up if they were of the other gender, reported that the boys "moaned and groaned . . . [showing] a great deal of distaste . . . associated with the thought of being a girl" (p. 248). Among a sample of third- and fourth-graders, Bussey and Perry (1982) found that boys were more rejecting than girls of object choices made by children of the other gender. These studies not only indicate how boys tend to respond to the category of "girls" but point to a general climate for girls of being avoided and distanced from by boys.

Ignoring, excluding, and devaluing may be said to represent portions of a continuum of negative responses to girls and women by boys and men that occur regularly in a sexist society or community. Elsewhere (B. Lott, 1993), I have suggested a model for such sexist responses in the form of a spiral, as shown in Figure 2.2, with humor and put-downs at the wide end, murder at the narrow end, and such behaviors as personal distancing, harassment, and physical abuse in between. That discrimination is represented by a wide variety of behaviors is a view shared by many. In the words of MacKinnon (1993, p. 56), these behaviors range "from contempt to genocide."

Feminist theory in many disciplines is concerned with analysis of sexist behaviors as part of its examination of women's lives. Such analysis begins with documentation and description, and moves toward explanation in terms of relationships with sociopolitical and personal antecedents and consequences. The model of sexist responses to women shown in Figure 2.2 may be considered an example of feminist analysis that attempts to reorder or reorganize familiar concepts and to suggest a new pattern reflecting the contemporary reality of women's experiences. Thus, feminist analysis includes deconstruction and reconstruction (Allen & Baber, 1992; DiLeonardo, 1991; Hare-Mustin & Marecek, 1990). Feminist analysis requires a focus not just on women, but on men's behavior. As Pleck (1977) has noted, "one of the most fundamental questions raised by the women's movement is not a question about women at all, but rather a question about men" (p. 13). How social class, ethnicity, sexual orientation, and other socially constructed categories affect or influence sexist responses to women, and mandate revisions in the model presented, are important questions that need to be addressed. I return to these questions later.

DOING GENDER

Feminist analysis suggests that interpersonal or face-to-face discrimination by men is part of what they do to establish or demonstrate their gender. As proposed by West and Zimmerman (1987), "a person's gender is not simply

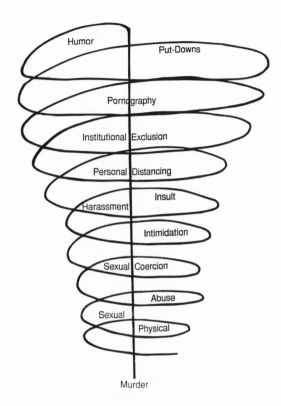

Humor

Put-Downs

Pornography

Institutional Exclusion

Personal Distancing

Insult

Harassment

Intimidation

Sexual Coercion

Abuse

Sexual

Physical

Murder

FIGURE 2.2. A model of sexist responses to women. From B. Lott (1993, p. 97). Copyright 1993 by National Education Association. Adapted by permission.

an aspect of what one is, but, more fundamentally, it is something that one *does*, and does recurrently, in interaction with others" (p. 140). We establish and maintain "the interactional scaffolding of social structure" (p. 147) by "doing gender"—that is, behaving like a woman or a man of one's time, place, and community. This proposition was presented earlier in somewhat different terms by Goffman (1979), who argued that women and men "learn to provide and to read depictions of masculinity and femininity and a willingness to adhere to a schedule for presenting these pictures" (p. 8). Doing gender is supported and facilitated by the differing positions occupied by women and men in social institutions, by widely accepted stereotypes, by observing the behavior of persons like oneself, and by acting in ways that are socially rewarded. As noted by Del Boca et al. (1986), "It is quite likely that a great deal of interaction between the sexes is scripted rather than individuated (i.e., attitude driven)" (p. 154). And Kahn (1984) has pointed out more specifically that persons who hold power (e.g., men in general in relation to women in general), attempt "to maintain a social and psychological distance from [the] inferior target of power . . . [which] can be clearly seen in men's behavior toward women" (p. 239). Thus, *to turn away and distance oneself from a woman is what a man does because he is a man*, and what boys do in relation to girls because they are boys. Such behavior is expected, is tacitly approved, often goes unnoticed, and contributes to the implicit definition or understanding of manliness in a sexist society.

That men (and women, too, of course) learn about themselves from observing how they behave is not a new idea. It is basic to Bem's (1972) self-perception theory, which posits that rather than acting on the basis of our feelings and beliefs, we often infer what our feelings and beliefs should be from our behavior and from the context or situation in which we are responding. There is considerable empirical support for this position. One example comes from a study by Kellerman, Lewis, and Laird (1989), in which mixed-gender pairs of persons who exchanged mutual unbroken gazes for 2 minutes, as instructed, subsequently reported increased feelings of attraction. Interestingly enough, the proposition that behavior influences thoughts and feelings is also a primary Marxist tenet. Marx argued in 1859 that "it is not the consciousness of men [*sic*] that determines their existence, but their social existence that determines their consciousness" (quoted in DiLeonardo, 1991, p. 31).

Does distancing behavior by a man or boy toward a woman or a girl always signify sexist discrimination? Perhaps not. For example, one colleague who read an early draft of this chapter recounted a story told to her of a man who, during his exercise jogs, crossed the street to avoid running behind a woman after one woman runner had been startled by finding him in back of her. A similar scenario later appeared in a "Miss Manners" column shared with me by a colleague. That some gender-related avoidance behavior may be maintained in particular circumstances by idiosyncratic reinforcements does not invalidate the general operational definition of interpersonal sexist discrimination as distancing behavior.

RELATIONSHIPS AMONG BEHAVIOR, ATTITUDES, AND BELIEFS

A focus on sexist behavior, as in the present chapter, requires some attempt to comment on the relationships among behavior, attitudes, and beliefs. These relationships, I suggest, are frequently presented in confusing ways, contributing to a lack of conceptual clarity and to the frustration often expressed over the common finding of low correlations. Even as late as the mid-1980s, McGuire referred to this situation "as the scandal of the field"

(1985, p. 251). More recently, Eagly and Chaiken (1993) have offered a more positive critique and presented evidence in support of their argument that high correlations between "attitudes and overt behavior can be produced by aggregating behaviors to create a measure that corresponds in generality to the attitude measure" (p. 216), and by manipulating appropriate mediating variables. They urge us to consider the influence on behavior of such nonattitudinal variables as habits, self-identity, and norms.

Although the size of attitude–behavior correlations can vary widely under differing conditions, the definition of "attitude" remains unclear despite the fact that, as Olson and Zanna (1993) note in their recent review, "attitudes and attitude change remain among the most extensively researched topics by social psychologists" (p. 118). In my view, a major source of confusion arises from those definitions of attitude that include behaviors, affect, and beliefs as components of attitude. Those who propose and utilize such a definition appear to lose sight of it when they typically go on to discuss correlations between attitudes and behaviors as though they had equal status as independent factors, and not as though one had been included as a component of the other.

A related source of confusion stems from the ambiguous position of the concept of "affect." Although all definitions of "attitude" include a reference to its pro-and-con nature, some define it entirely in affective terms, while others see affect as only one aspect of attitude. Identified with a learning- or behavior-oriented approach to attitudes, first articulated by Doob (1947), is its definition in affective terms. Thus, for example, in a paper on gender-related attitudes, Del Boca et al. (1986) refer to an attitude as "a positive–negative, pro–con, good–bad predisposition" with "affect . . . regarded as the core" (p. 134). The authors state clearly that "attitude is the degree of overall positive–negative feeling for or against an object" (p. 136).

Illustrative of the approach that views attitude as incorporating affect, belief, and action is the position of Eagly (1992), who defines an attitude as a "state internal to the person" that precedes and influences responses, which "can be cognitive, affective, or behavioral and overt or covert" (p. 694). As discussed more fully by Eagly and Chaiken (1993), an attitude is said to be some overriding internal response to an attitude object that is formed on the basis of "cognitive, affective, and behavioral processes" and subsequently "manifested in cognitive, affective, and behavioral responses" (p. 16). Although such a formulation permits the investigation of relationships among beliefs, feelings, and actions, with each independently and operationally defined, the investigation of relationships between attitude and behavior, or between attitude and affect, or between attitude and beliefs, becomes problematic because of the difficulty of assessing an attitude independently of its presumed components. Yet such relationships continue to be noted and discussed by those who define attitude as a multifaceted response. For example, in discussing research findings on evaluations of women and men (Eagly & Mladinic, 1994; Eagly, Mladinic, & Otto, 1991), Eagly and her colleagues take note of the poor relationships typically found between attitudes and behavior.

Zimbardo and Leippe (1991) also consider attitude to be "the overall summary evaluation that includes the other components," and as "an evaluative disposition" that is both based upon and can influence "cognitions, affective responses, and future intentions and behavior" (p. 32). These components of attitude are viewed as constituting an "attitude system." Despite this complex definition, Zimbardo and Leippe confuse the reader by sometimes treating attitudes more simply. Thus, for example, they point out that "we can have an attitude about something—liking or disliking it—even when the rest of the mental representation is practically devoid of beliefs and actual knowledge. This is true of many of our prejudices—the negative attitudes that we may develop about groups of people that we actually know little about" (p. 34). Implied by these statements, it seems to me, is that beliefs are not in fact a necessary component of attitude, and that an attitude (liking or disliking—i.e., affect) may be present without matching cognitions or beliefs. That Zimbardo and Leippe have a hard time sticking to their definition of an attitude as a system that includes beliefs and behavior can be further illustrated by statements in which the three concepts are treated as independent. For example, they point out that "behavior can be influenced *directly* by certain social stimuli, without first changing attitudes or beliefs" (p. 88).

Answers to the important question of whether or how attitudes, beliefs, and overt actions are independent or related are suggested by data from some recent studies that have focused on the seeming independence of affect and cognition. For example, in a situation in which students, sitting with eyes closed, visualized a positive interaction and a negative interaction with an emotionally close person, and then answered questions about feelings and beliefs, Wollman (1987) found only a low to moderate level of consistency between affective and cognitive measures. Results from a different empirical approach also support the proposition that affect and cognition are independent, and demonstrate that the latter can be influenced by the former. Target persons whose photos were subliminally paired with happy scenes were liked more than those whose photos were paired with scary scenes (Krosnick, Betz, Jussim, & Lynn, 1992) and, subsequent to the conditioning process, were judged to have more positive personality traits. The investigators, defining attitude as affect, concluded that "attitudes toward an object can be generated through processes other than deduction from beliefs about the attributes of the object" (p. 158). This approach is consistent with the argument presented by Zajonc (1980) that affect and cognition are independent reactions to a stimulus. It can be inferred from the way in which Zajonc used the term "affect" that he equated it with "attitude." Thus, he noted that "the dismal failure in achieving substantial attitude change through various forms of communication or persuasion is another indication that affect is fairly independent and often impervious to cognition" (p. 152). Edwards (1990) and Murphy and Zajonc (1993) are attempting to clarify affective–cognitive relationships, and Banaji and Greenwald (1993) are investigating the influence of unconscious processes on the separate categories of "stereotyped beliefs, prejudicial attitudes, and discriminatory behavior" (p. 55).

In an interesting study by Breckler (1984), utilizing three different measures each of affective, cognitive, and behavioral reactions to a live, caged snake, correlations were found to be only moderate. The three types of responses emerged as distinct, "suggesting," as noted by the investigator, "the practical importance of discriminating among them" (p. 1203). Similarly, Devine (1989) found that under certain conditions White college students who were low in verbally reported prejudice toward Blacks were as likely as those who were high in prejudice to indicate stereotyped beliefs, which, according to the investigator, could sometimes be automatically activated.

I define an attitude as a covert affective (or feeling) response to a stimulus, and suggest that cognitive (or belief) responses and overt action (or behavioral) responses to that same stimulus are acquired and maintained independently. Because an individual will frequently learn to feel, believe, and act toward a stimulus object under the same set of conditions, these three reactions will often be correlated. On the other hand, an individual may learn affective, cognitive, and behavioral reactions to a stimulus under different conditions; or, as is even more likely, these separate reactions may be maintained, or influenced by, separate sets of contextual cues and contingencies. Zimbardo and Leippe (1991) note, for example, that "it is the people in a social situation ... who are typically the most potent influences in that social context. Even strangers can cause us to behave in ways we would not if we merely paid attention to our own attitudes" (p. 189).

Illustrations of the relative independence of prejudicial attitudes, stereotyped beliefs, and discriminatory behavior come from a variety of sources. After reviewing the relevant literature, Crosby, Bromley, and Saxe (1980) concluded that discriminatory behavior directed toward Blacks by Whites in the United States (particularly when observed or assessed unobtrusively) was more prevalent than might be expected on the basis of attitude measures (survey data), or what European-Americans say they feel about African-Americans. Similar observations have been made about the discordance between what some men say they feel or believe about women and how they behave. Kahn (1984) has commented on "the failure of egalitarian men to act on their beliefs," and speculated that it is because men are "so used to exerting their power and confidence that they simply do not know how to act otherwise" (p. 242). Eagly and Mladinic (1994), while reporting that men tend to make favorable verbal evaluations of women, caution us against assuming that attitudes correspond directly with such complex social phenomena as women's lesser wages relative to men's and against assuming that discrimination is necessarily revealed or caused by negative attitudes or stereotypes.

Some studies have directly compared racist attitudes and behaviors of the same persons in the same situation. In an experimental study by Riches and Foddy (1989), for example, Australian college students were found to be less likely to accept influence in a joint decision task from a partner who spoke with a Greek accent than from a partner who spoke with an Anglo accent; however, when respondents were asked after the task for an explicit evaluation of their partners, no difference was found in the evaluations of Greek- and Anglo-accented persons. Had the investigators relied only on the verbal report of attitudes (or prejudice) and not also measured behavior (or discrimination), they would not have found anti-Greek bias. Comparable results were obtained in my study of mixed-gender pairs working on a laboratory task (B. Lott, 1987), to be described in a later section of this chapter.

The division of human experience into cognitions, affect, and behavior seems to be found in a large number of cultures. According to McGuire (1985, p. 242), "Human experience has been analyzed into knowing, feeling, and acting components so early and often that it may reflect a deep structure in Indo-European thought, central in the thinking of Hellenic philosophers . . . , in the Hindu . . . , and in the Zoroastrian." However, such an assumption about the components of human experience does not carry with it any assumptions about the ways in which they are related. In fact, our eagerness to find attitude–behavior consistencies may be a Western cultural phenomenon. This has been suggested by Slugoski and Ginsberg (cited by Sampson, 1991, p. 181), who reported "that in Japan, attitude–behavior consistency is not as valued a sign of integrity as it is in most western cultures, but rather is seen as a sign of immaturity and inconsiderateness. People are encouraged not to behave in accordance with their attitudes to avoid appearing insensitive and impolite."

An implicit recognition of the independence of attitudes and behavior is also found in the acceptance of civil rights legislation as a means of decreasing (or abolishing) discriminatory behavior toward members of low-power ethnic minority groups, disabled persons, and women. Regardless of how an individual feels about someone from a particular group (i.e., regardless of one's attitude), the law mandates nondiscriminatory behavior. As argued by Skinner (1987), "It is not enough to advise people how to behave in ways that will make a future possible; they must be given effective reasons for behaving in those ways, and that means effective contingencies of reinforcement now" (p. 785). Acceptance of the proposition that actions, attitudes, and beliefs are independent of one another does not necessarily lead to the expectation that they cannot influence one another. On the contrary, nondiscriminatory behavior (by oneself and others) is expected to lead to changed attitudes and beliefs by creating changed institutional practices and new situations of interpersonal interaction. As argued by Bem (1972) and supported by a sizable literature on self-perception theory, we learn about our feelings and beliefs by observing how we behave in particular situations.

In earlier work, I defined an attitude within the framework of learning theory as a fractional anticipatory goal response with stimulus and drive properties (B. Lott [Eisman], 1955; A. J. Lott & Lott, 1960, 1965). Such a response is covert and is evoked by a stimulus (object, person, or situation; actual or symbolic) in the presence of which an individual has had some positive or negative experience. The attitudinal response functions, then, as an anticipation of that same experience and can mediate overt responses such as verbal statements of like or dislike/pro or con, or approach and avoidance behaviors. Its drive property is derived from its strength and persistence, and contributes to its affective quality. Which behaviors will be mediated by an attitudinal response depends on conditions that influence response evocation (frequency of reinforcement, motivation, response competition, etc.). But certainly an atitude will mediate some behavior. However, overt responses to stimuli (objects, persons, situations) may be learned directly. I may turn away from X because X is asociated with painful or frustrating experiences (i.e., is aversive), and I am acting in a way that reflects my negative attitude toward X. Or I may turn away from (or exclude) X because I have learned, through modeling or direct reinforcement, that this is the appropriate, expected, normative way to behave. It seems likely that men's interpersonal discriminatory behavior toward women has been learned and maintained largely in the latter way.

DISTANCING BEHAVIOR

The use of interpersonal space as a dependent measure of discrimination was common in an earlier literature (see A. J. Lott & Lott, 1974) and dates back to the classic work of Bogardus (1925), who developed the Social Distance Scale 70 years ago as a measure from which prejudice toward ethnic/racial groups was inferred. There seems to be a general consensus or understanding in a variety of domains that distance between persons represents estrangement or avoidance, whereas closeness represents friendship and liking. (The extent to which this consensus may be limited to certain cultures is an important question requiring further study.) Schlenker and Leary, who investigated disaffiliative behaviors, include in their definition "keeping distant from others" (cited in Sampson, 1991, p. 234), and Landy (1983), in discussing drama therapy, mentions the interpretation of distancing as "a means of separating oneself from the other" (p. 175). A recently developed scale that measures interpersonal relationships (Aron, Aron, & Smollan, 1992) asks respondents to indicate which of seven diagrams of two circles describes a particular relationship. The diagrams differ in the extent to which the circles overlap or in the distance between their centers, representing different degrees of personal closeness. Anecdotal reports of personal experiences suggest that this approach has merit. For example, Graff (1993), in describing the behavior of a motel manager who showed her to the room with one double bed that she had requested for herself and another woman, wrote, "She dropped the key in my hand as if my skin were contagious—that gesture of willed distance every despised minority knows by heart" (p. 16).

As noted by Hendricks and Bootzin (1976), "the proximity of two individuals has become accepted as a 'presumptive index' of the affective relationship between them" (p. 172). Studies in which distancing is treated as an independent variable and its consequences are assessed have found that smaller distances between persons communicate positive relationshiops to observers (Mehrabian, 1968). In one investigation (Kelley, 1972), respondents from different backgrounds were asked to look at photos of therapists in different postures relevant to their clients and to judge how much they thought the therapist in each photo liked the client. It was found that a positive attitude toward the client was communicated by closer distances, eye contact, and leaning forward. Similarly, Abbey and Melby (1986) found that respondents judged two individuals seated together at a table as more likely to be friends as the distance between the two decreased.

In a review of research in which distancing was the dependent variable, Evans and Howard (1973) concluded that "the preponderance of data suggest that persons who are friendly with each other or wish to communicate a positive affect will tend to interact at smaller distances than those who are not friendly" (pp. 336–337). A sizable literature supports this conclusion. For example, it has been reported that college students in a laboratory situation placed themselves farther away from a disliked than from a liked confederate (Allgeier & Byrne, 1973); that students in a classroom whose seating positions were observed seven times during one semester consistently sat near preferred persons and tended to avoid sitting near nonpreferred persons (King, 1964); that among dyads observed in a sample of streets, parks, and markets, strangers were found generally to stand farther apart than acquaintances, friends, or relatives (Heshka &

Nelson, 1972); and that a sample of nonhandicapped college students avoided sitting next to a person in a wheelchair when there was an acceptable pretext for doing so (Snyder, Kleck, Strenta, & Mentzer, 1979).

Similarly, other investigators have found that friends approached each other and permitted approach at closer distances than strangers (Bell, Kline, & Barnard, 1988); that swim meet winners were touched, on average, six times more than losers (cited in Thayer, 1988); that persons said they would like to get closer to a stranger as a coworker, neighbor, or friend if that stranger was a winner than if the stranger was a loser (B. Lott & Lott, 1986); that individuals chose closer distances between chairs when they imagined themselves with a liked person (Gifford, 1982); and that Nigerian high school students seated themselves farther away from an interviewer they were led to expect would behave rudely than from an interviewer they expected would behave pleasantly (Ugwuegbu & Anusiem, 1982).

Some investigators have predicted and found that White persons in the United States tend to distance themselves from Black persons. For example, White students playing the role of job interviewer placed their chairs farther from Black than from White applicants (Word, Zanna, & Cooper, 1974); in another study (Hendricks & Bootzin, 1976), White students chose to sit farther away from a Black than from a White confederate when given a choice of empty seats. In the latter study, interestingly enough, when White students were instructed to approach confederates until they felt uncomfortable, and were observed by the investigator, color/ethnicity of the confederate did not influence their behavior.

In the above-cited studies, distancing in face-to-face situations was measured directly in terms of physical space, but other investigations have employed simulated distance measures such as the placement of figures on cardboard. Among such studies, research participants have been reported to place the greatest distance between pairs of strangers and the least betwen pairs of friends (e.g., Little, 1965), and to place themselves further away from "stigmatized" and disliked persons than from liked persons (e.g., Kleck et al., 1968). In a simulation study by Weinbaum and Gilead (1986), adults who were completing their high school requirements were asked to place various named items along a visualized 5-kilometer road and to indicate the distance from themselves. Disagreeable items such as their most fearsome teacher were placed farthest away.

In studies using symbolic or indirect measures of distancing or avoidance, college students were found to be less likely to wear a team badge if they had received feedback of failure on a team task than if they had received success feedback or no information (Snyder, Lassegard, & Ford, 1986); and the mean reaction time to overweight customers by shoe salespersons in an urban shopping mall was found to be significantly greater than that to thinner customers (Pauley, 1989). Ickes (1984) observed looking and smiling behavior in interracial dyads and found that White college students who had previously said that they tended to avoid persons not of their race looked and smiled at their Black partners less than did other White students.

Graumann and Wintermantel (1989) have proposed that speech (verbal acts) is an important but understudied domain in the investigation of interpersonal or "social" discrimination, which they define in terms of separation, distancing, accentuation of differences, and devaluing. For example, "members of a majority group may try to avoid close or personal contact with members of the minority, refuse to communicate with them directly or, if they have to deal with them, deny them equal standing and . . . [keep them] at a social distance." Thus, social discrimination, they argue, can be "actualized by doing something or refraining from doing something" (p. 184). Figure 2.3 graphically presents different categories for acts of social discrimination that these theorists assert can occur without noticeable prejudice.

DISTANCING RESPONSES TO WOMEN

The studies cited above support the proposition that distancing behavior is a widely used operational definition of interpersonal discrimination. But are distancing responses made more often to women than to men? The evidence suggests that this is generally the case. Pedersen and Sabin (1982), for example, found that college students who were approached for a brief survey when standing alone were more likely to move away from a woman than from a man. In an earlier field investigation (Barefoot, Hoople, & McClay, 1972), male students had been watched as they drank from water fountains when either a male or female confederate sat some distance away. When the confederate was a woman, a greater percentage of men were observed to drink farther away from her than closer to her. In two experiments (Zinkhan & Stoiadin, 1984; Stead & Zinkhan, 1986), mixed-gender pairs of confederates approached store clerks in different departments at the same time, and it was found that the man was served before the woman twice as often as the reverse. Other studies of clerk behavior have obtained similar results. For example, clerks in 576 small neighborhood groceries were observed to behave less positively to women than to men, both verbally and nonverbally (Rafaeli, 1989). One study utilizing an indirect measure (Bleda, Bleda, Byrne, & White, 1976) found that women were more likely than men to be reported as cheaters by college students working on a laboratory task. Another investigator (Buczek, 1986) found that a sample of students who heard audiotapes of clients interacting with a counselor recalled significantly less information about female than about male clients.

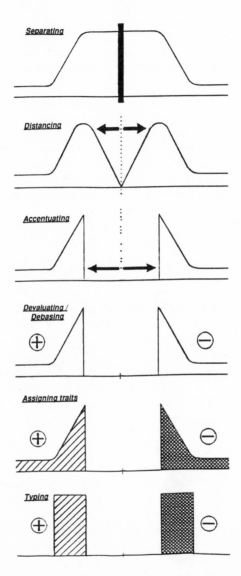

FIGURE 2.3. Functions of social discrimination suggested by Graumann and Wintermantel (1989, p. 185). The symbols + and − denote positive and negative, respectively. For each function of social discrimination, the distance between figures indicates the outcome; for example, "assigning traits" results in two clearly separated categories. The left half refers to one's "own" group and the right half to the "other" group.

A sizable literature has focused on judgments about the competence of women (see B. Lott, 1985a). Although many of these studies have utilized dependent measures that assess beliefs rather than overt behaviors, some have required respondents to make judgments with clear behavior implications, such as whether or not someone should be hired for a particular job. The devaluation of women's competence is a phenomenon that has been documented in a wide range of research settings; it is predictable from women's generally lower status in our society and our tendency to use status as a general or diffuse cue in making a variety of judgments, particularly in mixed-gender settings and in the absence of more specific information (Berger, Rosenholtz, & Zelditch, 1980; Carli, 1991). An example of the influence of status on judgments about women and men comes from a study by Banaji and Greenwald (1993) in which participants were first exposed to a list of names, half of women and half of men, half famous and half nonfamous; then, 2 days later, the participants were shown a new list consisting of all the previous names and an equal number of new names, and asked to judge each as famous or not. The authors found both that male names were more likely to be correctly identified as famous than female names, and that male names from the first list were more likely to be incorrectly identified as famous than female names. These findings were replicated in three experiments, with participants of both genders.

Some studies have reported different reactions to female and to male leaders. For example, Butler and Geis (1990), who assessed nonverbal responses, found that "female leaders [in four-person laboratory groups] received fewer pleased responses and more displeased responses from . . . group members than male leaders offering the same contributions . . . [and] Female leaders received more negative than positive responses compared to male leaders" (p. 54). Similarly, a study of reactions to leaders (Morrison & Stein, 1985) in a natural situation in which respondents participated in group training sessions found that male leaders were rated higher in competence and were more highly valued than female leaders. Focusing on the evaluation of leaders in laboratory studies involving primarily written descriptions of leaders, a meta-analysis of 61 investigations (Eagly, Makhijani, & Klonsky, 1992) found that there was a small tendency for women leaders to be evaluated more negatively than men, but that this tendency "to favor male leaders was stronger on the more general evaluative measures (i.e., perception of leader's competence and satisfaction with leader)" (p. 14). In addition, men respondents were found to be more likely than women to indicate greater valuation of men leaders. From another meta-analysis of 19 experiments, this time examining the impact of applicant gender on hiring recommendations (Olian, Schwab, & Haberfield, 1988), it was concluded that a preference for men over women in these laboratory studies was significant.

With respect to judgments of women and men in nonleadership roles, two reviews of the literature (Swim, Borgida, Maruyama, & Myers, 1989; Top, 1991) concluded that there is little or no overall tendency for men's products or performance to be evaluated more positively than women's. This conclusion, however, is questionable. The review by Top (1991) was of studies in which, according to the author, "the evaluations were without any consequences" (p. 103). The review by Swim et al. (1989) was primarily of studies using college student raters, and, even among these raters, there was a greater likelihood of positive responses to men in those experiments using resumés or applications as stimulus materials; this suggests that such bias is more likely to be manifested when the ratings are associated with potentially important decisions. We also know that even when oral or written evaluations are positive, they may not predict behavior in real situations. For example, in a study of 651 employees in five different companies (Gupta, Jenkins, & Beehr, 1983), it was found that regardless of how their work had been evaluated, women received the fewest promotions and men subordinates of men supervisors received the most frequent pay raises. A qualitative review of evaluations of women's competence (B. Lott, 1985a) suggested to me that women's competence is least likely to be devalued by college students doing simulated tasks and by persons who are actually familiar with the women and their work, whereas it is most likely to be devalued in realistic contexts by respondents such as personnel officers or employers, whose judgments may have some real consequences.

Some researchers have proposed that in the mass media, women are "symbolically annihilated" by underrepresentation and trivialization and by less facial prominence in photographs as compared to men. A study of four popular magazines from 1970 to 1984 (Nigro, Hill, Gelbein, & Clark, 1988) verified the hypothesis that facial prominence (the ratio of head size to body size) was consistently greater in men's photographs than in women's; in only one magazine, in 1980, was facial prominence in women's photos equal to that in men's. A later study (Zuckerman & Kieffer, 1994) confirmed the greater prominence of men's faces in four popular news magazines from January 1988 to January 1992 and on U.S. postage stamps.

In the studies mentioned above, distancing-related responses to women and men were examined or compared, but not the interaction between gender of respondents and gender of target persons. There are only a few investigations in which both gender of the actor and gender of the stimulus person have been treated as independent variables. The prediction from my model of sexism is that in relatively neutral situations men will be more likely to distance themselves from a woman than from a man, whereas women will not respond differentially on the basis of gender. Investigations that relate to this question and support the proposition have used a variety of dependent measures. For example, Gelfand, Hartmann, Walder, and Page (1973) had a female confederate in a field experiment act as a shoplifter in two drugstores, and found that twice as many men as women shoppers who had observed the incidents reported it to a store employee. In a very different setting, a laboratory study of mixed-gender dyads (Dovidio, Brown, Heltman, Ellyson, & Keating, 1988), men discussing a topic considered gender-neutral (vegetable gardening) were found to look at their women partners significantly less when their partners were speaking than was true of women with men partners. Another study (Hoffman, Tsuneyoshi, Ebina, & Fite, 1984), using speech as a measure of interpersonal behavior, randomly assigned college students to work in pairs on a drawing task with either a 9-year-old girl or a 9-year-old boy. Although the women participants did not respond differently to girls and boys on any of the dependent measures, the men were found to have spoken significantly less to girls than to boys. In an earlier investigation, Mathews and Cooper (1976) had pairs of same-gender and mixed-gender students participate in a teacher–learner task in which the teacher was instructed to provide false feedback to the learner. The results indicated that men lied to women more than was true for any other pairing.

Examination of data reported by Griffith, Sell, and Parker (1993) from a laboratory study of the allocation of rewards revealed an important difference between the behavior of women and men in dealing with same- and other-gender partners. Among allocators who had performed well on the laboratory task, men gave considerably more rewards to men partners than to women partners, whereas women rewarded same- and other-gender partners similarly. Finally, suggestive data have been reported by Hall (1984) on the contents of dreams studied across the world. He found in 29 of 35 samples that men reported dreaming more frequently about men than about women, whereas women reported dreaming equally of both; his findings led him to conclude that this difference occurs "on every continent; in a diversity of cultures . . . ; in all age groups; in dreams collected in the laboratory, in the classroom, and in the field by many different investigators over a period of 30 years" (p. 1115).

APPROACH RESPONSES TO WOMEN

Are there situations in which men tend to approach, and not to distance themselves from, women? Studies of the behavior of persons who enter the personal space of another in order to achieve some particular objective have generally reported that women's space is more likely to be intruded upon than men's, supporting the hypothesis of Henley (1977) that high-status persons are more likely to invade the personal space of persons in subordinate positions than vice versa. In one example of such a study (Buchanan, Juhnke, & Goldman, 1976), male and female confederates positioned themselves in front of the right and left selection panels on an elevator in a large office building, and it was found that men were more likely to violate the space of a woman than that of a man in order to press their floor button. Hall (1987) noted that studies using staged or projective measures tended to find that women were accorded smaller distances than men, but Stier and Hall (1984), who reviewed over 40 observational studies, reported no overall tendency for men to touch women more than for women to touch men. This conclusion is supported by the findings of a subsequent study in which pairs of persons were observed interacting in public places (Hall & Veccia, 1990).

It is to be expected, as noted earlier in this chapter, that touch and other approach behaviors will be dominant responses by men to women in certain situations. These should be ones in which approach behavior will be followed by positive consequences—satisfaction or pleasure, particularly from sexual stimulation, nurturance, or power enhancement. The important influence of power on social behavior is recognized and emphasized by feminist and other scholars. Wartenberg (1992), for example, notes "the failure of previous accounts of power to fully comprehend the role of power in the shaping of human life" (p. xi). Taking men's greater power into account in understanding interpersonal behavior leads to the expectation that where the reinforcement of this power can be achieved by touch or other approach behaviors, such behaviors may be stronger than avoidance or distancing. If by approaching a woman, a man can demonstrate to her, to himself, and/or to onlookers that he is "in charge," then such behaviors are likely.

Men have certainly learned to approach women with the expectation of nurturance or the expectation of sexual pleasure. In addition, men expect women to serve them reproductively (Dworkin, 1983; Tong, 1989). As argued by Janssen-Jurreit (1982), men need women in order to reproduce, and in both older and contemporary societies, fatherhood conveys the mark of manhood and gives meaning to life. Thus, there are significant rewards for men that are contingent upon reducing distance from, or approaching, women. In addition, for individual men interacting with individual women, particular and situation-based positive consequences may influence approach. Nevertheless, it is here proposed that in the absence of conditions in which positive consequences are expected (i.e., in relatively neutral situations), the dominant response toward women is one of exclusion, separation, and distancing. Although men can be expected to respond to women with a variety of approach behaviors under appropriate conditions, under relatively neutral circumstances men are more apt to avoid, withdraw, and separate themselves from women than from men, whereas women's distancing responses to women and men will not differ. With the assistance of students and colleagues, several investigations that test this general proposition have now been completed.

EMPIRICAL EVIDENCE

A Laboratory Demonstration

In the first study (B. Lott, 1987), the behavior of a sample of 80 European-American women and men college students toward same-gender and other-gender partners with whom they had no prior acquaintance was compared in a laboratory setting in which they participated in a domino construction contest. Each pair of same-gender or mixed-gender partici-pants was instructed to work together for 10 minutes and jointly build a structure with dominos (as they used to do "when they were children"). In this relatively neutral, task-focused situation, self-report paper-and-pencil measures did not reveal bias against other-gender partners in feelings or beliefs on the part of either women or men. However, the observations of trained observers (naïve about the hypothesis) who watched the pairs behind a one-way-vision window indicated that men more frequently made negative statements and turned away from their partners when the partners were women than when they were men, and that men also less frequently followed the advice of women partners than that of men part-ners. For the women, on the other hand, partner gender made no difference with respect to any of the measured behaviors. An additional, unantici-pated finding was that the domino structures built by mixed-gender pairs were significantly more often closer to the man than to the woman. This serendipitous result provides a kind of concrete, physical illustration of men's tendency to distance themselves from women.

In this study, no differences would have been found between men's responses to women and to other men if the data gathered had been restricted to self-reports of feelings and beliefs. Such measures did not reveal prejudice or stereotypes. Only observation of behavior revealed significant differences in the way men responded to men partners and to women partners, but no such differences in the behavior of women. These findings underscore the theoretical and practical necessity of separating the overt behavioral compo-nent of sexism from both the affective and cognitive.

A Study of Prime-Time Television

In a second study (B. Lott, 1989), 53 trained college student observers watched the behavior of women and men TV characters in face-to-face interaction with same- and other-gender persons on the television screen in episodes of weekly dramatic or comedy shows. If sexism is a dominant feature of present U.S. society, one would expect to find it reflected in the mass media which communicate to us so much about U.S. culture's ideology. It has been amply demonstrated that television in particular, in both programming and advertising, reinforces and perpetuates gender stereotypes (Bretl & Cantor, 1988; Davis, 1990; Liebert, Sprafkin, & Davidson, 1982; Steenland, 1988). But do the characters behave in ways that also illustrate the discrimination component of sexism? Do men, in other words, tend to be shown distancing or separating themselves from women?

To answer this question, women and men characters in 10 prime-time TV programs (found to be most popular with a sample of eighth graders) were observed interacting with same- and other-gender persons, and the frequency of distancing behaviors (as well as that of positive approach and aggressive approach behaviors) was recorded. Observers (naïve about the hypothesis) were preassigned on a random basis to watch four programs; for each program, the gender of the character to be observed was also preassigned. During the first segment of each TV program, the observer chose a character of the preassigned gender who was then monitored in interaction with other persons during the second 10- to 12-minute segment. Records of behavior were restricted to interactions between the focused-upon character and any single person. As predicted, men TV characters were observed more frequently to distance themselves from women than from men, whereas distancing responses by women TV characters were not related to the gender of the person they were with.

Individual Difference Correlates of Distancing Behavior

To assume that all men behave identically with respect to women would, of course, contradict human experience. One important objective, therefore, is to identify predictors or correlates of individual differences in men's distancing responses to women. One obvious approach is to relate measures of this behavior to the other components of sexism—that is, to measures of attitudes and/or beliefs.

In an effort to investigate connections among variables and to identify individual differences, a measure of simulated distancing behavior was developed, the Photo Choice Task (PCT). This task requires a participant to choose, from pairs of photographs of European-American middle-aged adults, the one who is preferred for a particular interaction. Participants respond to a series of 24 cards, each of which contains the photographs of two adults previously judged by a sample of raters as being of moderate and relatively equal attractiveness. Each card presents a question beginning with "Who would you choose . . . ," and the respondent is asked to select from the two photographs the person who is preferred. Eight sets of three cards present eight different service interactions (e.g., "Who would you choose as your real estate agent?", " . . . to elect to city council?", " . . . to ask for directions?"). For each different service interaction (relatively non-stereotyped by gender) there are three different cards—one showing the photographs of two women, one showing two men, and one card showing a woman and a man. Thus, on 8 of the 24 cards each respondent must make a choice between persons of different gender. (Twenty-two sets of the 24 cards are available, each containing the photographs of 48 different persons in completely randomized orders. An expanded PCT has since been developed that includes African-American faces; Maluso, 1992.)

Using these materials with a sample of 262 European-American respondents, my colleagues and I (B. Lott, Lott, & Fernald, 1990) found a predicted relationship between the number of men chosen over women on the PCT and the gender of the chooser, as well as a signifcant relationship between PCT choices of men over women and scores on measures of adversarial sex beliefs and sex stereotyping (Burt, 1980). Two samples of men, one under 30 and the other over 30, both chose more men over women on the PCT than would be expected by chance, while the choices of men by women over 30 were no different from chance, as predicted. The choices of men by women under 30, however, were at less than chance levels—possibly because, as persons preparing for careers, they were more sensitive to issues of job discrimination. Of additional interest is that when high, moderate, and low PCT scorers were compared, they were found to differ significantly in average score on both of the belief measures in the expected direction: The greater the choice of men over women on the PCT, the greater the respondent's adherence to adversarial sex beliefs and to sex role stereotypes. The same pattern of individual differences was found among women as among men, although the pattern was stronger for men.

These findings contribute to our knowledge about relationships between the cognitive and behavioral components of sexism and to our knowledge of individual differences. Other variables related to individual differences in distancing from women remain to be identified and investigated—variables pertaining both to persons and to situations.

A Field Experiment

Diane Maluso (1989) attempted to test the hypothesis of greater distancing by men toward women than toward other men in a natural field setting, and discovered the difficulty of assuming the existence of neutral conditions in real-life contexts. She had naïve observers watch women and men who, on their way to the university library, passed a table at which cards were being distributed. On the table was a large sign that read "URI

Descriptive Statistics," a similar sign reading "URI Background Information," or both signs. And handing out cards was either a woman undergraduate, a man undergraduate, or both. Careful counts were made of persons who stopped to take a card, and from whom, by gender. It was predicted that men would be most likely to take a card from a man than from a woman in the condition where there appeared to be a choice between different cards (or different surveys), since this would provide a situation in which discrimination could be masked. This testing strategy was adapted from Snyder et al. (1979), who investigated reactions to physically handicapped persons. What Maluso found was that the gender of the person handing out the card did indeed matter significantly more to men than to women, but in the reverse direction from what had been predicted: Men approached and picked up more cards from women than from men. Importantly, however, the variable of choice (between cards) mediated the findings only for men, as expected. Gender of the hander-outer made the most difference to men when a man and a woman were standing next to two different signs and presumably handing out different cards; it made the least difference where there was only one person handing out cards (either a woman or a man); with the two-person, one-sign condition falling in between. For the women, as predicted, gender of the hander-outer made no difference and did not influence their behavior. We suspect that the men in this study, the vast majority of whom were university undergraduates, discriminated in favor of women because sexual cues associated with gender remained, despite careful efforts to eliminate sexual cues by having the stimulus persons dress neutrally (simply, without jewelry, etc.).

A Train Station Study

In an investigation by Saris, Johnston, and Lott (in press), equal numbers of adult women and men sitting alone were approached randomly at four different train stations (two in Rhode Island and two in Connecticut) by either a female or male college student wearing a T-shirt that read either "Support University of Rhode Island Athletics" or "Support the Equal Rights Amendment" to create a $2 \times 2 \times 2$ design. The total of 240 participants were of various ages and ethnic backgrounds, with 40 in each of six different experimental conditions. Three women and three men college students were trained to approach participants, who were asked to fill out a questionnaire that included two simulated distance measures and a measure of attitudes toward egalitarian sex roles (Larsen & Long, 1988), which also contained filler items from a political ideology scale.

A Seating Measure, devised by the investigators, presents seven hypothetical situations, each involving a row of six seats in which four are empty while the second and fifth seats are occupied. In two rows the seats are occupied by two women (Rhoda and Julia), in two other rows by two men (Roger and James), and in three rows by a woman and a man. Participants are asked to place themselves in each row. Six of the hypothetical situations are considered sexually neutral (e.g., "You are in a diner and plan to order lunch," "You are at an airport terminal waiting for your flight") and are counterbalanced so that each situation appears with each possible gender combination. The seventh item, "You are in a bar and plan to order a drink," always presents Julia and Roger in the occupied seats and, as an item with probable sexual cues, is analyzed separately for comparison purposes. A Movie Choice Measure, also devised by the investigators, contains seven items in which the respondent is presented with a choice between two movies of different types (adventure, comedy, documentary, or drama). Each movie choice also involves placing oneself in a row of three seats, the first one of which is already occupied. For two items, the choice is between two movies where women are already seated; for two other items, both movie choices involve sitting near a man; and for three items, the choice is between a movie where a woman is already seated and a movie where a man is already seated.

Distancing was measured by counting the number of times a respondent chose to sit near a man instead of a woman in the five opportunities there were to do so (two from the Seating Measure and three from the Movie Choice Measure). Gender of respondent was found to have a significant influence on the seating choices made by men. For women respondents, as predicted, gender of the persons already seated in the hypothetical situations did not influence where they chose to sit. Almost half of the women chose to sit next to a man two out of five times, which was the median score for the total group of respondents. (The median was influenced by the unexpected statistically significant popularity of the name "Julia.") Men's choices, on the other hand, were influenced by gender of the persons seated. Most men were in the extreme categories; that is, they chose to sit near a man rather than near a woman either three or more times (above the median), or one or zero times (below the median). The influence of T-shirt and investigator gender were found only in combination and only for men respondents: The largest number of men distanced themselves from women on the simulated measures in the presence of a man investitgator who was wearing an ERA T-shirt.

In this study, the men differed from the women in having responded more extremely to the cue of gender—findings similar to those obtained in the field experiment by Maluso described above. When the women and men in this study were compared on just the proportions in the median score category, the difference between these proportions (.41 for women, .25 for men) was found to be statistically significant. Another indicator of the significance of gender as a cue for men's behavior came from examination of responses to the bar situation in the Seating Measure. Among the men, 65% chose to sit near a woman; in comparison, 50% of the women chose to sit near a woman and 50% near a man.

The results of the train station study support the conclusion that men are less likely to react neutrally to women than women are to men, with some tending to approach and others to distance. That the men who made simulated approach responses to women in this study were likely to be responding to women as sexual cues is suggested by the responses to the bar situation and by the findings of a sizable number of studies that men tend to ascribe more sexual meaning than women do to a variety of situations and behaviors. This has been reported for a sample of adolescents (Zellman, Johnson, Giarusso, & Goodchilds, 1979), as well as for samples of college students (Abbey, 1982; Abbey & Melby, 1986; Johnson, Stockdale, & Saal, 1991). One group of investigators (Saal, Johnson, & Weber, 1989), using three different methods, concluded that "men's 'thresholds'" for perceiving or attributing sexuality "may be reached more easily . . . than women's thresholds" (p. 275). Kowalski (1993), in a study of a large sample of college students, found corroborating evidence that men were more likely than women to see "mundane behaviors" such as smiling and eye contact as sexual in connotation, and that this was most true of men who endorsed traditional gender beliefs (stereotypes, adversarial sex relations, and rape myths). In the train study, however, when the respondents were divided into three groups on the basis of their distancing behavior—that is, those who distanced themselves from women (chose men above the median score), those who scored at the median, and those who approached women (chose men less than the median number)—no significant differences were found in scores on a measure of sex-role traditionality among the three groups of men or the three groups of women.

CONCLUSIONS

Considerable evidence supports the proposition that in current U.S. mainstream culture, gender is a more powerful cue for men's behavior than for women's. Men tend to approach women in situations appearing to have sexual, nurturant, or power-enhancing possibilities; men tend to distance themselves from women in relatively neutral situations. Men who distance from women have been found in some studies to be somewhat more likely than other men to adhere to sex role stereotypes, to self-report adversarial sex beliefs, and not to favor gender equality.

It may well be that experiencing and observing men's typical reactions constitute a major area of commonality among women. It is often noted that the search for "sameness" among women typically fails—a not surprising outcome, as MacKinnon (1989, p. 38) has pointed out in the face of "individual uniqueness, profound diversity (such as race and class), time, and place." But women in sexist cultures do share the conditions of low status and low power, as well as of men's typical responses to them. Of particular significance in women's lives may be those responses that define interpersonal sexist discrimination—responses that are likely to be the source of a wide range of negative experiences.

Nonetheless, despite the evidence presented in this chapter in support of a conceptualization of interpersonal sexist discrimination in terms of distancing behavior, we must be cautious about generalizing beyond the samples that have provided confirming evidence. These samples have been composed overwhelmingly, although not exclusively, of middle-class European-Americans. It is essential to determine whether it is only, or primarily, White men in the United States who have learned to "do gender" (display their manliness) by distancing from women, and whether it is only, or primarily, White women in the United States who tend to experience such reactions from men in relatively neutral situations.

Although some of the findings cited in this chapter, from studies of men in other countries, suggest similarity in the behaviors directed toward women in sexist societies, it is to be expected that cultural differences in the definitions of woman and man will be accompanied by differences in behaviors that are most linked to these definitions. It is well known, in addition, that cultures differ in degree of gender inequality, in men's power relative to women's, and in general sexism; these differences suggest that not all men everywhere will tend to distance themselves from women in neutral situations. The data presented in Chapter 7 of this volume by Landrine, Klonoff, Alcaraz, Scott, and Wilkins, from an exploratory study of one popular TV situation comedy featuring African-American actors, indicate that Black women may distance themselves more from Black men (and respond more aggressively to them) than Black men to Black women. Although these data are limited and very preliminary, they are certainly provocative.

Also pointing to the need for caution in generalizing from limited cultural samples are data from older societies. A study of the Mukogodo people of central Kenya (Cronk, 1993), for example, reveals a culture in which parents favor their daughters, not their sons. Although such "female-biased parental favoritism is very rare" (p. 272), a few other societies do exhibit it (e.g., the Kanjar people of Pakistan and northern India). Cronk argues that Mukogodo daughters are favored because they are more likely than sons to enhance the economic status of their families through bride price payments, and because they are more likely to marry (because their brothers are too poor to make such payments) and thus to have children. Evidence of this favoritism includes the more frequent taking of daughters than sons to health clinics by their parents and the longer time that daughters are breast-fed. It is of particular interest that Cronk's examples of favoritism, as he points out, focus "on the behavior of the parents. . . . Despite their behavior, most Mukogodo mothers claim to prefer sons rather than daughters. . . . [Thus] the Mukogodos' statements clearly do not reflect their behavior" (p. 279).

In an effort to examine experiences of men's distancing behavior among a sample of contemporary U.S. women differing in age, ethnicity, and income level, Therese Doyon, Karen Asquith, and I have asked samples of women of color and European-American women, aged over 35 and under 35, to respond to a number of questions on self-administered surveys. These questions deal with the frequency with which they find men turning away from them or excluding them, who the men are, the situations in which such behaviors occur, their experiences of sexist discrimination in general areas, and how they have responded to sexist treatment. This investigation is part of a necessary effort to identify cultural parameters for the issues raised in this chapter. Preliminary results suggest far more similarities than differences in reported experiences.

IMPLICATIONS FOR THE REAL WORLD
AND SOCIAL POLICY

If sexist behavior in actual or simulated interpersonal situations is only sometimes predictable from what men say they believe or feel about women, and must therefore be independently observed, then programs to change behavior must provide for the separate assessment of actions, attitudes, and cognitions, and must include planned strategies appropriate for each domain. Variables found to relate significantly to the increased (and decreased) probability of distancing responses to women will help us to understand how such behavior is learned and maintained, and will assist us in teaching what we know to others. We will need to study separately each of the components of sexism to understand their acquisition and maintenance, and to investigate the influence of situational or contextual factors on correlations among them.

With respect to the behavioral component, for example, it is to be expected that distancing or exclusion will vary with antecedent conditions, situational contexts, and individual differences. The general tendency for men to distance themselves from women should be more evident under some conditions and on the part of some men than others. From studies that will identify variables related to sexist discrimination can come suggestions for how change can be effected. For example, it is probable that boys and men who observe other boys and men displaying approach rather than avoidance behavior toward women in a variety of situations will behave similarly. It is also probable that boys and men who receive verbal encouragement and other positive reinforcement for displaying approach rather than avoidance behavior toward women will tend to repeat such behavior. Such findings would suggest clear strategies for change. Another strategy might involve simply "raising the consciousness" of men by sharing the results of investigations such as those reported in this chapter and/or exposing men to videotapes of their own behavior in face-to-face interactions with women in neutral situations.

Taking such a step-by-step approach to a major social problem like sexism permits us to concentrate on "small wins," and may temper the tendency to feel that our research is trivial in comparison to the complexity of such a vast, multifaceted issue. I agree with Weick (1984) that one reason social problems are so difficult to solve is that "people define these problems in ways that overwhelm their ability to do anything about them. Changing the scale of a problem can change the quality of resources directed at it" (p. 48). If we examine a social problem in terms of a series of small tasks that can be accomplished, then it may present itself as amenable to change by less than superhuman effort. Such an objective motivates the research program I have described.

It seems clear that public policy decisions based only on what men report they feel or believe about women may prove to be faulty if what men do in the presence of women reveals sexist discrimination while prejudice and stereotyped beliefs are not revealed by other measures. Observations of behavior, although costly and difficult, must be added to any body of evidence on which political, economic, and social decisions are made. Further, if we are concerned about eradicating sexism, we must plan programs directed toward changing actions as well as feelings and beliefs, and make sure that each component is independently assessed. Separating overt behavior from attitudes and beliefs is theoretically sound and empirically necessary, and it also increases the probability that we will understand more clearly and simply the conditions that influence each. This, in turn, should help us to make thoughtful and realistic suggestions about ways to improve social life.

ACKNOWLEDGMENTS

This chapter was largely completed while I was a visiting scholar at the Institute for Research on Women and Gender, Stanford University, during the winter and spring quarters of 1993. The nurturing and hospitable environment of the institute, and the helpful comments of my colleagues, are gratefully acknowledged. Earlier versions were presented at colloquia at the psychology departments of Yale University, the University of California at Berkeley, Stanford University, and the University of Rhode Island.

REFERENCES

Abbey, A. (1982). Sex differences in attributions for friendly behavior: Do males misperceive females' friendliness? *Journal of Personality and Social Psychology*, 42, 830–838.

Abbey, A., & Melby, C. (1986). The effects of nonverbal cues on gender differences in perceptions of sexual intent. *Sex Roles, 15*, 283–298.

Allen, K. R., & Baber, K. M. (1992). Ethical and epistemological tensions in applying a postmodern perspective to feminist research. *Psychology of Women Quarterly*, 16, 1–15.

Allgeier, A. R., & Byrne, D. (1973). Attraction toward the opposite sex as a determinant of physical proximity. *Journal of Social Psychology*, 90, 213–219.

Allport, G. W. (1954). *The nature of prejudice.* Reading, MA: Addison-Wesley.

Aron, A., Aron, E. N., & Smollan, D. (1992). Inclusion of Other in the Self Scale and the structure of interpersonal closeness. *Journal of Personality and Social Psychology, 63*, 596–612.

Banaji, M. R., & Greenwald, A. G. (1994). Implicit stereotyping and prejudice. In M. P. Zanna & J. M. Olson (Eds.), *The psychology of prejudice: The Ontario symposium. Vol. 7* (pp. 55–76). Hillsdale, NJ: Erlbaum.

Barefoot, J. C., Hoople, H., & McClay, D. (1972). Avoidance of an act which would violate personal space. *Psychonomic Science, 28*, 205–206.

Bell, P. A., Kline, L. M., & Barnard, W. A. (1988). Friendship and freedom of movement as moderators of sex differences in interpersonal distancing. *Journal of Social Psychology, 128*, 305–310.

Bem, D. J. (1972). Self-perception theory. In L. Berkowitz (Ed.), *Advances in experimental social psychology* (Vol. 6, pp. 1–62). New York: Academic Press.

Bennett, J. B., & Green, M. (1983). The subtler side of sexism. *Educational Record*, 64(1), 58–60.

Berger, J., Rosenholtz, S. J., & Zelditch, M. Jr. (1980). Status organizing processes. *Annual Review of Sociology, 6*, 479–508.

Bleda, P. R., Bleda, S. E., Byrne, D., & White, L. A. (1976). When a bystander becomes an accomplice: Situational determinants of reactions to dishonesty. *Journal of Experimental Social Psychology, 12*, 9–25.

Bogardus, E. (1925). Measuring social distance. *Journal of Applied Sociology, 9*, 299–308.

Breckler, S. J. (1984). Empirical validation of affect, behavior and cognition as distinct components of attitudes. *Journal of Personality and Social Psychology, 47*, 1191–1205.

Bretl, D. J., & Cantor, J. (1988). The portrayal of men and women in U.S. television commercials. *Sex Roles, 18*, 595–609.

Buchanan, D. R., Juhnke, R., & Goldman, M. (1976). Violation of personal space as a function of sex. *Journal of Social Psychology, 99*, 187–192.

Buczek, T. A. (1986). A promising measure of sex bias: The incidental memory task. *Psychology of Women Quarterly, 10*, 127–139.

Burt, M. R. (1980). Cultural myths and supports for rape. *Journal of Personality and Social Psychology, 38*, 217–230.

Bussey, K., & Perry, D. G. (1982). Same-sex imitation: The avoidance of cross-sex models or the acceptance of same-sex models? *Sex Roles, 8*, 773–784.

Butler, D., & Geis, F. L. (1990). Nonverbal affect responses to male and female leaders: Implications for leadership evaluations. *Journal of Personality and Social Psychology, 58*, 48–59.

Carli, L. L. (1991). Gender, status, and influence. *Advances in Group Processes, 8*, 89–113.

Cronk, L. (1993). Parental favoritism toward daughters. *American Scientist, 81*, 272–279.

Crosby, F., Bromley, S., & Saxe, L. (1980). Recent unobtrusive studies of black and white discrimination and prejudice: A literature review. *Psychological Bulletin, 87*, 546–563.

Davis, D. M. (1990). Portrayals of women in prime-time network television: Some demographic characteristics. *Sex Roles, 23*, 325–332.

Deaux, K., & Kite, M. (1993). Gender stereotypes. In F. L. Denmark & M. A. Paludi (Eds.), *Psychology of women: A handbook of issues and theories* (pp. 107–139). Westport, CT: Greenwood Press.

Del Boca, F. K., Ashmore, R. D., & McManus, M. A. (1986). Gender–related attitudes. In R. D. Ashmore & F. K. Del Boca (Eds.), *The social psychology of female–male relations: A critical analysis of central concepts* (pp. 121–163). Orlando, FL: Academic Press.

Devine, P. G. (1989). Stereotypes and prejudice: Their automatic and controlled components. *Journal of Personality and Social Psychology, 56*, 5–18.

DiLeonardo, M. (1991). Introduction: Gender, culture, and political economy. In M. DiLeonardo (Ed.), *Gender at the crossroads of knowledge* (pp. 1–48). Berkeley: University of California Press.

Doob, L. W. (1947). The behavior of attitudes. *Psychological Review, 54*, 135–156.

Dovidio, J. F., Brown, C. E., Heltman, K., Ellyson, S. L., & Keating, C. F. (1988). Power displays between women and men in discussions of gender-linked tasks: A multi-channel study. *Journal of Personality and Social Psychology, 55*, 580–587.

Dworkin, A. (1983). *Right-wing women*. New York: Perigee.

Eagly, A. H. (1992). Uneven progress: Social psychology and the study of attitudes. *Journal of Personality and Social Psychology, 63*, 693–710.

Eagly, A. H., & Chaiken, S. (1993). *The psychology of attitudes*. Orlando, FL: Harcourt Brace Jovanovich.

Eagly, A. H., Makhijani, M. G., & Klonsky, B. G. (1992). Gender and the evaluation of leaders: A meta-analysis. *Psychological Bulletin, 111*, 3–22.

Eagly, A. H., & Mladinic, A. (1994). Some answers from research on attitudes, gender stereotypes, and judgments of competence. In W. Stroebe & M. Hewstone (Eds.), *European review of social psychology* (pp. 1–35). New York: Wiley.

Eagly, A. H., Mladinic, A., & Otto, S. (1991). Are women evaluated more favorably than men? An analysis of attitudes, beliefs, and emotions. *Psychology of Women Quarterly, 15*, 203–216.

Edwards, K. (1990). The interplay of affect and cognition in attitude formation and change. *Journal of Personality and Social Psychology, 59*, 202–216.

Evans, G. W., & Howard, R. B. (1973). Personal space. *Psychological Bulletin, 80*, 334–344.

Feagin, J. R., & Feagin, C. B. (1978). *Discrimination American style: Institutional racism and sexism.* Englewood Cliffs, NJ: Prentice-Hall.

Ferguson, K. E. (1993). *The man question: Visions of subjectivity in feminist theory.* Berkeley: University of California Press.

Geffner, R., & Gross, M. M. (1984). Sex-role behavior and obedience to authority: A field study. *Sex Roles, 10,* 973–985.

Gelfand, D. M., Hartmann, D. P., Walder, P., & Page, B. (1973). Who reports shoplifters? A field–experimental study. *Journal of Personality and Social Psychology, 25,* 276–285.

Gifford, R. (1982). Projected interpersonal distance and orientation choices: Personality, sex, and social situation. *Social Psychology Quarterly, 45,* 145–152.

Goffman, E. (1979). *Gender advertisements.* New York: Harper & Row.

Graff, E. J. (1993, October 17). The double-bed principle. *New York Times Magazine,* pp. 14, 16.

Graumann, C. F., & Wintermantel, M. (1989). Discriminating speech acts: A functional approach. In D. Bar-Tal, C. F. Graumann, A. W. Kruglanski, & W. Storebe (Eds.), *Stereotyping and prejudice: Changing conceptions* (pp. 183–206). New York: Springer-Verlag.

Griffith, W. I., Sell, J., & Parker, M. J. (1993). Self-interested versus third-party allocations of rewards. *Social Psychology Quarterly, 56,* 148–155.

Gupta, N., Jenkins, G. D. Jr., & Beehr, T. A. (1983). Employee gender, gender similarity, and supervisor–subordinate cross-evaluations. *Psychology of Women Quarterly, 8,* 174–184.

Hall, C. S. (1984). "A ubiquitous sex difference in dreams" revisited. *Journal of Personality and Social Psychology, 46,* 1109–1117.

Hall, J. A. (1987). On explaining gender differences: The case of nonverbal communication. In P. Shaver & C. Hendrick (Eds.), *Sex and gender* (pp. 177–200). Beverly Hills, CA: Sage.

Hall, J. A., & Veccia, E. M. (1990). More "touching" observations: New insights on men, women, and interpersonal touch. *Journal of Personality and Social Psychology, 59,* 1155–1162.

Hare-Mustin, R. T., & Marecek, J. (1990). Gender and the meaning of difference: Postmodernism and psychology. In R. T. Hare-Mustin & J. Marecek (Eds.), *Making a difference: Psychology and the construction of gender* (pp. 22–64). New Haven: Yale University Press.

Hendricks, M., & Bootzin, R. (1976). Race and sex as stimuli for negative affect and physical avoidance. *Journal of Social Psychology, 98,* 111–120.

Henley, N. M. (1977). *Body politics.* Englewood Cliffs, NJ: Prentice-Hall.

Heshka, S., & Nelson, Y. (1972). Interpersonal speaking distance as a function of age, sex, and relationship. *Sociometry, 35,* 491–498.

Hoffman, C. D., Tsuneyoshi, S. E., Ebina, M., & Fite, H. (1984). A comparison of adult males' and females' interactions with girls and boys. *Sex Roles, 11,* 799–811.

Ickes, W. (1984). Compositions in black and white: Determinants of interaction in interracial dyads. *Journal of Personality and Social Psychology, 47,* 330–341.

Janssen-Jurreit, M. (1982). *Sexism: The male monopoly on history and thought.* New York: Farrar Straus Giroux.

Johnson, C. B., Stockdale, M. S., & Saal, F. E. (1991). Persistence of men's misperceptions of friendly cues across a variety of interpersonal encounters. *Psychology of Women Quarterly, 15,* 463–475.

Kahn, A. (1984). The power war: Male response to power loss under equality. *Psychology of Women Quarterly, 8,* 234–247.

Kellerman, J., Lewis, J., & Laird, J. D. (1989). Looking and loving: The effects of mutual gaze on feelings of romantic love. *Journal of Research on Personality, 23,* 145–161.

Kelley, F. D. (1972). Communicational significance of therapist proxemic cues. *Journal of Consulting and Clinical Psychology, 39,* 345.

King, M. G. (1964). Structural balance, tension, and segregation in a university group. *Human Relations, 17,* 221–225.

Kleck, R., Buck, P. L., Goller, W. L., London, R. S., Pfieffer, J. R., & Vukcevic, D. P. (1968). Effect of stigmatizing conditions on the use of personal space. *Psychological Reports, 23,* 111–118.

Kowalski, R. M. (1993). Inferring sexual interest from behavioral cues: Effects of gender and sexually relevant attitudes. *Sex Roles, 29,* 13–36.

Krosnick, J. A., Betz, A. L., Jussim, L. J., & Lynn, A. R. (1992). Subliminal conditioning of attitudes. *Personality and Social Psychology Bulletin, 18,* 152–162.

Landy, R. J. (1983). The use of distancing in drama therapy. *The Arts in Psychotherapy, 10,* 175–185.

Larsen, K. S., & Long, E. (1988). Attitudes toward sex-roles: Traditional or egalitarian? *Sex Roles, 19,* 1–12.

Libby, M. N., & Aries, E. (1989). Gender differences in preschool children's narrative fantasy. *Psychology of Women Quarterly, 13,* 293–306.

Liebert, R. M., Sprafkin, J. N., & Davidson, E. S. (1982). *The early window: Effects of television on children and youth* (2nd ed.). New York: Pergamon.

Little, K. B. (1965). Personal space. *Journal of Experimental Social Psychology, 1,* 237–247.

Lott, A. J., & Lott, B. (1960). The formation of positive attitudes toward group members. *Journal of Abnormal and Social Psychology, 61,* 297–300.

Lott, A. J., & Lott, B. (1965). Group cohesiveness as interpersonal attraction: A review of relationships with antecedent and consequent variables. *Psychological Bulletin, 64,* 259–309.

Lott, A. J., & Lott, B. (1968). A learning theory approach to interpersonal attitudes. In A. G. Greenwald, T. C. Brock, & T. M. Ostrom (Eds.), *Psychological foundations of attitudes* (pp. 67–88). New York: Academic Press.

Lott, A. J., & Lott, B. (1972). The power of liking: Consequences of interpersonal attitudes derived from a liberalized view of secondary reinforcement. In L. Berkowitz (Ed.), *Advances in experimental social psychology* (Vol. 6, pp. 109–148). New York: Academic Press.

Lott, A. J., & Lott, B. (1974). The role of reward in the formation of positive interpersonal attitudes. In T. L. Huston (Ed.), *Foundations of interpersonal attraction* (pp. 171–192). New York: Academic Press.

Lott [Eisman], B. (1955). Attitude formation: The development of a color preference response through mediated generalization. *Journal of Abnormal and Social Psychology, 50,* 321–325.

Lott, B. (1985a). The devaluation of women's competence. *Journal of Social Issues, 41*(4), 43–60.

Lott, B. (1985b). The potential enrichment of social/personality psychology through feminist research, and vice versa. *American Psychologist, 40* 155–164.

Lott, B. (1987). Sexist discrimination as distancing behavior: I. A laboratory demonstration. *Psychology of Women Quarterly, 11,* 47–58.

Lott, B. (1989). Sexist discrimination as distancing behavior: II. Primetime television. *Psychology of Women Quarterly, 13,* 341–355.

Lott, B. (1990). Dual natures or learned behavior. In R. T. Hare-Mustin & J. Marecek (Eds.), *Making a difference: Psychology and the construction of gender* (pp. 65–101). New Haven, CT: Yale University Press.

Lott, B. (1991). Social psychology: Humanist roots and feminist future. *Psychology of Women Quarterly, 15,* 505–519.

Lott, B. (1993). Sexual harassment: Consequences and remedies. *Thought and Action, 8*(2), 89–103.

Lott, B. (1994). *Women's lives: Themes and variations in gender learning* (2nd ed.). Pacific Grove, CA: Brooks/Cole.

Lott, B., & Lott, A. J. (1985). Learning theory in contemporary social psychology. In G. Lindzey & E. Aronson (Eds.), *The handbook of social psychology* (3rd ed., Vol. 2, pp. 109–136). New York: Random House.

Lott, B., & Lott, A. J. (1986). Likability of strangers as a function of their winner/loser status, gender, and race. *Journal of Social Psychology, 126,* 503–511.

Lott, B., Lott, A. J., & Fernald, J. L. (1990). Individual differences in distancing responses to women on a photo choice task. *Sex Roles, 22,* 97–110.

Maccoby, E. E. (1988). Gender as a social category. *Developmental Psychology, 24,* 755–765.

MacCorquodale, P., & Jensen, G. (1993). Women in the law: Partners or tokens? *Gender and Society, 7,* 582–593.

MacKinnon, C. A. (1989). *Toward a feminist theory of the state.* Cambridge, MA: Harvard University Press.

Maluso, D. (1989). *Intergender distancing behavior: A field experiment.* Unpublished master's thesis, University of Rhode Island.

Maluso, D. (1992). *Interventions to lessen racist prejudice and discrimination among college students.* Unpublished doctoral dissertation, University of Rhode Island.

Mathews, K. E. Jr., & Cooper, S. (1976). Deceit as a function of sex of subject and target person. *Sex Roles, 2,* 29–38.

McGuire, W. J. (1985). Attitudes and attitude change. In G. Lindzey & E. Aronson (Eds.), *The handbook of social psychology* (3rd ed., Vol. 2, pp. 233–346). New York: Random House.

Mehrabian, A. (1968). Inference of attitudes from the posture, orientation, and distance of a communicator. *Journal of Consulting and Clinical Psychology, 32,* 296–308.

Morrison, T. L., & Stein, D. D. (1985). Member reaction to male and female leaders in two types of group experience. *Journal of Social Psychology, 125,* 7–16.

Murphy, S. T., & Zajonc, R. B. (1993). Affect, cognition, and awareness: Affective priming with optimal and suboptimal stimulus exposures. *Journal of Personality and Social Psychology, 64,* 723–739.

Nigro, G. N., Hill, D. E., Gelbein, M. E., & Clark, C. L. (1988). Changes in the facial prominence of women and men over the last decade. *Psychology of Women Quarterly, 12,* 225–235.

Olian, J. D., Schwab, D. P., & Haberfield, Y. (1988). The impact of applicant gender compared to qualifications on hiring recommendations: A meta-analysis of experimental studies. *Organizational Behavior and Human Decision Processes, 41,* 180–195.

Olson, J. M., & Zanna, M. P. (1993). Attitudes and attitude change. *Annual Review of Psychology, 44,* 117–154.

Pauley, L. L. (1989). Customer weight as a variable in salespersons' response time. *Journal of Social Psychology, 129,* 713–714.

Pedersen, D. M., & Sabin, L. (1982). Personal space invasion: Sex differentials for near and far proximities. *Perceptual and Motor Skills, 55,* 1060–1062.

Pleck, J. H. (1977). Men's power with women, other men, and society: A men's movement analysis. In D. V. Hiller & R. Sheets (Eds.), *Women and men: The consequences of power.* Cincinnati: Office of Women's Studies, University of Cincinnati.

Rafaeli, A. (1989). When clerks meet customers: A test of variables related to emotional expression on the job. *Journal of Applied Psychology, 74,* 385–393.

Riches, P., & Foddy, M. (1989). Ethnic accent as a status cue. *Social Psychology Quarterly, 52,* 197–206.

Riley, P. J. (1981). The influence of gender on occupational aspirations of kindergarten children. *Journal of Vocational Behavior, 19,* 244–250.

Rowe, M. P. (1973, December). *The progress of women in educational institutions: The Saturn's rings phenomenon* [Mimeograph]. Cambridge, MA: Massachusetts Institute of Technology.

Saal, F. E., Johnson, C. B., & Weber, N. (1989). Friendly or sexy? *Psychology of Women Quarterly, 13,* 263–276.

Sampson, E. E. (1991). *Social worlds—personal lives.* San Diego: Harcourt Brace Jovanovich.

Saris, R., Johnston, I., & Lott, B. (in press). Women as cues for men's approach or distancing behavior: A study of interpersonal sexism. *Sex Roles.*

Skinner, B. F. (1987). Whatever happened to psychology as the science of behavior? *American Psychologist, 42,* 780–786.

Snyder, C. R., Lassegard, M. A., & Ford, C. E. (1986). Distancing after group success and failure: Basking in reflected glory and cutting off reflected failure. *Journal of Personality and Social Psychology, 51,* 382–388.

Snyder, M. L., Kleck, R. E., Strenta, A., & Mentzer, S. J. (1979). Avoidance of the handicapped: An attributional ambiguity analysis. *Journal of Personality and Social Psychology, 37,* 2297–2306.

Stead, B. A., & Zinkhan, G, M. (1986). Service priority in department stories: The effects of customer gender and dress. *Sex Roles, 15,* 601–611.

Steenland, S. (1988). *Prime-time women: An analysis of older women on entertainment television.* National Commission on Working Women, 1325 G Street, N.W., Washington, DC 20005.

Stier, D. S., & Hall, J. A. (1984). Gender differences in touch: An empirical and theoretical review. *Journal of Personality and Social Psychology, 47,* 440–459.

Stroebe, W., & Insko, C. A. (1989). Stereotype, prejudice, and discrimination: Changing conceptions in theory and research. In D. Bar-Tal, C. F. Graumann, A. W. Kruglanski, & W. Stroebe (Eds.), *Stereotyping and prejudice: Changing conceptions* (pp. 3–36). New York: Springer-Verlag.

Swim, J., Borgida, E., Maruyama, G., & Myers, D. G. (1989). Joan McKay versus John McKay: Do gender sterotypes bias evaluations? *Psychological Bulletin, 105,* 409–429.

Tavris, C. (1992). *The mismeasure of woman.* New York: Simon & Schuster.

Thayer, S. (1988, March). Close encounters. *Psychology Today,* pp. 31–36.

Thorne, B. (1993). *Gender play: Girls and boys in school.* New Brunswick, NJ: Rutgers University Press.

Tong, R. (1989). *Feminist thought.* Boulder, CO: Westview Press.

Top, T. J. (1991). Sex bias in the evaluation of performance in the scientific, artistic, and literary professions: A review. *Sex Roles, 24,* 73–106.

Ugwuegbu, D. C. E., & Anusiem, A. U. (1982). Effects of stress on interpersonal distance in a simulated interview situation. *Journal of Social Psychology, 116,* 3–7.

Word, C. O., Zanna, M. P., & Cooper, J. (1974). Avoidance behaviors as measures of discrimination in interpersonal situations. *Journal of Experimental Social Psychology, 10,* 109–120.

Wartenberg, T. E. (Ed.). (1992). *Rethinking power.* Albany: State University of New York Press.

Weick, K. E. (1984). Small wins: Redefining the scale of social problems. *American Psychologist, 39,* 40–49.

Weinbaum, J., & Gilead, S. (1986). Distancing behavior and imagery in the school aversive. *Journal of Mental Imagery, 10*(1), 75–80.

West, C., & Zimmerman, D. H. (1987). Doing gender. *Gender and Society, 1,* 125–151.

Wollman, N. (1987). Consistency between affect and cognition in interpersonal attraction. *Journal of Mental Imagery, 11,* 119–124.

Wolman, C., & Frank, H. (1975). The solo woman in a professional peer group. *American Journal of Orthopsychiatry, 45,* 164–171.

Young, I. M. (1992). Five faces of oppression. In T. E. Wartenberg (Ed.), *Rethinking power* (pp. 174–195). Albany: State University of New York Press.

Zajonc, R. B. (1980). Feeling and thinking: Preferences need no inferences. *American Psychologist, 35,* 151–175.

Zellman, G. L., Johnson, P. B., Giarusso, R., & Goodchilds, J. D. (1979, September). *Adolescent expectations for dating relationships: Consensus between the sexes.* Paper presented at the meeting of the American Psychological Association, New York.

Zimbardo, P. G., & Leippe, M. R. (1991). *The psychology of attitude change and social influence.* New York: McGraw-Hill.

Zinkhan, G. M., & Stoiadin, L. F. (1984). Impact of sex role stereotypes on service priority in department stores. *Journal of Applied Psychology, 69,* 691–693.

Zuckerman, M., & Kieffer, S. C. (1994). Race differences in face-ism: Does facial prominence imply dominance? *Journal of Personality and Social Psychology, 66,* 86–92.

3

Shaking Hands
with a Clenched Fist
Interpersonal Racism

DIANE MALUSO

You cannot shake hands with a clenched fist.
—INDIRA GANDHI (October 19, 1971; quoted in Partnow, 1977, p. 210)

Despite decades of legal and educational reform, racism remains a serious social problem in the United States. Research
findings have demonstrated that in the wake of the civil rights
movement, racism has not declined but has merely changed
forms. The changed, more subtle forms of racism prevalent today have
developed despite widespread efforts to educate European-Americans
about the stereotypical nature of their beliefs about Americans of Asian,
African, and Latin heritage, as well as Native Americans. Racist acts persist
despite the almost universal conclusion among educators that the construct
of "race" at best serves to divide humans artificially and inaccurately into
mutually exclusive groups, and at worst has perpetuated racism. Any
efforts to combat racism must explore methods of intervention that are
likely to result in an actual decrease in both institutional and interpersonal
discrimination. Where should limited resources be directed in order to be
most effective in changing the prejudices, stereotypes, and discriminatory
behaviors of European-Americans toward members of other ethnic

groups? How can we best measure racist discrimination so that we might ascertain the outcome of interventions? In what ways do racism interventions differentially affect the lives of women and men of color? This chapter explores issues relevant to these questions.

INTERPERSONAL RACISM DEFINED AND ILLUSTRATED

Historically, psychological definitions of "social attitudes" have stressed the relationship between negative thoughts and feelings toward members of groups and discriminatory behavior toward those people. As early as the 1920s, researchers in social science began measuring attitudes toward ethnic minorities; by the 1940s, major theoretical frameworks such as Myrdal's (1944) were being developed. By the 1970s, social scientists had developed definitions of racism that distinguished institutional from interpersonal racism. Jones (1972), for example, suggested that racism was practiced "by individuals and institutions with the intentional or unintentional support of the entire culture" (p. 172). Wilson (1973) specified three levels of racism: institutional, collective, and individual (or interpersonal). According to Wilson, "institutional racism" occurs when a subordinate racial group is denied equal participation in "associations or procedures that are stable, organized, and systematized (e.g., the electoral process, residential patterns, and formal education)" (p. 34). "Collective racism" refers to less formal group and societal norms that reinforce collective acts, such as demonstrations against Blacks moving into White neighborhoods. "Individual racism," as defined by Wilson, is "a given person's set of attitudes (that members of the minority group are culturally or biologically inferior to the dominant group and therefore should be exploited or discriminated against)" (p. 34).

The analysis of interpersonal racism that seems to have had the most durable impact was developed by Allport (1954). He distinguished among the attitudinal, belief, and behavioral components of "prejudice," and suggested that this distinction was important because some programs attempting to decrease racism were only successful in changing beliefs, not behaviors. These distinctions have remained important in contemporary social-psychological conceptualizations of racism.

In the present discussion, racism is understood to consist of three independent but positively related constructs: prejudice (defined as hostility toward ethnic minorities); stereotypical beliefs about minorities; and overt discriminatory behaviors toward minorities that achieve distance from them. Interpersonal racist discrimination is operationalized as distancing behavior, following the rationale provided by Lott (Chapter 2, this volume) for interpersonal sexist discrimination and by Snyder, Kleck, Strenta, and Mentzer (1979) for interpersonal discrimination against the physically handicapped. Allport (1954) suggested that interpersonal discrimination exists on a continuum from mild to severe forms of expression ranging from anti-locution through avoidance, exclusion, and physical attack to extermination. Duckitt (1993), in a review of the literature, noted that there are expressions of interpersonal discrimination even milder than those proposed by Allport. Some of these are failure to make eye contact or to interact verbally (Bielby, 1987), negative voice tone (Weitz, 1972), and failure to respect personal space (Brown, 1981).

One important aspect of this (as well as other) definitions of racism is its directional nature: that is, racism is directed toward persons of color by Whites. The antecedents and consequences of racism, thus understood, are very different from the antecedents and consequences of negative beliefs, attitudes, and behaviors of low-status persons about and toward members of oppressor or powerful groups. In other words, "reverse racism" is an oxymoron. Although members of oppressed groups can certainly feel hostility toward their oppressors, hold stereotypical beliefs about them, and behave in ways that will distance themselves from their oppressors, an understanding of racism requires consideration of the power differential between Whites and persons of color, and the resulting inequities in society. Since European-Americans control more of society's resources than African-Americans, for example, the avoidance of Blacks by Whites serves to deny Blacks access to resources (e.g., higher education, employment, housing, adequate health care), whereas the avoidance of Whites by Blacks does not similarly limit the access of Whites to such resources. Unless one considers racism as a purely theoretical construct existing in a vacuum, it is theoretically and methodologically unsound to equate the attitudes, beliefs, and behaviors *toward* the oppressed with those *of* the oppressed.

It has been found that people do indeed distinguish the distancing behaviors of the more powerful from those of the less powerful. In a series of investigations of asymmetry in prejudice attribution (Rodin, Price, Bryson, & Sanchez, 1990), three types of discriminatory behaviors directed toward the less powerful by the more powerful were identified by respondents as more indicative of prejudice than the same behaviors directed toward the more powerful by the less powerful. The negative attitudes toward Blacks of Whites who excluded Blacks from a sports team, who derogated the general and intellectual capabilities of Blacks, and who gave preferential housing or restaurant seating to a White over a Black were seen as more extreme than were the negative attitudes toward Whites of Blacks who engaged in the same behaviors toward Whites. Rodin and her colleagues found similar patterns of attributions of "prejudice" among women and men, old and young people, and straights and gays.

The proposition that the affective, cognitive, and behavioral components of a "social attitude" are independent constructs was tested by Bagozzi (1978), who demonstrated that these constructs can be independently learned and elicited. According to Bagozzi, affect toward (or feeling about) an object is acquired through the systematic pairing of positive or negative stimuli with the attitude object (classical conditioning). Cognitions are formed through the processing of information and problem solving. Finally, Bagozzi maintained that behaviors toward an attitude object are learned instrumentally. He used structural modeling analyses to examine the construct validity of the three components (Bagozzi, 1978), and suggested that theoretical models should reflect the independence of these attitudinal, belief, and behavioral constructs. The utility of such a tripartite model lies in its breadth and in its ability to differentiate the attitudinal, belief, and behavioral components of a social "ism."

A large body of empirical evidence suggests that racist stereotyping, prejudice, and discrimination, although independent constructs, are generally positively related. The relationship between prejudice and discrimination has been especially widely studied and discussed. According to Allport (1954), "It is true that any negative attitude tends somehow, somewhere to express itself in action. . . . The more intense the attitude, the more likely it is to result in vigorously hostile action" (p. 14). Not all have agreed with Allport, however. Duckitt (1993) notes that the relationship between prejudice and discrimination has been seriously questioned because the relationship is weak, inconsistent, and complex, and because discrimination is more likely to be influenced by situational factors than by the presence of prejudice. Although some social scientists (e.g., Bowser, 1985; Feagin & Eckberg, 1980) have suggested that these empirical problems render the relationship between prejudice and discrimination so slight that there can be little predictive value in studying prejudice, Duckitt's (1993) review of the literature suggests a different interpretation. According to Duckitt, the social-psychological studies that do not find a significant and positive relationship between prejudice and discrimination are those that involve structured tasks with well-defined expectations and goals. In these studies, it is likely that clear normative criteria for equitable and fair behavior are salient. The studies that do find a prejudice–discrimination relationship, however, are those that involve informal social interaction, usually measured by friendliness or choosing partners for some activities. In these situations, discrimination may be facilitated because an individual's personal likes and dislikes are more salient and seem permissible.

The relationship between stereotypes and discrimination has also generated interest. Some studies have demonstrated that racial/ethnic stereotypes adhered to by individuals have a differential effect on their interpretation of behaviors exhibited by members of majority and minority groups.

For example, one study of Whites' interpretations of ambiguous shoving behavior (Duncan, 1976) found that Whites interpreted the same shove as hostile or violent when performed by a Black actor and as playful when performed by a White actor. In a similar study, Sagar and Schofield (1980) found that both Black and White schoolchildren who viewed videotaped interactions of Black and White actors rated ambiguous bumping in a hallway by Blacks as more threatening than the same bumping behavior by Whites. Devine (1989) broadened this line of research to include the mediating effect of prejudice (attitudes) on the relationship between stereotypes (cognitions) and discrimination (behaviors). Devine demonstrated that individuals, regardless of their degree of prejudice toward members of ethnic minorities, are knowledgeable about ethnic minority stereotypes, and that such stereotypes are automatically activated in the presence of a minority group member. Devine also demonstrated that less prejudiced persons are likely to inhibit automatically activated stereotypes and to replace them with thoughts incongruent with the stereotypes.

The potential danger for members of ethnic minorities of Whites' negative interpretations of their behavior is illustrated in several studies. For example, an archival study of White attendants' behavior in physically restraining White and non-White adolescent patients in a psychiatric hospital (Bond, DiCandia, & MacKinnon, 1988) found that although there was no difference in the number of violent acts performed by White and Black patients, Blacks were four times more likely to be physically restrained than Whites. In a laboratory study, Donnerstein and Donnerstein (1976) found that White college students administered more electric shock to male target persons represented as Black than to ones represented as White, and that the White participants' stereotypes of Blacks as aggressive were positively correlated with their shock-administering behavior. One proposed explanation for the greater aggression of Whites toward Blacks in such studies is that adherence to racial stereotypes inhibits empathic responses by Whites to Black target persons. Baron (1979), for example, found that pain cues elicited by a suffering victim of the same ethnicity as an attacker led to restrained aggression, whereas the same cues elicited by a victim of a different ethnicity had no such restraining effect.

Environmental variables have been found to mediate the relationships among prejudice, stereotypical beliefs, and discriminatory behaviors. One important example of such a mediator is situational demand. Contemporary theorists almost unanimously adhere to the position that the salience of the cultural norm of egalitarianism will inhibit expressions of racism. An extensive review of unobtrusive measures of racism led Crosby, Bromley, and Saxe (1980) to conclude that this norm is made salient in the presence of Black investigators, in situations where behavior is not anonymous, and in self-report measures of attitudes and stereotypical beliefs. Supporting this conclusion are findings from a recent investigation of the effects of normative influence on the expression of racism (Blanchard, Lilly, & Vaughn, 1991). White female undergraduate students expressed stronger anti-racist opinions if exposed to a strong anti-racist normative influence in the form of overheard statements than if exposed to a normative influence indicating a strong acceptance of racism. Similarly, Frey and Gaertner (1986) found that a sample of 130 White female university students only refused to help Black recipients when the failure to help would not be perceived by others as socially inappropriate.

RESEARCH METHODOLOGIES

One important contribution of social-psychological investigations of interpersonal racism has been consideration of the reactivity associated with self-reported measures of social attitudes and beliefs. Two types of methodologies that have been effectively used to avoid such reactivity are archival research and unobtrusive measures of interpersonal behavior. Archival research has been particularly useful in understanding the experiences of non-Whites as they come in contact with various public institutions. For example, the punishments received by Black and White children in a south Florida school district during 1987–1988 were analyzed via an assessment of school discipline records by McFadden, Marsh, Price, and Hwang (1992). They found that Black students received more corporal punishment and were suspended from school more often than White students. Only 36.7% of the discipline referrals were of Black students; yet Blacks received 54.1% of the corporal punishment and 43.9% of the school suspensions, but only 23% of the less severe internal suspensions (which still allowed students to attend classes).

One of the best-known areas of research in which archival methodologies have been extensively used is the study of Blacks' experiences with the U.S. legal system. Archival research on prison sentencing has more consistently shown patterns of racist discrimination than have methods employing self-report measures such as those used in simulation studies (Nickerson, Mayo, & Smith, 1986). In an early study of over 3,500 Texas state prison inmates, Bullock (1961) found that Blacks got longer jail sentences when their victims were White than when their victims were Black. Gerard and Terry (1970, cited in Nickerson et al., 1986) found that Blacks in Missouri were more likely to receive prison sentences than Whites who had committed the same crimes, and that Whites received probation more than twice as often as Blacks. An ambitious archival study by the Rand Corporation (Petersilia, 1983), which examined the 1980 data arrest and sentencing data of 1,400 men imprisoned in California, Texas, and Michigan, concluded that when other factors such as crime committed and ethnicity of victim were held constant, non-Whites received longer sentences than did Whites.

Archival research has also been used to study the experiences of Blacks with mental health care providers. In one such study, Sue, McKinney, Allen, and Hall (1974) analyzed the experiences of clients in a large number of community mental health centers; they found that Blacks were less likely to be seen by psychologists, psychiatrists, and social workers, and more likely to be seen by paraprofessionals, than were White clients. Sue (1977) also found that Asian-American and Native American clients in community mental health centers were less likely to see psychologists and more likely to see nonprofessionals than were Whites. Flaherty and Meagher (1980) analyzed the inpatient treatment records of 66 Black and 36 White patients diagnosed with schizophrenia. They determined that Blacks were hospitalized for fewer days than Whites, had fewer inpatient privileges than Whites, were less likely to receive occupational and recreational therapy than Whites, were restrained and secluded significantly more often than were Whites, and were medicated twice as many days as were Whites. Similar results were obtained in an early archival study conducted by Singer (1967), who examined the treatment records of Blacks and Whites hospitalized for mental disorders during a 4-year period, and found that Blacks were less likely than Whites to receive intense psychotherapy and more likely than Whites to receive only drug therapy.

Crosby et al. (1980) reported that unobtrusive studies of interpersonal racism show that anti-Black behaviors continue to occur even though self-reports indicate that interpersonal racist attitudes have decreased. Crosby and her colleagues recommended that assessments of the incidence of discriminatory behavior, of adherence to stereotypical beliefs, and of prejudice must be based on unobtrusive measures of these constructs. Other researchers have agreed with this suggestion and have demonstrated that self-reports of stereotypical beliefs about Blacks (and other ethnic minorities) are subject to participant reactivity (Lobel, 1987; Devine, 1989); that is, participants tend to underreport adherence to racial stereotypes in order to appear socially acceptable. Others have shown that self-reports of prejudice against Blacks are also subject to participant reactivity (Katz & Hass, 1988; Gaertner & Dovidio, 1986), and that unobtrusive measures of distancing behaviors of Whites toward Blacks yield more consistent results than do self-report measures (Gaertner & Dovidio, 1986).

Several researchers have turned to naturalistic observation to obtain unobtrusive measures of racist discrimination. Thus, one study operationalized racist discrimination as avoidance of a Black clerk by White customers (McCormick & Kinloch, 1985). Another study (Word, Zanna, & Cooper, 1974) of interracial distancing found that White men interviewing Black and White confederates sat farther away from Blacks than from Whites, made more verbal errors when speaking to Blacks than to Whites, and terminated the interviews of Blacks sooner than the interviews of Whites. Hendricks and Bootzin (1976) found that, given a choice of seats, a sample of 80 White women were more likely to sit farther away from Black women and men than from White women and men.

Although racism and sexism are intertwined in U.S. society and in everyday behavior, current research on racism and sexism is often limited to the study of one or the other. Rarely are the differential behaviors and attitudes directed toward Black men and women included in studies of racism, and rarely are gender comparisons included in analyses of racist behaviors and attitudes of Whites. The empirical evidence that does exist indicates important gender differences in the experiences of Blacks. In a study of children who received services from child guidance clinics (Jackson, Farley, Zimet, & Waterman, 1978), Whites were found to have received more intense forms of contact (such as individual psychotherapy) than Blacks. In addition, even though Black girls were diagnosed as having more severe psychopathology than Black boys or Whites, they were the most likely to receive only diagnostic procedures with no follow-up treatment. Finally, Black girls received fewer numbers of hours of treatment than Black boys or White children. In a study of interracial distancing among peers, Damico and Sparks (1986) found that among 677 sixth-, seventh-, and eighth-graders attending two desegregated schools, Black girls but not Black boys were isolated from social interactions with White classmates.

A notable critique of research on racism and sexism is that of Smith and Stewart (1983), who have proposed that the limitations of studying sexism and racism separately can be corrected by studying the different experiences of Black women and other gender–ethnic groups. They have suggested that such studies must reflect the social contexts in which racism and sexism occur, and must consider the interaction of ethnicity and gender. I would add that the examination of White women's and men's differential attitudes, beliefs, and behaviors directed toward women and men members of ethnic minorities is also necessary to increase our understanding of racism. Some recent research is beginning to address these gender–race interactions. Carter (1990), for example, found that although White women and White men exhibit racist beliefs and attitudes, they may do so in different ways, and that White women in particular may be most racist when they deny the importance of race in their interactions with members of other ethnicities. A recent study of college students' racist attitudes and self-reported discrimination (Quall, Cox, & Schehr, 1992), found that White women reported less participation in discriminatory practices than did White men, and that White women were more accepting of racial minorities than White men, but that the self-reported acceptance and the self-reported participation in discriminatory practices were poorly correlated for both White women and men. The decontextualization of discrimination has been a major limitation in empirical investigations of racism. One of the most vocal critics of context stripping has been Jones (1983),who argues that most studies of racism do not even really involve reactions to Black people (who are typically presented only symbolically), and that even when they do, the contact is too brief for any interactive effects to be studied. Jones has urged more use of naturalistic observation in order to study the actual discriminatory behaviors of individuals in real-life situations. Chidester (1986) has also argued that studies employing simulated interracial dyads are usually stripped of context and lack external and construct validity.

Despite a growing awareness of the need for unobtrusive measures of racism and for realistic, long-term interactions between Black and White research participants, most research still depends almost exclusively on self-reports as measures of attitudes and beliefs, and on brief interactions between strangers in laboratory settings as indicators of discrimination. The need for new, unobtrusive measures and innovative research settings in the study of racism cannot be overly emphasized.

STUDIES OF INTERVENTIONS TO DATE

The most extensively studied interventions designed to reduce racist prejudice, stereotyping, and discrimination are based on Allport's (1954) contact theory of intergroup relations. This theory postulates that racism

> may be reduced by equal status contact between majority and minority groups in the pursuit of common goals. The effect is greatly enhanced if this contact is sanctioned by institutional supports . . . and provided it is of a sort that leads to the perception of common interests and common humanity between members of the two groups. (p. 281)

The necessary conditions for prejudice reduction suggested by contact theory are as follows: Interracial contact must be sustained; individuals must be of equal status; individuals must work toward common goals; there must be an absence of competition for scarce resources; and there must be strong support from relevant authorities (Cook, 1988).

Contact theory has received a great deal of empirical attention and support. A national sample of White adults, for example, was surveyed by Jackman and Crane (1986) in a study of friendship patterns. Only 21% of those surveyed could name an acquaintance who was Black, and only 9% of those surveyed could name a "good friend" who was Black. Those

Whites who did have Black friends or acquaintances were less likely to say that they preferred to live in an all-White neighborhood, and were less likely to believe that Whites were more intelligent than Blacks. Especially striking is the finding that Whites whose Black friends or acquaintances were of a higher socioeconomic status than themselves were even less likely to prefer an all-White neighborhood or to believe that Whites are more intelligent than Blacks. Cook (1990) found that cooperative, equal-status contact between Black and White adults resulted in increased favorable beliefs about, and liking for, Blacks by formerly prejudiced Whites. Whites who experienced such contact with Blacks demonstrated increased readiness to extend equality in housing, education, and employment. Sigelman and Welch (1993) examined the data from 1,315 Whites who participated in a 1989 ABC News–*Washington Post* poll, and found that Whites who had social contacts with Blacks were more likely to support racial interactions than those who did not. Whites who had Black friends and who lived in neighborhoods with Blacks had the greatest likelihood of endorsing the importance of people sending their children to racially mixed schools, attending racially mixed churches, living in racially mixed neighborhoods, socializing with members of other races outside of work, and having close friends of other races.

Contact theory is the framework for "cooperative learning" educational techniques, which have been credited with improving intergroup relations in classrooms (Slavin, 1985). Cooperative learning techniques involve assigning White and non-White children to "interdependent teams that cooperate to complete classroom assignments" (Sears, Peplau, & Taylor, 1991, p. 434). In a review of cooperative education, Slavin (1983) concluded that academic performance of all students was increased in 63% of cooperative classrooms, compared to 4% of traditional classrooms. A program that increased the interracial contact among 80 fourth- and fifth-graders in a desegregated school was found to increase the students' acceptance of members of another ethnicity, to decrease their racial preconceptions, and to increase their willingness to consider reducing the social distance between themselves and a member of another ethnicity (Colca, Lowen, Colca, & Lord, 1982). A recent study (Vohra, Rodolfa, de la Cruz, & Vincent, 1991) found that White college students in a semester-long cross-cultural training program for peer counselors who met regularly with members of ethnic minorities increased their awareness of the effects of racism and rated the meetings highly.

Less optimistic findings were reported by Sampson (1986) from his study of the effects of desegregation on racist attitudes and expectations among college students attending an "elite, predominantly white, desegregated" university. Sampson found that the attitudes of Whites toward Blacks were more negative at the end of the freshman year than at the beginning, possibly because of the lower status of Black students and the lack of interaction among White and Black students.

Most interventions directed at reducing racism are of the educational type and typically involve strategies that directly or indirectly address racial stereotypes—that is, strategies that focus on the cognitive (belief) aspect of racism. Some social scientists have suggested that educational approaches addressing prejudice (i.e., those emphasizing attitudes and values) are more effective in reducing racism than those primarily addressing beliefs. Katz and Hass (1988), for example, investigated value conflict and racism, and argued that racism can be mediated by an educational approach that stresses the relationship between egalitarian values and the rights of ethnic minority groups. Further support for the effectiveness of educational interventions that focus on prejudice has been provided by Furuto and Furuto (1983), who found a workshop addressing racist attitudes to be more useful than a workshop addressing stereotypes in reducing self-reports of prejudice toward various ethnic groups among White university students in Hawaii.

Others have suggested that the most effective educational programs for reducing prejudice are those that involve simulation or role playing. Byrnes and Kiger (1990), for example, found that college students who participated in a 3-hour prejudice reduction simulation game ("Blue Eyes—Brown Eyes") were less prejudiced 3 weeks later, whereas those students who experienced a lecture on prejudice reduction and those who viewed others playing "Blue Eyes—Brown Eyes" on film did not self-report less prejudice. Bruin (1985) has argued that the use of simulation games in workshops allows participants to see the importance of the dominant culture's role in shaping their opinions of ethnic minorities. Conflicting evidence has been offered by Sedlacek, Troy, and Chapman (1976), who found that of three interventions to decrease racism and sexism among college students, a role-playing game was preferred by students and a movie format inspired participants with a desire to act against racism or sexism, but students who participated in a discussion group with a leader-led workshop gained the most knowledge.

Barnard and Benn (1988) examined the relationship between workshop group composition and the effectiveness of workshops in reducing prejudice. They found that participation in a workshop discussion about racism reduced prejudice in a sample of 74 White male undergraduates, whether or not others in the discussion group held beliefs similar to those of the participants. Other researchers have argued that an important factor in the effectiveness of educational programs to reduce prejudice is that of the program leadership. Lowenstein (1985), for example, in a study of prejudice among girls and boys living in a therapeutic community in the United Kingdom, found that those who attended workshops on racial tolerance manifested a reduction in prejudice that was maintained for at least 6 months. Lowenstein argued that the status of the group leader and the overall atmosphere of support for the workshop from other staff members were the main contributors to prejudice reduction.

A few newer interventions have combined interracial contact with an educational component. A particularly innovative intervention, developed by Clayton-Pederson of Vanderbilt University, includes an interactive computer-controlled videodisk package called "Diversity Opportunity Tool" (Wilson, 1994). Participants view a scene in which there is some sort of interpersonal discrimination occurring; instead of just passively watching a videotape, they are called upon to analyze the situation and choose, via a computer keyboard, different courses of action. Participants can then see the likely consequences of their responses and gain confidence from practicing ways to confront discriminatory behaviors. Following their interaction with the videodisk, students participate in small-group discussions that foster dialogue among members of various ethnicities. According to Clayton-Pederson and others who have used the Diversity Opportunity Tool package, the strength of this intervention lies in a combination of the interactivity of the role-playing video component and the permission to discuss sensitive issues gained from the discussion component. Another multimethod technique, developed at Mount Holyoke College, is a semester-long course called "The Psychology of Racism" (Tatum, 1992). In this course, the students discuss the issues of stereotyping, prejudice, and discrimination, while also focusing on the process involved in becoming aware of those issues. The combination of content with process is the particular strength of this model, which involves weekly classroom meetings of students who are of various ethnicities. According to Tatum, White students in her classes gain a great deal of understanding of students of color, whereas the latter grow to appreciate the behaviors of White students who are struggling with the issues of racism and ethnic identity.

Several questions relative to interventions designed to reduce racism remain unexplored. The relative merits of the contact and educational methods of racism reduction are not well addressed in the literature to date and have not been tested. In addition, although the negative impact of traditional status differences between Whites and Blacks has been well documented in tests of Allport's contact theory (e.g., Sampson, 1986; Bond et al., 1988), the impact of Whites' contact with Blacks of higher status (e.g., leadership positions) is a relatively unexplored area. One recent study of the dynamics of mixed-race mentor–protégé relationships in industry (Thomas, 1993) examined the behaviors and attitudes of 18 Black–White pairs of middle-level managers, but only included two pairs in which the mentor was Black and the protégé White. In both of those cases, the mentors were men and the protégés were women. All other pairs consisted of White mentors and Black protégés. Especially important is the question of whether interventions designed to reduce interpersonal racism are as effective in reducing racism directed toward Black women as they are in reducing racism directed toward Black men. Whether Whites' contact with high-status non-Black (e.g., Hispanic) minority group members generalizes to attitudes and behaviors directed toward Blacks also merits attention. I addressed these questions in the first of the three experiments described below.

NEW RESEARCH

Experiment 1: A Comparison of Interventions to Lessen Racist Discrimination

The first study evaluated the effects of intense contact with a high-status minority person group leader and of participation in a discussion-format cultural diversity workshop on the racist prejudice and discriminatory behaviors of White college students. The effects of three independent variables were investigated: (1) ethnicity of a student group leader (Black, Hispanic, or White); (2) participation in the cultural diversity workshop; and (3) gender of participants.

Prejudice and discrimination, two components of racism, were the dependent variables. Prejudice was operationalized as self-reported responses to a revised version of the Modern Racism Scale (MRS; McConahay, 1986) and was assessed before and after the interventions. Discrimination was operationalized by choice of Whites versus Blacks on a version of the Photo Choice Task (PCT; Lott, Lott, & Fernald, 1990), and was measured only after the interventions.

Method

Participants. Students attending orientation for new students at a mid-sized Northeastern university during the summer of 1991 were participants (Ps) in this study. During each of six 2-day sessions, 21 groups of approximately 15 students each engaged in a variety of academic and student-life-oriented activities designed to prepare them for their first year of college attendance. The mean age of all entering students was 18, and 94.9% were European-Americans. Although data were obtained from all orientation attendees, only the data from European-American students who completed both the pre- and posttest portions of data collection are included in this study (*n* = 356; 257 women, 99 men).

Procedure. Each orientation group of approximately 15 students was directed by a student orientation leader who led meetings, assisted and encouraged students, and escorted student groups during their 2-day visit to the campus. Among the student orientation leaders, 3 were African-American, 14 were European-American, and 4 were Hispanic-American. Ps completed a pretest Entering Student Questionnaire during the first day of each orientation session in an auditorium setting. Embedded in the 44-item questionnaire was the MRS. During the second day of each orientation session, some Ps attended a 50-minute cultural diversity workshop designed to facilitate attitude and behavioral change toward ethnic minorities, while other Ps attended a similar 50-minute workshop addressing either alcohol awareness or date rape issues. All of the educational workshops were 50-minute-long presentations to groups of approximately 45 students. Approximately 12 weeks after orientation (the third and fourth weeks of the fall semester), Ps in large introductory classes were asked to complete a posttest MRS as well as the PCT.

Instruments

1. *The Modern Racism Scale (MRS).* Four of the items from the MRS developed by McConahay (1986) were included in the pre- and posttest questionnaires. Although the MRS requires agreement or disagreement with belief statements, it is considered an indicator of attitude (i.e., of racist prejudice). As originally designed, the MRS consisted of seven statements with which respondents were asked to agree or disagree along a 5-point scale ranging from "strongly disagree" to "strongly agree." Because of space and time considerations as well as concern for the appropriateness of items for this population, only four of the seven original items were used in this study. Three were used as originally written by McConahay, and a fourth item was used in a revised form. The item that was revised was originally written, "Over the past few years, blacks have gotten more economically than they deserve." The revised item reads, "Recently, Blacks have gotten further than they deserve through special programs and laws." Scale scores on the revised MRS used in this study range from 4 to 20, with a high score indicating a high degree of racist prejudice and a low score indicating a low degree of racist prejudice.

2. *The Photo Choice Task—Racism (PCT-R).* This measure is a revised version of the PCT developed by Lott and her colleagues (Lott et al., 1990) as a simulated measure of sexist discrimination. Pairs of faces were projected onto a screen in the front of a classroom by means of a photographic slide projector. Ps were administered the PCT-R in large classroom settings and recorded their responses on computer answer forms. A total of 128 different faces were randomly grouped into 64 pairs. For each pair Ps were asked, "Who would you choose . . . , " followed by one of eight phrases: " . . . as your pharmacist?", " . . . as your attorney?", " . . . as your real estate agent?", " . . .

as your accountant?", " . . . to give your child driving lessons?", " . . . to ask for directions?", " . . . to give you advice?", " . . . to elect to city council?"

On each trial, Ps indicated their choice of face on a computer answer sheet by selecting (A) for the face appearing on the left or (B) for the face on the right. Choices were between a Black woman and White woman; a Black man and White man; a Black man and Black woman; a White man and White woman; two Black women; two Black men; two White women; or two White men. In order to study differential responses to male and female stimulus persons, two subscales served as dependent variables in this study, the PCT-RW and PCT-RM. Scores for the PCT-RW were calculated from responses to the eight presentations in which there was a choice between a Black woman and a White woman, and ranged from 0 to 8, with 1 point assigned to each choice of a White woman over a Black woman. Scores for the PCT-RM were similarly calculated from responses to the eight presentations in which there was a choice between a Black man and a White man.

Results

PCT-Results. Photo choices were analyzed (1) to determine whether Whites were chosen over Blacks with greater than chance frequency (i.e., significantly greater than a score of 4); and (2) to test for differences among group mean scores for Ps whose group leader had been either Black, Hispanic, or White, and who either did or did not attend a cultural diversity workshop. Only Ps who had experienced both a Black group leader and a workshop did not choose significantly more White women than Black women on the PCT-RW, while Ps whose group leaders had been White or Hispanic and Ps whose group leader had been Black but who had not attended a workshop were more likely to choose a White woman over a Black woman. Scores on the PCT-RW were also significantly related to the ethnicity of group leader: Ps whose group leader had been Black chose fewer White women over Black women than did those whose group leader had been White or Hispanic. Workshop participation was not related to scores on the PCT-RW, and there was no interaction between ethnicity of group leader and workshop participation. PCT-RM scores were related to ethnicity of group leader, regardless of workshop participation. Only Ps whose group leader had been Black did not choose significantly more White men than Black men on the PCT-RM, while Ps whose group leader had been White or Hispanic were more likely to choose a White man over a Black man. Participation in a cultural diversity workshop was not, by itself, related to selection of White or Black men; nor was the ethnicity of group leader significantly related to scores on the PCT-RM; and there was no interaction between ethnicity of group leader and workshop participation.

The influences of participant gender and stimulus person gender on photo choices were analyzed by a mixed-design 2 × 2 analysis of variance (ANOVA) in which gender of participant was the between-subject variable and gender of stimulus person (scores on the PCT-RW and PCT-RM) was the within-subject variable. Figure 3.1 shows the frequency distributions of Ps' scores (regardless of gender) on the PCT-RW and PCT-RM. A significant main effect was found for gender of stimulus person, $F (1, 317) = 32.82, p < .0001$. Participants, regardless of gender, tended to distance from Black women to a greater degree than they distanced from Black men. No significant effect was found for participant gender or for the interaction between participant gender and stimulus person gender.

MRS Results. MRS scores of Ps who had experienced either a Black, Hispanic, or White group leader and who either did or did not attend a cultural diversity workshop were analyzed to determine (1) differences between pre- and postintervention MRS mean scores, and (2) differences among postintervention MRS group mean scores, using preintervention MRS scores as a covariate. MRS scores could range from 4 to 20, with a midpoint of 12. No significant differences were found between pre- and postintervention MRS scores for any of the

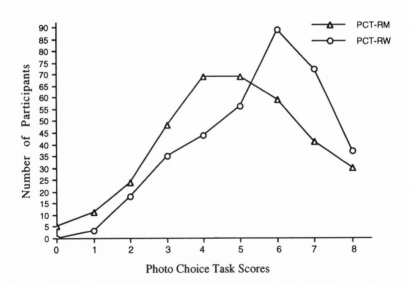

FIGURE 3.1. Frequency distributions for choice of White women over Black women and choice of White men over Black men (PCT-RW and PCT-RM scores).

experimental groups; that is, neither group leader ethnicity, workshop participation, nor the ethnicity–workshop interaction was significantly related to postintervention scores on the MRS. All group means were below the scale's midpoint of 12, indicating that Ps, on the average, reported a low degree of prejudice regardless of group leader ethnicity or of workshop participation.

Relationships among the PCT-R and MRS Results. Pearson correlation coefficients were calculated for all dependent measures. As predicted, high scores on the postintervention MRS were significantly and positively correlated with greater choice of Whites over Blacks (women or men) on the PCT-R. Choices of Black and White men were positively and significantly correlated with choices of Black and White women. The relationship between MRS scores and choices of White men over Black men was twice as strong as that between MRS scores and choices of White women over Black women.

Additional Analyses. Concern about the possible underreporting of prejudice, as indicated by relatively low mean scores on the postintervention MRS for all experimental groups, led to additional analyses of this variable. Participants were divided into three groups on the basis of their scores on the PCT-RW and PCT-RM. Ps who chose 0–2 White women over Black women (out of 8) on the PCT-RW were categorized as low discriminators; Ps who chose 3–5 White women were categorized as medium discriminators; and Ps who chose 6–8 White women were categorized as high discriminators. Participants were similarly categorized as low, medium, and high discriminators on the basis of their PCT-RM scores (i.e., their choices of White men over Black men). One-way ANOVAs were performed, and significant differences were found among the low, medium, and high choosers of White men on postintervention MRS scores. High choosers of White men were more prejudiced than medium or low choosers of White men, and medium choosers of White men were more prejudiced than low choosers of White men. No significant differences, however, were found among low, medium, and high choosers of White women on postintervention MRS scores.

Discussion

Contact with High-Status Minority Persons. The hypothesis that contact with a high-status Black person would decrease discrimination toward Blacks was supported by data from the PCT-R. The only nonracist choices of Black and White men on the PCT-RM (not different from chance) were made by Ps who had contact with a high-status Black orientation leader. Contact with a high-status Black leader, in conjunction with participation in a cultural diversity workshop, resulted in the only nonracist (not different from chance) choices of photos of White and Black women on the PCT-RW. In addition, although Ps who had contact with a Black orientation leader made racist choices of women, their choices were significantly less racist than those of Ps who had contact with a White orientation leader.

This study's findings relevant to contact with Hispanic leaders suggest that the effects of contact with high-status non-Black minority persons do not generalize to behaviors and attitudes directed toward Blacks. Contact with a Hispanic orientation leader resulted in a greater-than-chance likelihood of distancing oneself from a Black woman or a Black man, as measured by the PCT-R than contact with a Black orientation leader. Ps who had experienced contact with a Hispanic orientation leader showed greater distancing from Blacks than Ps who had experienced contact with a White orientation leader. Although this was not statistically significant, it suggests that contact with a high-status Hispanic does not decrease and may increase racist discrimination directed toward Blacks. Why this might be the case was not addressed in this study and requires further investigation.

Participation in a Cultural Diversity Workshop. The findings of this study do not support the use of a single discussion-format workshop as an effective racism intervention. There was no indication that such a workshop decreased Whites' likelihood of distancing from Black women or men. This lack of effectiveness occurred despite the considerable resources invested in developing the workshop and despite the high ratings given the cultural diversity workshop by students. Participants who had attended the single 50-minute workshop were later just as likely to distance themselves from Black women and men, while reporting a low degree of prejudice, as were students who had not attended the workshop.

That a combination of interventions (e.g., workshop and contact) is more likely to succeed in changing attitudes and behaviors toward Blacks is partly supported by this study. Contact with a high-status Black person resulted in nonracist behavior of Whites toward Black men (as measured by the PCT-RM), regardless of Whites' workshop participation, but only the combination of contact with a high-status Black and participation in a cultural diversity workshop resulted in nonracist behavior of Whites toward Black women (as measured by the PCT-RW). It would seem that decreasing racist responses toward Black women is more difficult, and may require more intervention, than decreasing racist behavior toward Black men.

Relationship between Racist Discrimination and Prejudice. The findings of significant positive correlations among measures of discrimination and prejudice are consistent with previous research. Overall correlations indicated that a higher degree of self-reported prejudice was associated with a greater likelihood of choosing Whites over Blacks on the PCT-R. It is important to note that the relationship between discrimination toward Black men (PCT-RM scores) and prejudice (MRS scores) was twice as strong as the relationship between discrimination toward Black women (PCT-RW scores) and prejudice (MRS scores). One possible explanation for this difference is that respondents to the MRS, the prejudice measure, are making judgments about Black men rather than about Black men and women considered together.

The relationship between distancing (discrimination) and prejudice is clarified by examining the mean differences in self-reported prejudice among low, medium, and high choosers of White men and women over Black men and women. High choosers of White men were more prejudiced than medium or low choosers of White men, and medium choosers of White men were more prejudiced than low choosers of White men. Differences in self-reported prejudice among low, medium, and high choosers of White women over Black women, however, were not statistically significant. In other words, individual differences among Whites in their likelihood of distancing themselves from Black men were positively related to individual differences in attitudes toward Blacks, whereas individual differences in Whites' likelihood of distancing themselves from Black women were not related to individual differences in attitudes toward Blacks. These findings support the suggestion that respondents, when asked about their attitudes toward Blacks, may be considering only Black men rather than both Black men and women.

Gender and Racism. Gender was considered in this study as both a stimulus and a participant variable. As a participant variable, gender was not systematically related to racism; no significant differences in the behavior or attitudes of White women and men toward Blacks were found on any dependent measure. Gender was, however, an especially noteworthy stimulus variable. The differential distancing from Black women and Black men by Whites is an important finding of this study. The pattern of distancing found in these data suggest strongly that Black women are discriminated against to an even greater degree than are Black men. The likelihood of Whites' choosing White women over Black women was greater than their likelihood of choosing White men over Black men, regardless of intervention or of participant's gender. Moreover, while contact with a high-status Black resulted in nonracist choices of Black and White men, the only group of participants to make nonracist choices of Black and White women were those who had experienced both interventions—contact with a high-status Black and the workshop. These findings are congruent with those of Damico and Sparks (1986), who reported that Black girls were the most excluded group in desegregated middle schools, and supports the suggestion of Smith and Stewart (1983) that the interaction of ethnicity and gender should be considered in investigations of racism and sexism.

Measures of Prejudice and Distancing. The MRS appears to lack the sensitivity necessary to test the effects of the racism interventions used in this study; both pre- and postintervention scores on the MRS were generally low. Scores on the MRS were most useful as indicators of group differences among low, medium, and high choosers of Blacks over Whites, contributing to an understanding of individual differences among Whites who discriminate against Blacks. However, MRS scores did not significantly vary following contact with high-status Blacks or Hispanics, or following participation in a cultural diversity workshop. These findings support the conclusion of previous researchers (e.g., Crosby et al., 1980; Gaertner & Dovidio, 1986; Katz & Hass, 1988) that the use of self-report measures of racism is problematic.

The PCT-R, perhaps because of its oblique nature, was more sensitive to racism interventions than the MRS. It is likely that the inclusion of masking items (slides in which both persons were of the same ethnicity) caused Ps to be unaware of the intent of the research and therefore to express a wider (and probably more accurate) range of responses. Use of the PCT-R is not limited to studying only choices of Black and White women and men. If other images are substituted for those used in this study, the PCT-R can be easily adapted to measuring distancing from other ethnic groups (e.g., Hispanic-Americans, Native Americans), toward people of varying ages, or toward other groups of interest.

These findings, and those of other researchers, suggest that racism is best studied with unobtrusive measures. Even a self-report measure that has been shown to be minimally reactive, the MRS, was a less discerning tool than a measure that did not alert participants to the nature of the research. The use of the PCT as a research tool in the study of interpersonal racist discrimination seems promising. One potential avenue of study is to determine whether distancing as measured by the PCT-RW and PCT-RM (which are simulated measures of behavior) correlates with other unobtrusive measures of racist discrimination in actual interpersonal situations. The separation of photo choices into the PCT-RW and PCT-RM provides an opportunity to use the PCT-R in the study of racist and sexist discrimination as well as of various gender–ethnicity interactions. Two additional studies were undertaken to examine such interactions.

Experiment 2: Investigation of Gender–Ethnicity Interactions Using the PCT-R

In order to further explore the intricacies of gender and ethnicity as they relate to interpersonal discrimination, the PCT-R scores of Black, Asian, Latina, and White women were examined for group mean differences. Relationships between PCT-R scores and self-reported racist prejudice were also examined within each subsample.

Method

Participants. In this study, Ps were 30 Asian, 31 Black, 20 Latina, and 46 White female college students attending a New England women's college and recruited through introductory classes and student organizations. Students were paid a small sum or given class credit for their participation.

Procedure. All Ps completed the PCT-R and the MRS using Macintosh LC II computers. Scanned photo images and scale items were displayed via the computer screen, and Ps responded by choosing appropriate keys on the computer keyboard. Participants were assured both privacy and confidentiality.

Results

The PCT-R data from Black, Asian, Latina, and White women were compared and indicate that Ps' ethnicity was related to choices of Blacks and Whites on the PCT-R. Only White and Asian women chose significantly more White men over Black men on the PCT-RM and chose more White women over Black women on the PCT-RW, whereas Latina and Black women did not choose more Whites than Blacks. MRS scores were not positively correlated with choices of Black and White women for any group of participants, regardless of ethnicity, and only for White women was a higher degree of self-reported prejudice associated with a greater likelihood of choosing White men over Black men on the PCT-RM ($r = .39, p < .01$). In general, all participants reported a low degree of racist prejudice, although the MRS scores of Asians were significantly higher (but still below the scale median) than those of Blacks.

Experiment 3: PCT-R Response Latencies as Measures of Interpersonal Discrimination

The use of a computer for the presentation of the PCT-R allows for the measure of PCT-R response latencies as an unobtrusive measure of behavior. The third experiment examined the influence of racist prejudice on the speed with which photo choices were made. Devine (1989) studied the influence of racist prejudice on the speed with which individuals endorsed racist stereotypes, and found that less prejudiced individuals took longer to endorse stereotypes than did more prejudiced individuals. Devine suggested that the conflict between racial stereotypes and belief in racial equality that is experienced by less prejudiced people causes them to take longer to endorse negative stereotypes than more prejudiced people. In a separate line of research, it has been demonstrated that persons who endorse gender schemas are more quick to describe themselves in gender-appropriate terms than in non-gender-appropriate terms (Markus, Crane, Bernstein, & Siladi, 1982). Specifically, Markus et al. found that individuals with a masculine schema were faster to judge whether or not they were aggressive, dominant, and leader-like than they were to judge whether or not they were gentle, emotional, and sensitive. Conversely, those with a feminine schema were faster to judge whether or not they were gentle, emotional, and sensitive than to judge whether or not they were aggressive, dominant, and leader-like.

Method

Participants. In this study, Ps were 34 White male college students, and 31 Black, 30 Asian, 20 Latina, and 46 White female students, attending schools in a New England state and recruited through introductory classes. Students were given class credit for their participation.

Procedure. All Ps completed the PCT-R and the MRS using Macintosh LC II computers. Scanned photo images and scale items were displayed via the computer screen, and Ps responded by choosing appropriate keys on the computer keyboard. Both the responses and the latency times were recorded by the computer (although Ps were unaware that latencies were being measured).

Results

In order to examine the relationships between the self-reported racist prejudice and gender stereotype measures and the PCT-R response latencies, a median split was performed on MRS scores. Data were collapsed across ethnicity and gender, since the only individual differences in the relationship between prejudice and PCT-R response latencies were of concern. PCT-R response latencies of high and low scorers on the MRS were compared by means of a *t* test. As hypothesized, high MRS scorers (more racially prejudiced persons) took significantly longer to choose Black men over White men than to choose White men over Black men on the PCT-RM. Low MRS scorers (less racially prejudiced persons) exhibited no such differences in their PCT-R response latencies. Paradoxically, high MRS scorers took longer to choose White women over Black women than to choose Black women over White women. Once again, the utility of the self-reported MRS scores in predicting racist discrimination directed toward Black women is in question.

SUMMARY AND POLICY IMPLICATIONS

Empirical evidence has shown that the nature of interpersonal racism is changing. The newer conceptualizations of "aversive racism" (Kovel, 1970; Gaertner & Dovidio, 1986), "symbolic racism" (Kinder & Sears, 1981), "modern racism" (McConahay, 1986), "regressive racism" (Griffin & Rogers, 1977), and "ambivalent racism" (Katz, 1981) suggest that the old-fashioned "redneck" (or Archie Bunker) type of openly discriminatory behavior and openly verbalized negative stereotypes has decreased. These beliefs and behaviors have been replaced by feelings that minority groups are too demanding and getting more than they deserve (Gaertner & Dovidio, 1986), and that "blacks are violating cherished values and making illegitimate demands for changes in the racial status quo" (McConahay & Hough, 1976, p. 38). Lani Guinier, whose nomination as head of the Justice Department's Office of Civil Rights was withdrawn by President Clinton, has noted the often polite verbal and behavioral codes that mask more open racism. She has suggested that significant inroads against racism will not take place unless people "start speaking openly about the unpleasant but real racial divisions in this society" (cited in Rich, 1993, p. 26). There is good reason to believe that coded racist beliefs are expressed in such behaviors as opposition to welfare and affirmative action programs. Direct anti-ethnic sentiments are replaced by opposition to symbols associated with ethnicities (such as "busing" and "welfare"). Ellis Cose (cited in Rampersad, 1994, p. 6) describes these more subtle racist behaviors as "soul-destroying slights," and maintains that the "often hurtful and seemingly trivial encounters of daily existence are in the end what most of life is." Kovel (1970) described this more hidden type of racist discrimination (which he labeled "aversive") in the following manner:

> The aversive racist is the type who believes in white race superiority and is more or less aware of it but does nothing overt about it. He tries to ignore the existence of black people, tries to avoid contact with them, and, at most, tries to be polite, correct and cold in whatever dealings are necessary between the races. (p. 54)

A basic assumption in new theories of racism is that Whites' opposition to policies such as affirmative action and mandatory school busing is an indication that they possess prejudice against people of color, that is concealed by a superficial commitment to change the status quo (Katz & Hass, 1988). There is considerable empirical support for this conclusion from studies such as that by Sears and Allen (1984) on opposition to school busing. Another study, of a random sample of 1,504 European-American adults (Kluegel & Smith, 1982) found that Whites perceived widespread reverse discrimination, and believed that Blacks' opportunities in recent years have improved. In a 1981 national poll (Smith & Dempsey, 1983), non-Black respondents placed Blacks at the top of a list of those who have "too much power and influence over our country's policies" (p. 598) and are most likely to try to "push in where they are not wanted (p. 598)." The new research presented in this chapter provides strong support for the position that Blacks continue to be distanced from by others in our society. Whites, regardless of what they say about their feelings toward Blacks, tend to avoid Blacks for various types of interpersonal interactions. The research presented here also indicates that other non-Blacks (e.g., Asian-Americans) also avoid Blacks for social interactions.

At the beginning of this chapter I have asked the question, "How can we best measure racist discrimination so that we might ascertain the outcome of interventions?" The research presented here indicates that unobtrusive measures of interpersonal racist discrimination are proving most useful in increasing our understanding of the patterns of distancing to which people of color are exposed. The use of measures such as the PCT-R, in conjunction with self-report measures of prejudice and stereotyping, provides one way of examining the relationships among racist prejudice, stereotyping, and discrimination. Measures such as the MRS, however, should be used with caution, since it seems that they are more likely to be measuring prejudice toward Black men than toward Black women. As one of a set of measures, self-reports can provide valuable confirmatory information, but they must be used cautiously in studies that rely on analyses of group differences for hypothesis testing.

The revisitation of Allport's (1954) contact theory has been a productive area of research. Especially interesting has been a reconsideration of the relative status of the people of color with whom Whites come in contact. The findings presented here suggest that exposing European-Americans to high-status African-Americans during cooperative, intense interaction is likely to decrease later avoidance of African-Americans. Important work remains to be done to further define the intersection of class and race.

Important, too, is the pattern of findings regarding generalizability. Theories and interventions of racism directed toward Black men do not help us to understand the greater likelihood of Black women's being discriminated against. When studying racism directed toward Blacks, one must remember that Blacks are of two genders, and that the relationship between racism and sexism must not be ignored if there is any hope of changing racism directed toward Black women. In what ways do racism interventions differentially affect the lives of women and men of color? We must not assume that all interventions improve behaviors of Whites toward women of color. On the contrary, the research presented here seems to indicate that, despite intervention, women of color continue to be discriminated against by others. In addition, the findings from the intervention study presented in this chapter suggest that to be most effective, interventions should target behaviors toward specific minority groups rather than attempting to change racist behaviors directed toward all underrepresented groups at once. If true behavioral change is to occur, creative methods of interracial contact among individuals must be sought.

After more than two decades, affirmative action policies have still not resulted in getting large numbers of people of color into high-level positions (Crosby, 1993). Despite the threat of federal sanctions, college administrators have responded to a lack of funds by questioning the worth of affirmative action. Crosby (1993) suggested that despite the cost and difficulty in designing good affirmative action policies, they are worth instituting. She noted that institutions that do not invest in such policies may "find themselves paying a high price in alienation and campus unrest" (p. B2). The research presented in this chapter suggests that some inexpensive and specific changes are likely to result in improved intergroup relations. In university settings, for example, affirmative action practices similar to those employed to increase ethnic diversity among faculty members could be used to increase the presence of high-status student employees and staff persons who are members of underrepresented groups. Institutions could increase the placement of such students as peer counselors, residence hall coordinators and assistants, academic tutors, freshman orientation staff persons, teaching assistants, and so forth. In addition, students who are members of underrepresented groups should be encouraged to occupy voluntary high-status positions in student government, club leadership, and the like.

If institutions of higher education in the United States hope to be central forces for change in an increasingly pluralistic society, then educators must seriously consider the frequency and context of intergroup contact among college students. African-American, Asian-American, Hispanic-American, Native American, and other traditionally underrepresented groups of students who are avoided by European-American students in social interactions are not receiving the full benefit of the college experience. The same is true of those who do the distancing (i.e., European-American students). A single educational workshop is not likely to change the racist behaviors of participants; yet that is the intervention of choice at many, perhaps most, institutions. It is not enough to change curricula to address the needs of minority students if peer interactions serve to keep them marginalized. Desegregated classrooms cannot accomplish what integrated social interactions can. The use of interracial learning teams has been one of the most successful strategies for decreasing racism in classrooms, but it has hardly been used at the postsecondary level. It seems likely, however, that assigning ethnically diverse college students to project groups can lead to a reduction in racist discrimination.

Racism in the United States is escalating; budgetary problems notwithstanding, institutions can no longer afford the consequences of interventions that fail to change behavior. Strategies that best succeed in improving intergroup relations are likely to be ones that are grounded in theoretically based empirical research, and that address both racism and sexism. Such strategies will require the creative commitment of institutional administrations and resources.

ACKNOWLEDGMENTS

This chapter is partly based on a doctoral dissertation completed in the Department of Psychology at the University of Rhode Island in 1992. Additional research was conducted while I was a visiting assistant professor of psychology and education at Mount Holyoke College during the 1992–1993 academic year. The support of my colleagues, and the capable and dedicated contributions of my students there, were instrumental in the completion of this research. Portions of this chapter were presented in a talk at the Association for Women in Psychology's 1993 annual conference in Atlanta, Georgia, and in colloquia at Mount Holyoke College, the University of Hawaii, and the East–West Center, Honolulu, Hawaii.

REFERENCES

Allport, G. W. (1954). *The nature of prejudice*. Reading, MA: Addison-Wesley.
Bagozzi, R. P. (1978). The construct validity of the affective, behavioral, and cognitive components of attitude by analysis of covariance structures. *Multivariate Behavioral Research, 13*, 9–31.
Barnard, W. A., & Benn, M. S. (1988). Belief congruence and prejudice reduction in an interracial contact setting. *Journal of Social Psychology, 128*(1), 125–134.
Baron, R. A. (1979). Aggression, empathy, and race: Effects of victim's pain cues, victim's race, and level of instigation on physical aggression. *Journal of Applied Social Psychology, 9*, 103–114.
Bielby, W. T. (1987). Modern prejudice and institutional barriers to equal employment opportunity for minorities. *Journal of Social Issues, 13*(1), 79–84.

Blanchard, F. A., Lilly, T., & Vaughn, L. A. (1991). Reducing the expression of racial prejudice. *Psychological Science, 2*, 101–105.

Bond, C. F., DiCandia, C. G., & MacKinnon, J. R. (1988). Responses to violence in a psychiatric setting: The role of patient's race. *Personality and Social Psychology Bulletin, 14*(3), 448–458.

Bowser, B. P. (1985). Race relations in the 1980s: The case of the United States. *Journal of Black Studies, 15*, 307–324.

Brown, C. E. (1981). Shared space invasion and race. *Personality and Social Psychology Bulletin, 7*(1), 103–108.

Bruin, K. (1985). Prejudices, discrimination, and simulation/gaming: An analysis. *Simulation and Games, 16*(2), 161–173.

Bullock, H. A. (1961). Significance of the racial factor in the length of prison sentences. *Journal of Criminal Law, Criminology, and Police Science, 52*, 411–417.

Byrnes, D. A., & Kiger, G. (1990). The effect of a prejudice-reduction simulation on attitude change. *Journal of Applied Social Psychology, 20*(4), 341–356.

Carter, R. T. (1990). The relationship between racism and racial identity among White Americans: An exploratory investigation. *Journal of Counseling and Development, 69*, 46–50.

Chidester, T. R. (1986). Problems in the study of interracial interaction: Pseudo-interracial dyad paradigm. *Journal of Personality and Social Psychology, 50*, 74–79.

Colca, C., Lowen, D., Colca, L. A., & Lord, S. A. (1982). Combating racism in the schools: A group work pilot project. *Social Work in Education, 5*(1), 5–16.

Cook, S. W. (1988). The 1954 social science statement and school desegregation: A reply to Gerard. In P. A. Katz & D. A. Taylor (Eds.), *Eliminating racism: Profiles in controversy* (pp. 237–256). New York: Plenum.

Cook, S. W. (1990). Toward a psychology of improving justice: Research on extending the equality principle to victims of social injustice. *Journal of Social Issues, 46*, 147–161.

Crosby, F. (1993, December 15). Affirmative action is worth it. *Chronicle of Higher Education*, pp. A22, B2.

Crosby, F., Bromley, S., & Saxe, L. (1980). Recent unobtrusive studies of Black and White discrimination and prejudice: A literature review. *Psychological Bulletin, 87*, 546–563.

Damico, S. B., & Sparks, C. (1986). Cross-group contact opportunities: Impact on interpersonal relationships in desegregated middle schools. *Sociology of Education, 59*, 113–123.

Devine, P. G. (1989). Stereotypes and prejudice: Their automatic and controlled components. *Journal of Personality and Social Psychology, 56*(1), 5–18.

Donnerstein, E., & Donnerstein, M. (1976). Research in the control of interracial aggression. In R. G. Geen & E. C. O'Neal (Eds.), *Perspectives on aggression* (pp. 133–168). New York: Academic Press.

Duckitt, J. (1993). Prejudice and behavior: A review. *Current Psychology: Research and Reviews, 11*(4), 291–307.

Duncan, B. L. (1976). Differential social perception and attribution of intergroup violence: Testing the lower limits of stereotyping of Blacks. *Journal of Personality and Social Psychology, 34*, 590–598.

Feagin, J. R., & Eckberg, D. R. (1980). Discrimination: Motivation, action, effects, and context. *Annual Review of Sociology, 6,* 1–20.

Flaherty, J. A., & Meagher, R. (1980). Measuring racial bias in inpatient treatment. *American Journal of Psychiatry, 137*(6), 679–682.

Frey, D. L., & Gaertner, S. L. (1986). Helping and the avoidance of inappropriate interracial behavior: A strategy that perpetuates a nonprejudiced self-image. *Journal of Personality and Social Psychology, 50*(6), 1083–1090.

Furuto, S. B., & Furuto, D. M. (1983). The effects of affective and cognitive treatment on attitude change toward ethnic minority groups. *International Journal of Intercultural Relations, 7*(2), 149–165.

Gaertner, S. L., & Dovidio, J. F. (1986). The aversive form of racism. In J. F. Dovidio & S. L. Gaertner (Eds.), *Prejudice, discrimination, and racism* (pp. 61–89). Orlando, FL: Harcourt Brace Jovanovich.

Griffin, B. Q., & Rogers, R. W. (1977). Reducing interracial aggression: Inhibiting effects of victim's suffering and power to retaliate. *Journal of Psychology, 95,* 151–157.

Hendricks, M., & Bootzin, R. (1976). Race and sex as stimuli for negative affect and physical avoidance. *Journal of Social Psychology, 98,* 111–120.

Jackman, M. R., & Crane, M. (1986). "Some of my best friends are black . . . ": Interracial friendship and whites' racial attitudes. *Public Opinion Quarterly, 50,* 459–486.

Jackson, A. M., Farley, G. K., Zimet, S. G., & Waterman, J. M. (1978). Race and sex as variables for children involved in treatment. *Psychological Reports, 43,* 883–886.

Jones, J. M. (1972). *Prejudice and racism.* Reading, MA: Addison-Wesley.

Jones, J. M. (1983). The concept of race in social psychology: From color to culture. In L. Wheeler & P. Shaver (Eds.), *Review of personality and social psychology* (Vol. 4, pp. 127–149). Beverly Hills, CA: Sage.

Katz, I. (1981). *Stigma: A social psychological analysis.* Hillsdale, NJ: Erlbaum.

Katz, I., & Hass, R. G. (1988). Racial ambivalence and American value conflict: Correlational and priming studies of dual cognitive structures. *Journal of Personality and Social Psychology, 55*(6), 893–905.

Kinder, D. R., & Sears, D. O. (1981). Prejudice and politics: Symbolic racism versus racial threats to the good life. *Journal of Personality and Social Psychology, 40,* 414–431.

Kluegel, J. R., & Smith, E. R. (1982). Whites' beliefs about blacks' opportunity. *American Sociological Review, 47*(4), 518–532.

Kovel, J. (1970). *White racism: A psychological history.* New York: Pantheon.

Lobel, S. A. (1987). Effects of personal versus impersonal rater instructions on relative favorability of thirteen ethnic group stereotypes. *Journal of Social Psychology, 128*(1), 29–39.

Lott, B., Lott, A. J., & Fernald, J. (1990). Individual differences in distancing responses to women on a photo choice task. *Sex Roles, 22,* 97–110.

Lowenstein, L. F. (1985). Investigating ethnic prejudices among boys and girls in a therapeutic community for maladjusted children and modifying some prejudices: Can basic prejudices be changed? *School Psychology International, 6*(4), 239–243.

Markus, H., Crane, M., Bernstein, S., & Siladi, M. (1982). Self-schemas and gender. *Journal of Personality and Social Psychology, 42*, 38–50.

McConahay, J. B. (1986). Modern racism, ambivalence, and the Modern Racism Scale. In J. F. Dovidio & S. L. Gaertner (Eds.), *Prejudice, discrimination, and racism* (pp. 91–125). Orlando, FL: Harcourt Brace Jovanovich.

McConahay, J. B., & Hough, J. C. (1976). Symbolic racism. *Journal of Social Issues, 32*, 23–45.

McCormick, A. E., & Kinloch, G. C. (1985). Interracial contact in the customer–clerk situation. *Journal of Social Psychology, 126*, 551–553.

McFadden, A. C., Marsh, G. E., Price, B. J., & Hwang, Y. (1992). A study of race and gender bias in the punishment of school children. *Education and Treatment of Children, 15*(2), 140–146.

Myrdal, G. (1944). *An American dilemma: The Negro problem and modern democracy.* New York: Harper.

Nickerson, S., Mayo, C., & Smith, J. (1986). Racism in the courtroom. In J. F. Dovidio & S. L. Gaertner (Eds.), *Prejudice, discrimination, and racism* (pp. 255–278). Orlando, FL: Harcourt Brace Jovanovich.

Partnow, E. (Ed.). (1977). *The quotable woman* (Vol. 2). Los Angeles: Pinnacle Books.

Petersilia, J. (1983). *Racial disparities in the criminal justice system.* Santa Monica, CA: Rand Corporation.

Qualls, R. C., Cox, M. B., & Schehr, T. L. (1992). Racial attitudes on campus: Are there gender differences? *Journal of College Student Development, 33*, 524–529.

Rampersad, A. (1994, January 9). Another day, another humiliation [Review of *The rage of a privileged class*]. *New York Times Book Review*, p. 6.

Rich, F. (1993, November 7). Public stages: Stepin in it. *New York Times Magazine*, pp. 24, 26.

Rodin, M. J., Price, J. M., Bryson, J. B., & Sanchez, F. J. (1990). Asymmetry in prejudice attribution. *Journal of Experimental Social Psychology, 26*, 481–504.

Sagar, H. A., & Schofield, J. W. (1980). Racial and behavioral cues in black and white children's perceptions of ambiguously aggressive acts. *Journal of Personality and Social Psychology, 39*, 590–598.

Sampson, W. A. (1986). Desegregation and racial tolerance in academia. *Journal of Negro Education, 55*(2), 171–184.

Sedlacek, W. E., Troy, W., & Chapman, T. (1976). An evaluation of three methods of racism–sexism training. *Personnel and Guidance Journal, 55*, 196–198.

Sears, D. O., & Allen, H. M. (1984). The trajectory of local desegregation controversies and whites' opposition to busing. In N. Miller & M. B. Brewer (Eds.), *Groups in contact: The psychology of desegregation* (pp. 123–151). New York: Academic Press.

Sears, D. O., Peplau, L. A., & Taylor, S. E. (1991). *Social psychology* (7th ed.). Englewood Cliffs, NJ: Prentice Hall.

Sigelman, L. & Welch, S. (1993). The contact hypothesis revisited: Black–white interaction and positive racial attitudes. *Social Forces, 71*(3), 781–795.

Singer, B. D. (1967). Some implications of differential psychiatric treatment of Negro and white patients. *Social Science and Medicine, 1*, 77–83.

Slavin, R. E. (1983). When does cooperative learning increase student achievement? *Psychological Bulletin, 94*, 429–443.

Slavin, R. E. (1985). Cooperative learning: Applying contact theory in desegregated schools. *Journal of Social Issues, 41*(3), 45–62.

Smith, A., & Stewart, A. J. (1983). Approaches to studying racism and sexism in Black women's lives. *Journal of Social Issues, 39*(3), 1–15.

Smith, T. W., & Dempsey, G. R. (1983). The polls: Ethnic social distance and prejudice. *Public Opinion Quarterly, 47*, 584–600.

Snyder, M., Kleck, R., & Strenta, A., & Mentzer, S. J. (1979). Avoidance of the handicapped: An attributional ambiguity analysis. *Journal of Personality and Social Psychology, 37*, 2297–2306.

Sue, S. (1977). Community mental health services to minority groups. *American Psychologist, 32*, 616–624.

Sue, S., McKinney, H., Allen, D., & Hall, J. (1974). Delivery of community mental health services to black and white clients. *Journal of Consulting and Clinical Psychology, 42*(6), 794–801.

Tatum, B. D. (1992). Talking about race, learning about racism: The application of racial identity development theory in the classroom. *Harvard Educational Review, 62*(1), 1–24.

Thomas, D. A. (1993). Racial dynamics in cross-race developmental relationships. *Administrative Science Quarterly, 38*, 169–194.

Vohra, S., Rodolfa, E., de la Cruz, A., & Vincent, C. (1991). A cross-cultural training format for peer counselors. *Journal of College Student Development, 32*, 82–84.

Word, C. O., Zanna, M. P., & Cooper, J. (1974). Avoidance behaviors as measures of discrimination in interpersonal situations. *Journal of Experimental Social Psychology, 10*, 109–120.

Weitz, S. (1972). Attitude, voice, and behavior: A repressed affect model of interracial interaction. *Journal of Personality and Social Psychology, 24*, 14–21.

Wilson, D. L. (1994, January 19). Diversity on a disk: Vanderbilt develops multimedia package to foster racial and ethnic sensitivity. *Chronicle of Higher Education*, pp. A23–A25.

Wilson, W. J. (1973). *Power, racism, and privilege: Race relations in theoretical and sociohistorical perspectives*. New York: Macmillan.

4

Interpersonal
Heterosexism

J. L. FERNALD

DEFINING HETEROSEXISM

"Heterosexism" has been defined (Herek, 1990) as an "ideological system that denies, denigrates, and stigmatizes any nonheterosexual form of behavior, relationship, or community" (p. 316). To this definition I would add the denial, denigration, and stigmatization of nonheterosexual *persons*. Like other forms of oppression, heterosexism is manifested both in discriminatory social customs and institutions, and in individual behaviors that discriminate against individual lesbians and gay men. Perhaps two of the most obvious examples of institutional heterosexism are the refusal of all 50 of the United States to legally recognize marriage between two persons of the same gender, and the U.S. military's policy forbidding gay and lesbian personnel to disclose their sexual orientation. These and numerous other cultural and institutional practices systematically exclude and marginalize gay men and lesbians, and confer upon them the symbolic status of "other." It is this symbolic status, Berk (1990) has noted, that is the key ingredient of all hate crimes—the most extreme and violent acts of interpersonal discrimination against members of disesteemed subordinate groups. Although this chapter focuses on interpersonal heterosexist discrimination, it is assumed that such discrimination occurs within the cultural context of pervasive institutional heterosexism, and that both institutional and interpersonal heterosexism create and maintain a climate of hostility for lesbians and gay men.

Social scientists have used multiple terms to refer to negative responses to lesbians and gay men, including "homoerotophobia" (Churchill, 1967), "homophobia" (Smith, 1971; Forstein, 1988; Morin & Garfinkle, 1978; Weinberg, 1972), "homosexphobia" (Levitt & Klassen, 1974), "homonegativism" (Hudson & Ricketts, 1980; VanderStoep & Green, 1988), "homosexism" (Hansen, 1982; Lehne, 1976), and "homosexual bias" (Fyfe, 1983). "Homophobia" is most often used in the psychological and popular literature and in the mass media. This term is rooted in Churchill's (1967) study of attitudes toward homosexuality, in which he coined the term "homoerotophobia" to refer to a pervasive cultural fear of homosexual eroticism or behavior (Neisen, 1990; Nungesser, 1983). "Homophobia" first appeared in the psychological literature in an article by Kenneth Smith (1971) who used it to label a dimension of personality in individuals who endorsed negative attitudes toward homosexuals. The term was popularized by Weinberg (1972) who defined it as a "dread of being in close quarters with homosexuals" (p. 4).

Although the concept of homophobia has been instrumental in helping to shift the research focus in psychology away from etiological explanations of homosexuality toward studies of attitudinal bias against lesbians and gay men, it has recently been criticized. Specifically, Haaga (1991) has pointed out that the suffix "-phobia" inaccurately reflects the nature of anti-gay/lesbian attitudes. Whereas a phobia is an intense, irrational and persistent fear, the affect most closely associated with anti-gay/lesbian attitudes is primarily anger or disgust, not fear (Ernulf & Innala, 1987; Haaga, 1991). Furthermore, expression of anti-lesbian/gay attitudes in a culture in which homosexuality is condemned and/or ignored is not only not irrational, but in some situations actually confers benefits on the individual who expresses them (Herek, 1986a). Hostility toward lesbians and gay men is also unlike a phobia in that phobics perceive their fears as excessive or unreasonable, whereas persons who express hostility toward lesbians and gay men usually perceive their anger as justified. In addition, phobics are often motivated to change their condition, but gay men, lesbians, and their supporters are the ones who are invested in changing anti-gay/lesbian attitudes.

Because the term "homophobia" is misleading, and because it has been so broadly used as a descriptor of a wide variety of negative emotions, attitudes, and behaviors, as well as a cultural phenomenon and a personality dimension, some have suggested it no longer be used (Fyfe, 1983; Haaga, 1991; MacDonald, 1976; Neisen, 1990). As MacDonald (1976, p. 24) pointed out, "a term that means everything has little utility . . . [and] . . .

such usage is likely to lessen our objectivity and inhibit us in our attempts to find other explanations for negative reactions to homosexuality." It has been argued that anti-gay/lesbian attitudes reflect a culturally entrenched prejudice, more akin to other such prejudices (e.g., sexism and racism) than to a phobia (Haaga, 1991; Hansen, 1982; Herek, 1984, 1986a, 1990; Lehne, 1976; Neisen, 1990). Finally, whereas the behavior associated with phobias is avoidance, anti-lesbian/gay attitudes, like other prejudices, are associated with both avoidance and aggression.

To borrow from Lott's social-psychological conception of sexism (Lott, 1987 and Chapter 2, this volume), it is here proposed that interpersonal heterosexism is composed of the related but independent dimensions of prejudice, stereotypes, and discrimination. In the language of social-psychological behavior theory (see Lott & Lott, 1985), heterosexist prejudice refers to negative attitudes toward (i.e., dislike of) lesbians and gay men; heterosexist stereotypes are widely shared and socially sanctioned beliefs about gay men and lesbians that are used to justify anti-gay/lesbian hostility; and heterosexist discrimination includes face-to-face overt behaviors that distance, avoid, exclude, or physically violate lesbians and gay men. Most psychological research on heterosexism, regardless of the term used, has focused on attitudes and beliefs. The question of how heterosexists actually behave in face-to-face situations with lesbians and gay men has been relatively underresearched. This is particularly true with respect to investigations of aggression against lesbians and gay men. This omission in the literature is particularly glaring, given that anti-gay/lesbian behavior in the "real world" often takes the form of violence. This chapter reviews the literature documenting anti-lesbian/gay prejudice and its correlates, and stereotypes of gay men and lesbians; however, it focuses particularly on interpersonal heterosexist discrimination. After all, as Plasek and Allard (1984) have pointed out, it is ultimately in actions, not in words, that a society is libertarian or repressive.

HETEROSEXIST PREJUDICE

Finding of Surveys and Opinion Polls

There is evidence of ambivalence in today's publicly expressed attitudes about homosexuality and the rights of gays and lesbians. On the one hand, support for civil rights for gays and lesbians has been increasing, and endorsement of restrictions on gay and lesbian expressions of free speech have been decreasing since at least the late 1960s. On the other hand, there has been no corresponding decline in moral and social sanctions against homosexuality (Dejowski, 1992). Analysis of data collected in large public opinion polls suggests that beliefs about legal rights for lesbians and gay men have been getting more liberal. For example, Gallup polls among Canadians showed an increase from 42% in 1968 to 70% in 1977 in those who favored the decriminalization of homosexual acts between consenting adults, and an increase from 52% in 1977 to 70% in 1985 in those who supported the passage of human rights legislation that would prohibit discrimination on the basis of sexual orientation (cited in Rayside & Bowler, 1988). Public support for gay equality rights has been increasing in Great Britain and the United States as well. Although a majority of U.S. residents surveyed in 1970 by the Institute for Sex Research (see Levitt & Klassen, 1974) believed that gays should be barred from the ministry (77%), teaching school (77%), practicing medicine (68%), and government service (67%), 65% of U.S. residents surveyed in a Gallup poll in 1983 said they thought that "homosexuals should have equal rights in terms of job opportunities" (cited in Rayside & Bowler, 1988, p.651). In 1979, 73% of those surveyed in Great Britain agreed with a similar statement (cited in Rayside & Bowler, 1988). Public willingness to endorse restrictions on expression by gays and lesbians has also been decreasing. Data from the General Social Surveys (GSS) found, among independent nationally representative samples of approximately 1,500 English-speaking adults in the United States from 1973 through 1988, a gradual but linear decline in support for proposals to remove gay-positive books from library shelves, to dismiss gay and lesbian college teachers, and to prohibit public speaking by gays and lesbians (Dejowski, 1992).

Although support for legal equality rights has obtained majority support, most U.S., Canadian, and British respondents continue to believe that homosexuality is morally wrong. The Institute for Sex Research survey conducted in the United States in 1970 found that nearly half believed that "homosexuality is a social corruption that can cause the downfall of civilization" (Levitt & Klassen, 1974, p. 34), and 84% felt that homosexuality is obscene and vulgar. Sixty-nine percent of Canadians in 1980, and 69% British respondents in 1985, agreed (Rayside & Bowler, 1988). It appears that beliefs about the morality of homosexual behavior has remained consistent over the past 20 years. U.S. Gallup polls from 1973 to 1989 found that approximately 70% of respondents believed that sexual relations between two adults of the same sex are always wrong, with no more than a 4% variation in that rate in any year (Smith, 1990). GSS data indicate a slight increase from 1973 to 1988, when just over 75% of respondents believed that same-sex sexual relations are "always" or "almost always" wrong (Dejowski, 1992). Among a sample of 1,880 self-identified completely heterosexual, never-married teenage males in the United States who responded to the 1988 National Survey of Adolescent Males, almost 89% agreed "a lot" that they found the thought of two men having sex with each other disgusting, and 38.5% disagreed "a lot" with the idea of personally being able to befriend a gay person, while only 12% agreed "a lot" with this notion (Marsiglio, 1993). Recent studies have also documented a prevalence of anti-lesbian/gay attitudes among college dormitory residents (D'Augelli & Rose, 1990), students in a counseling program (McDermott & Stadler, 1988), and doctors and nurses (Douglas, Kalman, & Kalman, 1985).

In 1944 Myrdal described the "American dilemma" as the deep cultural and psychological conflict among the American people between American ideals of dignity of the individual, basic equality of all people, and inalienable rights to freedom, justice, and equality of opportunity on the one hand, and discrimination against and denial of opportunity to Blacks and others in a racist society on the other hand. It may well be that the ambivalent attitudes expressed by many U.S. residents in regard to the rights of gay men and lesbians reflect a similar dilemma.

Correlates of Anti-Lesbian/Gay Attitudes

Much of the research in the area of attitudes toward gay men and lesbians has focused on identifying correlates of negative attitudes (Herek, 1984). In an attempt to develop a personality profile of "homophobic" individuals, Smith (1971), for example, found that anti-gay attitudes were related to authoritarianism, status consciousness, and sexual rigidity. Endorsement of anti-gay/lesbian attitudes has also been shown to be positively related to sexual conservatism (Dunbar, Brown, & Amoroso, 1973; Minnigerode, 1976) and sex guilt (Dunbar, Brown, & Amoroso, 1973). The relationship between heterosexist attitudes and authoritarianism has been confirmed by other researchers (Hood, 1973; Herek, 1988; Karr, 1978; Larsen, Reed, & Hoffman, 1980; MacDonald & Games, 1974; Newman, 1989). In a sample of college students, Kurdek (1988) found anti-gay/lesbian attitudes to be inversely related to principled moral reasoning. That is, participants who held positive attitudes toward gay men and lesbians were more likely to reason about moral dilemmas in terms of individually constructed principles rather than in terms of rules that uphold the conventional social order. Kurdek (1988) concluded that heterosexist attitudes are part of a larger system of beliefs about conventional social order.

Other research has found a link between traditional religiosity and endorsement of anti-gay/lesbian attitudes (Alston, 1974; Bowman, 1979; Cameron & Ross, 1981; Glassner & Owen, 1976; Hansen, 1982; Henley & Pincus, 1978; Herek, 1988; Irwin & Thompson, 1977; Larsen et al., 1980; Nyberg & Alston, 1976–1977; VanderStoep & Green, 1988). Henley and Pincus (1978) found that persons who identified themselves as belonging to one of the three major Western religions (Catholicism, Protestantism, or Judaism) expressed more negative attitudes toward gays than those who self-identified as nonreligious, whereas others (Alston, 1974; Nyberg & Alston, 1976–1977) have reported that Protestants and Catholics are more prejudiced against gays than either Jews, followers of "other" religions, or the nonreligious. For example, in the Nyberg and Alston (1976–1977) sample, 79% of the Protestants and 74% of the Catholics, as opposed to 32% of the Jews and 37% of the nonreligious, believed that sexual relations between two adults of the same sex is "always wrong." In the studies that have examined the relationship between religiosity and gay-negative attitudes, religiosity is primarily operationalized as adherence to a major religion, membership in a particular Protestant denomination, or frequency of church attendance; thus, these studies have failed to address which specific aspect or aspects of religiosity are predictive of anti-gay/lesbian attitudes. In an effort to do that, VanderStoep and Green (1988) conducted a path-analytic study and found that religiosity, as measured by religious belief, religious knowledge, religious practice, and religious experience, significantly predicted "ethical conservatism," which in turn significantly predicted anti-gay/lesbian attitudes. These findings suggest that ethical (moral) conservatism is an important direct predictor of anti-gay/lesbian attitudes, and also acts as an intervening variable between religiosity and heterosexist attitudes. It appears, then, that persons who endorse anti-lesbian/gay attitudes are more likely to be both sexually and ethically conservative.

In addition to being more generally conservative, individuals with heterosexist attitudes have also been found to express more racist attitudes than individuals with more positive attitudes toward gays (Ficarrotto, 1990; Henley & Pincus, 1978). In order to empirically test the proposition supported by many gay activists that gays are marginalized in much the same way that Blacks and women are, Henley and Pincus (1978) compared attitudes toward Blacks, women, and gays. Respondents in their sample who endorsed anti-lesbian/gay attitudes did indeed also endorse more racist and more sexist attitudes. In order to compare the relative explanatory power of a sexual conservatism theory of "homophobia" with an intergroup prejudice theory, Ficarrotto (1990) analyzed correlations among erotophobia (sexual conservatism), sexism, racism, and anti-lesbian/gay attitudes. Sexual conservatism (as measured by a scale of erotophobia) and social prejudice (as measured by scales of racism and sexism) were found to be independent and equal predictors of negative attitudes toward gays. These findings provide empirical support for the conceptualization of heterosexism as a social prejudice, but also suggest that anti-gay/lesbian attitudes have a dimension of sexual conservatism that may not be associated with other social prejudices.

Demographic variables that are associated with anti-lesbian/gay attitudes include age, education, and geographic region. People raised in the U.S. Midwest and South, in rural areas and small towns, and in the Canadian prairies tend to be more anti-lesbian/gay than those raised in other regions of the United States and Canada and in and urban areas (Hansen, 1982; Irwin & Thompson, 1977; Levitt & Klassen, 1974; Nyberg & Alston, 1976–1977; Stephan & McMullin, 1982). Education has generally been found to be positively associated with less anti-lesbian/gay attitudes (Hansen, 1982; Irwin & Thompson, 1977; Levitt & Klassen, 1974), but the results for age have been inconsistent. Although being younger has been found to be associated with more positive attitudes toward gays by Bowman (1979), Irwin and Thompson (1977), and Nyberg and Alston (1976–1977), it has also been found to be related to more negative attitudes in studies by Hudson and Ricketts (1980), Kurdek (1988), and Whitley (1987).

Friendship, personal contact, or previous association with a gay person have also been identified as factors associated with more positive attitudes toward lesbians and gay men (Hansen, 1982; Herek, 1988; Glassner & Owen, 1976; Millham, San Miguel, & Kellogg, 1976; Whitley, 1990). Although the studies cited above do not help us decide whether knowing a gay person is a cause or an effect of reduced prejudice, the contact hypothesis literature on racial prejudice (Allport, 1954; Amir, 1966; Stephan, 1985) leads us to expect that under favorable conditions, contact with a lesbian or a gay man may reduce prejudice. We have known for a long time, beginning with the work of Allport (1954), that contact with persons of equal or higher status reduces prejudice, whereas contact with persons of lower status creates and maintains it. Conditions that reduce prejudice have been found to include personal interactions between individuals from different social groups (Wilder, 1986), pleasant or rewarding contact (Amir, 1966), and cooperative interactions in functionally important activities (Amir, 1966; Sherif, Harvey, White. Hood, & Sherif, 1988). These findings suggest that intimate, pleasant, and functionally important contact with lesbians and gay men of equal or higher status may reduce anti-gay/lesbian prejudice, whereas contact under unfavorable conditions or with lower-status persons may exacerbate prejudice.

Three studies have examined the consequences of different attributions for homosexuality on affective responses to gay men and lesbians (Aguero, Bloch, & Byrne, 1984; Ernulf, Innala, & Whitam, 1989; Whitley, 1990). Consistent with attribution theory, which holds that reactions to a stigma are moderated by perceived controllability of the stigma (Weiner, Perry, & Magnusson, 1988), Whitley (1990) found that a significant proportion of the variance in respondents' attitudes toward gay men and lesbians was accounted for by belief in the controllability of homosexuality. Those who believed that homosexuality is controllable were found to be more anti-gay/lesbian than those who believed that it is uncontrollable. Similarly,

Ernulf et al. (1989) found that respondents from Hawaii, Arizona, the Philippines, and Sweden who believed that "homosexuals are born that way" were more tolerant of gays than respondents who believed that "homosexuals learn to be that way" or "choose to be that way." The magnitude of the differences was small, and the investigators caution that "it would be an exaggeration to conclude that all people who believe that homosexuals are 'born that way' are tolerant of homosexuals" (p. 1009).

Aguero et al. (1984) also found that among "erotophiles" (persons expressing positive affect to sexual arousal), a hypothetical gay target person was disliked most by individuals who were high in general negative affect toward homosexuality *and* who believed that homosexuality is a "learned problem." "Erotophobes" (persons expressing negative affect to sexual arousal), on the other hand, were equally likely to dislike the gay target person, regardless of whether they believed that homosexuality is learned or innate. Among sexual conservatives (erotophobes), who are more likely to be anti-gay/lesbian than sexual nonconservatives (erotophiles), belief about the etiology of homosexuality may be irrelevant. Furthermore, when considering the impact of explanations for homosexuality on attitudes toward gay men and lesbians, one should keep in mind that according to attribution theory, perceived controllability leads to negative affective responses only when the event (i.e., homosexuality) is perceived negatively (Weiner, 1986). When an event is perceived to be positive, perceived controllability will elicit positive affect. Therefore, while adherence to an innate model may attenuate anti-gay/lesbian attitudes in some people, it will only do so to the extent that being gay is perceived as a negative event or a stigma. When being gay or lesbian is perceived positively or neutrally, the perception of controllability should enhance liking of lesbians and gay men or should have no effect.

Gender Belief Correlates of Anti-Lesbian/Gay Attitudes

Since lesbians and gay men are widely viewed as violating prescribed gender roles, it is not surprising that restrictive gender beliefs have consistently been shown to be related to anti-gay/lesbian attitudes. In a study of beliefs about the male role, Thompson, Grisanti, and Pleck (1985) found that of four predictors, endorsement of a traditional male sex role was most strongly predicted by anti-gay/lesbian attitudes. Similarly, Dunbar, Brown, and Amoroso (1973) found that anti-gay/lesbian attitudes were positively related to the endorsement of stereotypes of masculinity and femininity. Hostile attitudes toward gays have been shown to be correlated with traditional, restrictive beliefs about sex roles and with anti-feminist attitudes in numerous other studies (Brown & Amoroso, 1975; Dunbar, Brown, & Vuorinen, 1973; Herek, 1988; Kite & Deaux, 1986; Krulewitz & Nash, 1980;

Kurdek, 1988; Laner & Laner, 1979, 1980; Lieblich & Friedman, 1985; MacDonald & Games, 1974; MacDonald, Huggins, Young, & Swanson, 1973; Millham & Weinberger, 1977; Minnigerode, 1976; Newman, 1989; Stark, 1991; Smith, Resick, & Kilpatrick, 1980; Weinberger & Millham, 1979), providing strong evidence for the contention that hostility toward gays serves to maintain and reinforce traditional sex roles.

In an attempt to determine the relative importance of traditional sex role ideology and sexual conservatism for anti-gay/lesbian attitudes, Mac-Donald et al. (1973) correlated relevant measures. Both sexual conservatism and restrictive sex role beliefs were positively correlated with anti-lesbian/gay attitudes, but correlations between sex role beliefs and gay/lesbian attitudes remained significant even when sexual conservatism was partialed out, whereas sexual conservatism was not a significant predictor of anti-gay/lesbian attitudes when sex role beliefs were partialed out. The investigators concluded that anti-lesbian/gay attitudes are more highly associated with support for a double standard for women and men than with nonpermissive attitudes toward premarital sex. Similarly, Minnigerode (1976) found that sexual conservatism and anti-feminist attitudes independently predicted anti-lesbian/gay attitudes, but that anti-feminist attitudes were a better predictor than sexual conservatism. In a study of attitudes toward lesbians (Newman, 1989), heterosexual women's anti-lesbian attitudes were predicted by gender role beliefs, parents' attitudes, authoritarianism, and media and educational exposure to homosexual themes, whereas heterosexual men's anti-lesbianism was significantly predicted solely by conservative sex role attitudes. These findings suggest that the most important dimension of heterosexism is traditionality of gender beliefs.

Gender as a Correlate of Anti-Lesbian/Gay Attitudes

Although some studies have reported no gender differences in anti-lesbian/gay attitudes (Glenn & Weaver, 1979; Hudson & Ricketts, 1980; Irwin & Thompson, 1977; Kite & Deaux, 1986; Levitt & Klassen, 1974; MacDonald, 1974; Newman, 1989; Smith, 1971), most studies have found more negative attitudes among heterosexual men than among heterosexual women (Aguero et al., 1984; Brown & Amoroso, 1975; Cuenot & Fugita, 1982; Glassner & Owen, 1976; Gurwitz & Marcus, 1978; Hansen, 1982; Herek, 1988; Kite, 1984; Kurdek, 1988; Laner & Laner, 1979; Larsen et al., 1980; Lieblich & Friedman, 1985; Millham et al., 1976; Minnigerode, 1976; Nyberg & Alston, 1976–1977; Steffensmeier & Steffensmeier, 1974; Storms, 1978; Weis & Dain, 1979; Whitley, 1988). A meta-analysis of studies reporting gender comparisons published before 1983 (Kite, 1984) revealed a small gender-of-respondent effect, with men being somewhat more anti-gay/lesbian than women. Two variables found to be related to effect size were sample size and year of publication. More recent studies have tended to show greater gender differences, which Kite attributes to the use of progressively more reliable instruments; however, smaller gender differences were reported in studies employing larger samples, suggesting that obtained differences were influenced by sampling error or participant selection. Most of the smaller studies employed college students.

Whitley (1988) has suggested that gender differences in anti-gay/lesbian attitudes are dependent on the way in which the attitudes are operationalized. In order to test the hypothesis proposed by Morin and Garfinkle (1978) that gender differences are found only when attitude questions deal with personal threat or anxiety, as opposed to general beliefs about homosexuals, Whitley (1988) compared heterosexual women's and men's responses to scale items assessing attitudes toward the following: contact with same-gender homosexuals, contact with other-gender homosexuals, homosexual advances, and the social role of gender-unspecified homosexuals. He found no gender differences in personal responses to homosexual advances, contrary to the Morin and Garfinkle (1978) prediction. Items dealing with homosexual advances elicited the strongest negative responses from both genders, suggesting that heterosexist women and heterosexist men feel equally negative about being the target of a homosexual advance. Similarly, Kite (1984) found no difference in effect size between studies that assessed attitudes with scales predominantly employing personal anxieties (e.g., "I would not want to be close to a homosexual") and studies that assessed attitudes with scales predominantly employing general beliefs about homosexuality (e.g., "I believe homosexuality is always wrong"). On the other hand, Whitley (1988) did find that heterosexual men were more negative than women about the social roles of gender-unspecified homosexuals (e.g., "I believe homosexuals should be banned from military service"). Gender differences in beliefs about the social roles of gay men and lesbians may be attributable to men's greater endorsement of traditional sex role ideology. Studies have consistently reported that heterosexual men are more likely to adhere to traditional sex role beliefs than heterosexual women (Brown & Amoroso, 1975; Kurdeck, 1988; MacDonald & Games, 1974; Smith et al., 1980; Stark, 1991).

Anti-gay/lesbian attitudes are also affected by the gender of the homosexual stimulus person (Herek, 1988; Kite, 1984; Whitley, 1988). A number of studies have reported a tendency to respond more negatively to a same-gender gay person (Herek, 1988; Millham et al., 1976; Millham & Weinberger, 1977; Smith et al., 1980; Whitley, 1988). For example, Gentry (1987) found that respondents preferred greater social distance from same-gender than from other-gender homosexuals; and heterosexual men were found to be more negative toward gay men, but less negative toward lesbians, than were women (Whitley, 1988; Smith et al., 1980). Kite's (1984) meta-analysis, on the other hand, revealed that men were more negative toward gay men than women were, but that there was little gender difference in attitudes toward lesbians. In three studies employing samples from six college campuses, Herek (1988) found that across samples, there was a tendency for participants to respond more negatively to same-gender targets than to other-gender stimulus persons, but that the effect was more pronounced among men. He found that, overall, men were both more anti-gay and anti-lesbian than women, and that differences in attitudes toward lesbians and gay men were significant only for male respondents. In all of the studies that have examined the interaction of gender of respondent and gender of homosexual target, the greatest negativity has been reported for heterosexual men toward gay men.

Even in studies that do not distinguish between gay male and lesbian targets, gender differences probably reflect respondents' assumptions about the gender of the homosexual stimulus person. Black and Stevenson (1984) reported that when responding to items pertaining to gender-unspecified homosexuals, 75% of the male respondents and 41% of the female respondents were thinking only of gay men; 25% of the men and 53% of the women were thinking of both gay men and lesbians; and 6% of the women and none of the men were thinking only of lesbians. If this pattern holds for other groups, reported gender differences in studies assessing attitudes to gender-unspecified homosexuals probably reflect, at least in part, a gender-of-respondent × gender-of-target interaction.

Summary

In summary, stronger anti-lesbian/gay attitudes are associated with greater sexual and ethical conservatism and with greater adherence to beliefs about conventional social order, including both racist and sexist beliefs. Anti-gay/lesbian attitudes are most strongly related to gender role beliefs. Gender differences in personal anxiety about and general attitudes toward homosexuality are small or nonexistent. Men appear, however, to endorse more social role restrictions on gays and lesbians; this is probably related to men's greater adherence to traditional gender role beliefs. Men also tend to be more anti-gay than anti-lesbian. More pro-lesbian/gay attitudes are associated with having been raised in an urban area or in the U.S. Northeast or Far West; more education; and friendship, personal contact, or previous association with a gay man or lesbian. Those who believe that homosexuality is uncontrollable also hold slightly more positive attitudes than those who believe homosexuality is controllable; however, these differences are small and appear not to attenuate anti-gay/lesbian bias in those who are sexually conservative.

HETEROSEXIST STEREOTYPES

Most investigations of lesbian and gay male stereotypes have involved asking participants to complete adjective checklists with respect to typical homosexuals (Taylor, 1983). The data suggest that lesbians and gay men are widely perceived as sex role deviants, as psychologically unhealthy individuals, and to a lesser extent as dangerous persons. In an early study (Simmons, 1965), 72% of a sample of 134 respondents were found to believe that gender-unspecified homosexuals are sexually abnormal; 52% believed that they are perverted; and 40% believed that they are mentally ill and maladjusted. In other studies, 68% (Steffensmeier & Steffensmeier, 1974) and 86.7% (Rooney & Gibbons, 1966) of respondents agreed that gender-unspecified homosexuals are psychologically disturbed. Among a sample of 72 heterosexuals (Jenks, 1988), the average estimate of the number of gays who need psychological counseling because they are gay was 83.3%. Ten percent of the Simmons (1965) sample, 37% of the Steffensmeier and Steffensmeier (1974) sample, and 69.1% of the Rooney and Gibbons (1966) sample believed that homosexuals are dangerous. The latter two studies made explicit that homosexuals are dangerous because they prey on young children; thus more heterosexuals may believe gays and/or lesbians to be dangerous when child sexual abuse is made salient. The Steffensmeiers found that dangerousness was attributed more to gay men than to lesbians. It is important to note that these three studies were conducted before the identification of AIDS, which can be expected to influence the perception of gays as dangerous.

The most pervasive continuing belief about lesbians and gay men is that they are gender deviants. Herek (1984, 1986b) notes that gay men are commonly perceived as stereotypically feminine, whereas lesbians are commonly perceived as stereotypically masculine. In a national survey, almost 70% of respondents "strongly" or "somewhat" agreed that "homosexuals act like the opposite sex" (Levitt & Klassen, 1974, p. 35). Responding to a list of 84 items, a sample of 538 undergraduates attributed sensitivity (a characteristic usually associated with women) to homosexuals more than any other characteristic (Staats, 1978). Responding to open-ended questions, 38% of 189 female nursing students expressed the belief that lesbians try to seduce heterosexual women, perhaps reflecting their belief that lesbians are sexually assertive or aggressive (a characteristic usually associated with men), and 31% suggested that lesbians were identifiable by their "aura of masculinity" (Eliason, Donelan, & Randall, 1992).

A number of studies have compared the attributes assigned to lesbians and gay men with attributes assigned to heterosexual women and men. Lesbians and gay men were consistently found to be rated higher in attributes stereotypically associated with the other gender, and lower in attributes stereotypically associated with their own gender, than their same-gender heterosexual counterparts. In one study (Taylor, 1983), a sample of 103 nonstudent adults aged 17 to 64 rated "gay men" higher than "men" in traits from the Femininity scale of the Personal Attributes Questionnaire, and "lesbians" higher than "women" in traits on the Masculinity scale. In another study (Weissbach & Zagon, 1975), a videotaped interviewee was rated as significantly weaker, more feminine, more emotional, more submissive, and more conventional when he was labeled gay than when he was not. Gurwitz and Marcus (1978) found that, compared to heterosexual men, gay men were perceived as less aggressive, less strong, poorer leaders, more clothes-conscious, more gentle, more passive, and more theatrical, as well as less calm, dependable, honest, and religious, than heterosexual men. Similarly, Gross, Green, Storck, and Vanyur (1980) found that a sample of female and male introductory psychology students rated heterosexual men as more aggressive, dominant, competitive, strong, and stable than gay men, who were rated as more gentle, theatrical, and liberated. Heterosexual women were perceived as more conservative and stable than lesbians who were perceived as more dominant, direct, forceful, strong, liberated, and nonconforming. Stereotypes were found to be stronger for same-gender homosexual targets. Support for a "cross-gendered" stereotype of homosexuality has been reported by others (Karr, 1978; Laner & Laner, 1979, 1980; Page & Yee, 1985; Weinberger & Millham, 1983).

INTERPERSONAL HETEROSEXIST DISCRIMINATION

Interpersonal discrimination against lesbians and gay men takes many forms, which range from jokes and put-downs to murder. Lott (1993 and Chapter 2, this volume) has suggested a model for interpersonal sexist discrimination in the form of a spiral, with the most common and relatively least dangerous behaviors at the wide end; the least common and most lethal at the narrow end; and distancing from, harassment of, and physical abuse of women somewhere in between. A similar model could be used to conceptualize interpersonal heterosexist discrimination. There is a clear difference in the frequency and the dangerousness of jokes that degrade gay men and lesbians and physical "gay-bashing," but all discriminatory behavior contributes to a climate of hostility and reinforces the subordinate status of gay men and lesbians in our culture.

An excellent example of the meaning conveyed by something as seemingly innocuous as an anti-gay joke comes from the 1993 film *Philadelphia*, in which a gay man with AIDS is fired from his job at a prestigious law firm. The gay attorney with AIDS, played by Tom Hanks, talks about how relieved he was that he hadn't revealed his homosexuality when he heard a senior partner tell an anti-gay joke. The anti-gay joke signified that it was unsafe for the gay lawyer to "come out" at work. That the partners fire him when they discover that he is gay and has AIDS demonstrates that his fears were well founded.

Although most of the psychological research on interpersonal heterosexism has focused on prejudice and stereotypes, some empirical evidence and much anecdotal evidence suggests that negative responses to gay men and lesbians in face-to-face interactions are prevalent. Distancing from, harassment of, and violence against lesbians and gay men are common.

Distancing Responses to Lesbians and Gay Men

Lott (Chapter 2, this volume) presents evidence that distancing behavior is an often used index of a negative response to another person and a reasonable definition of interpersonal discrimination. Studies that have examined distancing responses as a function of sexual orientation of a target clearly support the proposition that heterosexuals are more likely to distance themselves from persons perceived to be lesbian or gay than from those perceived (presumed) to be heterosexual. For example, Morin, Taylor, and Kielman (cited in Morin & Garfinkle, 1978) found that although participants expressed more positive attitudes toward homosexuals when they were interviewed by an experimenter who wore a "Gay and Proud" button and who was introduced as a member of the Association of Gay Psychologists than when they were interviewed by an experimenter who was introduced as a graduate student and who wore no button, the participants nevertheless positioned their chairs significantly farther from gay and lesbian interviewers than from graduate student interviewers. Male participants reacted to the gay male experimenter with approximately three times more physical distance than female participants reacted to the lesbian experimenter. Another interview study (Cuenot & Fugita, 1982) found that female and male college students who responded to questions posed by interviewers who were labeled gay or lesbian spoke more rapidly than students who responded to the same interviewers when they were not so labeled. The authors attributed the more rapid speech pattern to situational anxiety. Participants of the same gender as interviewers labeled gay or lesbian also indicated a greater desire to avoid the interviewers than when they were not labeled. In another experiment, Karr (1978) found that men perceived male confederates as less masculine and preferred them less as fellow participants in any future experiment when they were labeled gay than when they were not so labeled, and participants who scored high on a measure of "homophobia" sat farther away from confederates when they were labeled gay than when they were not.

Additional evidence of interpersonal heterosexist discrimination is provided by a study of helping behavior conducted by Gray, Russell, and Blockley (1991) in Great Britain. In this study shoppers were approached by a person wearing a T-shirt bearing a pro-gay slogan or by a person wearing a plain T-shirt, and were asked for change for a pound. Help was less likely to be given to the pro-gay person. Although help was more often given when the request was justified by an explanation that change was needed for an important phone call, justification did not attenuate the bias against helping the pro-gay confederate.

Other studies have employed simulated anticipated-interaction measures to investigate the influence of a homosexual label on potential distancing responses. In these studies, participants are typically presented with information about a fictitious target person (including the target person's sexual orientation), and then asked how well they like the target person and how willing they would be to have future interactions with the target person. In one such study (Krulewitz & Nash, 1980), male students were given a questionnaire supposedly completed by a bogus male partner, who was sometimes identified as gay. The men in this study were found to be less attracted to, and less willing to interact with, the target person when he was labeled gay than when he was not. Using the same procedure, Kite and Deaux (1986) found that among a sample of male college students, participants who were informed that their (bogus) partner was gay liked their partner less well, sought less information about their partner, and disclosed less information about themselves to their partner than did uninformed participants. These responses were more likely among participants who expressed more intolerant attitudes toward homosexuality than among those who expressed more tolerance.

In another anticipated-interaction study, Gurwitz and Marcus (1978) presented female and male introductory psychology students with a bogus questionnaire and showed them a 3-minute taped interview of a male target who was sometimes labeled gay and sometimes not. Participants liked the heterosexual target more than the gay target, thought that a friendship with the heterosexual target was more likely, and preferred the heterosexual target as a possible resident on their dormitory floor. When they thought that they would have to interact with the target in the future, male and female participants thought that a friendship with the heterosexual target was more likely than when they did not expect to meet the target. Only female participants thought a friendship more likely when a future interaction with the gay target was expected than when they did not expect to meet him. Male participants, on the other hand, thought a friendship with a gay target less likely when they thought they would have to meet him than when they thought they would not. In a similar study (Gross et al., 1980), male and female introductory psychology students were presented with written information about, and a videotaped interview with, a target labeled gay or lesbian. Targets were rated more negatively and in a more stereotypically cross-gendered manner when a sexual orientation label was revealed than when it was not.

Another, more subtle indicator of the tendency for heterosexuals to distance themselves from lesbians and gay men may be the tendency among heterosexuals to perceive gay men and lesbians as dissimilar to themselves. In one study (Shaffer & Wallace, 1990), male and female students evaluated the placement file of a (fictitious) male stimulus person whose file was varied by sexual orientation (gay or heterosexual) and the extent to which his attitudes and preferred activities were similar to those of a "typical" college student (similar or dissimilar). Participants did in fact perceive the stimulus person to be more similar to themselves when he had "typical" attitudes and preferred activities than when he had "atypical" attitudes and preferred activities. However, the stimulus person was presumed to be dissimilar "in other ways" when he was gay, but not when he was heterosexual. Attitudinally similar stimulus persons were judged more attractive as employees than attitudinally dissimilar stimulus persons, regardless of sexual orientation; however, attitudinal similarity significantly enhanced the social desirability of the heterosexual stimulus person, but not of the gay stimulus person. Krulewitz and Nash (1980) also found that participants perceived their (bogus) male partners as more dissimilar to themselves when they were gay, even when the information provided about them was manipulated so that they were very similar to participants.

Because simulated anticipated interaction studies do not allow participants to actually interact with targets, the information provided by these studies is limited. Ultimately, such simulated measures only provide verbal indicators of potential distancing from lesbians and gay men.

Harassment and Violence

Early in the morning of July 2, 1990, three young men, Daniel Doyle, Eric Brown, and Esat Bici, bludgeoned and stabbed to death Julio Rivera, a 29-year-old gay man, as he was returning home from a friend's apartment in Queens, New York (Pooley, 1991). According to Daniel Doyle's taped confession, the three young men, after 4 hours of beer drinking at Doyle's family's home, armed themselves with a carpenter's hammer, a wrench, and a kitchen knife; walked to a convenience store to buy more beer; and then went to the schoolyard of P.S. 69, a known pickup spot used by gay men. Doyle, then a 20-year-old student at Union College, left the grounds to buy himself another beer. When he returned to the schoolyard he saw Esat Bici " . . . swinging the hammer . . . as hard and as fast as he could" into Julio Rivera's head. According to the coroner's report, Rivera was struck 10 blows to the head with the claw end of the hammer. Doyle said he then tried to break up the "scuffle" by hitting Rivera in the face with his fist and kicking him in the stomach. When Rivera, who was bent over in a defensive posture, still did not go down, Eric Brown handed Doyle a knife, which Doyle used to stab Rivera in the back. At that point, Bici resumed hitting Rivera with the hammer, and Brown swung a wrench up and into the face of the crouching Rivera. Then the three ran away. Rivera, who was unknown to the murderers, died in the hospital several hours later.

The murder of Julio Rivera was not an isolated incident. In July 1991, a 27-year-old banker was slain by two carloads of teenagers as he left a gay bar in Houston, Texas (Garcia & Wright, 1991). In October 1992, Seaman Alan Schindler of the U.S. Navy was found dead, with eight broken ribs, a battered skull, and a lacerated penis, in a public restroom near the Yokosuka naval base in Japan, where his ship, the U.S.S. *Belleau Wood*, was berthed (Salholz, with McCormick, McKillop, & Hill, 1993). A shipmate, Navy Airman Charles E. Vins, pleaded guilty to a lesser charge in exchange for his testimony implicating Airman Apprentice Terry Helvey, also of the U.S.S. *Belleau Wood*. In January, 1993, four teenage high school students were arrested for beating a man in a known gay area of Laguna Beach, California, so badly that hospital authorities were unable to identify the victim's race (Billiter & Crouch, 1993).

Anti-gay/lesbian violence is traumatic, often causing the victims to experience physical and emotional pain, fear, and anger. Perhaps most devastating is the need many victims feel to restrict their movements through the world. One victim described his range of reactions to being gay-bashed in one of several handwritten statements featured in an art exhibit by Fazzino and Bostrom (1993):

> I got bashed riding my bike to [a local gay bar]. I was going dancing—riding sort of oblivious. . . . Out of the side of my eye I saw two guys running towards me. . . . I got scared for a second before woosh . . . one guy hit me on the back with a tire iron, knocked me off my bike, and then hit me on the ground on my back. . . . I reacted. . . . running at me—he hit me on the side of the head—I got pissed and ran at him. I forgot to be scared—then he and his friend ran to their car—cause another guy in a car saw what was happening and drove at them. I was lucky . . . he drove them off—and then came and picked me up and put my bike in the back of his car and took me home. I was fine driving home, sort of dazed. I got out of the car, got my bike, he drove off and then I freaked . . . crying, fucked up, wanting to break something.
>
> I called a friend. She took me to [the hospital]. I had contusions. The check-up cost $87. I filed a police report. I spent a month wanting to move to San Francisco. I might.

I fucking hated it. It was full of shit to have it happen. I've never punched anyone. The guys who did it are assholes. Fucked up shits. The society that condones it by pretending stuff like it doesn't happen is hateful.

I was lucky. I have a friend who was bashed in the same area with a baseball bat. He lost six teeth and part of his ear. He moved.

I don't ride my bike far at night anymore. (Included in Fazzino & Bostrom, 1993; used here by permission of the author)

Although it is clear that anti-gay/lesbian violence can have a profound impact on the victims, it also affects all gay men and lesbians, and indeed all of U.S. society. According to the NGLTF (1994),

As with other other bigoted attacks, each anti-gay episode sends a message of hatred and terror intended to silence and render invisible not only the victim but all lesbians, gay men, and bisexuals. In effect, such violence denies gay people, and all who are potential targets their full measure of equality, including the rights to speak out, associate, and assemble. Left unchecked, these crimes of hate create an atmosphere of intolerance that undermines not only the lesbian and gay community but the democratic and pluralistic foundation of society. (p. 40)

Anti-gay/lesbian violence is pervasive today in the United States (Berrill, 1990; Berrill & Herek, 1990; Bohn, 1984). According to a 1986 U.S. Department of Justice study of bias-related crime, gays and lesbians are probably the most frequent victims of hate violence in the nation (Finn & McNeil, 1987). In the first national study focusing exclusively on anti-lesbian/gay violence, gay and lesbian organizations in eight U.S. cities (Atlanta, Boston, Dallas, Denver, Los Angeles, New York, Seattle, and St. Louis) surveyed 1,420 gay men and 624 lesbians attending gay pride events during June 1983 (National Gay Task Force [NGTF], 1984). Of those surveyed, 19% reported having been physically assaulted (punched, hit, kicked, or beaten); 44% had been threatened with physical violence; and 94% had experienced some type of victimization (including verbal harassment, vandalism, being spat upon, chased, followed, or pelted with objects) at least once in their lives because they were known or perceived to be gay or lesbian. Eighty-four percent reported knowing other gay men or lesbians who had been physically victimized because of their sexual orientation. Other surveys of lesbian and gay samples have also found anti-lesbian/gay harassment and violence to be widespread. Kevin Berrill (1990) of NGLTF compiled the results of studies conducted in the cities of Baltimore, Boston, Chicago, the District of Columbia, Minneapolis, Richmond, and San Francisco, and in the states of Alaska, Maine, New Jersey, New York, Pennsylvania, Vermont, and Wisconsin. Berrill noted that 52% to 87% of respondents said they had been verbally harassed; 21% to 27% had been pelted with objects; 13% to 38% had been chased or followed; 10% to 20% had experienced vandalism; 9% to 24% had been physically assaulted; and 4% to 10% had been assaulted with an object or a weapon because of their known or perceived sexual orientation. Between 51% and 79% of the respondents reported that they feared for their safety, and between 76% and 88% expected to be the target of anti-gay/lesbian violence or harassment at some time in the future.

As alarmingly high as these rates of victimization are, gay men and lesbians who live in areas with a highly visible gay community may be at an even greater risk. A survey conducted by the Philadelphia Lesbian and Gay Task Force in 1992 found that among Philadelphia residents, 16% of lesbians and 24% of gay men had been threatened, chased, punched, hit, or assaulted; and 50% of the lesbians and 65% of the gay men reported that they had been harassed because of their sexual orientation in the preceding 12 months alone. Thirty-five percent of the lesbians and 57% of the gay men had been threatened, chased, or physically assaulted; and 74% of the lesbians and 89% of the gay men had been harassed at least once during their lives because of their sexual orientation (NGLTF, 1993). Among a sample surveyed during a gay pride celebration in Los Angeles in June 1992, 28% said that they had experienced some type of assault or physical abuse in the preceding 12 months because they were gay (NGLTF, 1993). A full 20% of the respondents claimed to have been harassed three or more times during the year, experiencing what the Los Angeles Gay and Lesbian Community Services Center refered to as a "continual barrage of harassment" (NGLTF, 1993, p. 18).

Although aggression against lesbians and gay men is not a new phenomenon, its frequency may be increasing. The number of reports of anti-lesbian/gay violence and harassment to police departments and to lesbian and gay community and victim assistance organizations has risen dramatically in recent years. The New York City Police Department Bias Investigating Unit recorded a 79% increase in reported anti-gay/lesbian crime from 1987 to 1988, and an additional 9% increase from 1988 to 1989 (Collins, 1989; Senzel, 1990). Surveys of lesbians and gay men in Philadelphia found that twice as many respondents had been victims of anti-lesbian/gay criminal violence in a 12-month period in 1986–1987 (Gross, Aurand, & Adessa, 1988) as in a 12-month period in 1983–1984 (Aurand, Adessa, & Bush, 1985). Gross et al. (1988) attribute the change partially to having a more representative sample in the second study and partially to a real rise in victimization levels over the 3-year period between the surveys. Between 1988 and 1993 there has been a 127% increase in the total number of anti-gay/lesbian episodes (including harassment, threats, vandalism, and violence) documented by victim service agencies in the five cities (Boston, Chicago, Denver, Minneapolis/St. Paul,

New York City, and San Francisco) that have reported annually to NGLTF since 1988 (NGLTF, 1994).

Aggression against gays is usually thought of in terms of street violence, but it is also pervasive on college campuses (Berrill, 1990; Herek, 1989; NGLTF, 1989, 1990). Lesbian, gay, and bisexual student organizations on 40 college campuses reported 1,329 anti-lesbian/gay incidents to NGLTF in 1989 (NGLTF, 1990). Asked about whether there had been a change in victimization rates on campus between 1988 and 1989, 70% of the groups said that they felt the problem had grown or stayed the same, 23% were unsure, whereas only 7% of the groups felt that anti-gay/lesbian harassment and violence had decreased. On every college campus where a study has been conducted, pervasive anti-gay/lesbian physical and verbal abuse has been documented (Herek, 1989). In one such study conducted at Pennsylvania State University (D'Augelli, 1989), questionnaires were distributed at lectures, films, social events, and organizational meetings of campus gay and lesbian groups. Of the 125 self-identified gay men, lesbians, and bisexuals who responded, 76% had been verbally harassed at least once; 26% had been threatened with physical violence at least once; 22% had been chased or followed; 5% had been spat upon; and 4% had been punched because of their known or perceived sexual orientation at some point during their college careers. Similar rates of victimization have been documented at Rutgers University (see Berrill 1990), Yale University (Herek, 1986c), the University of Massachusetts at Amherst (Yeskel, 1985), and the University of Illinois at Urbana–Champaign (see Berrill, 1990), suggesting that anti-lesbian/gay violence and harassment are part of college life.

Younger gay and lesbian students are also at risk for anti-lesbian/gay violence and harassment. Berrill (1990) cites studies indicating that between 33% and 49% of gay and lesbian respondents reported having been victims of gay-related harassment, threats, and/or violence while in high school and junior high school. At the Hetrick–Martin Institute, a New York City community-based program that provides services to mostly minority gay and lesbian teenagers and their families, records of the first 500 youths seeking services in 1988 were examined for reported instances of anti-lesbian/gay aggression (Hunter, 1990). Forty percent of the sample had experienced violent physical assault; of these, 44% reported that the assault was gay-related. Sixty-one percent of the gay related violence had occurred in the respondents' families, while the remaining 39% was committed by persons other than family members. Although these data report only physical violence, Hunter, who is employed at the center, believes that emotional and verbal abuse are probably even more common. Among the youths who had been physically assaulted, 41% of the girls and 36% of the boys had attempted suicide. Gay and lesbian youths constitute one of the highest-risk groups for adolescent suicide; they are at even higher risk than pregnant teenagers and runaways (Hunter, 1990). Gay and lesbian youths are two to three times more likely to attempt suicide than other youths, and as many as 30% of teen suicides are believed to be related to lesbian or gay status (D'Augelli & Rose, 1990).

Differential patterns of victimization of gay men and of lesbians were evidenced in all of the studies discussed by Berrill (1990). Gay men are more likely than lesbians to experience anti-gay violence and intimidation (including being assaulted with or without weapons, pelted with objects, spat upon, chased, or followed), to be threatened with violence, to be verbally harassed by persons other than family members, and to be victimized by police because of their sexual orientation. Lesbians, on the other hand, are more likely than gay men to be verbally harassed by family members, to be discriminated against (the type of discrimination was not reported), and to fear anti-lesbian violence. Gay men and lesbians are equally likely to be physically assaulted by family members because of their sexual orientation. Gender differences have also been found in the settings in which anti-gay/lesbian violence occurs (Comstock, 1989). Gay men are more often victimized in schools, and in public gay-identified areas, whereas lesbians are more often victimized in non-gay-identified public settings and at home.

Berrill (1990) attributes the greater likelihood of most types of aggression against gay men than against lesbians to several factors. First, men in general are more likely than women to be victims of violent crime. In addition, the vastly greater number of public establishments (e.g., bars, restaurants) serving exclusively or primarily gay men as opposed to lesbians may increase gay men's public visibility, thus increasing their risk for violence. Gay men may also be at greater risk because they tend to recognize their sexual orientation as much as 6 years earlier than lesbians (Aurand et al., 1985; Gross et al., 1988), thus increasing the percentage of their lives in which they might encounter anti-gay violence. The 1983 NGTF (NGTF, 1984) study found that lesbians appear to decrease their risk for anti-lesbian victimization by avoiding certain locations or refraining from public displays of affection with lovers or same-gender friends. Furthermore, because violence against lesbians is more likely to occur in non-gay-identified areas, anti-lesbian violence and harassment may be difficult to distinguish from more general anti-woman violence and harassment (Berrill, 1990). Finally, higher rates of most types of victimization of gay men may reflect relatively greater negativity toward gay men than toward lesbians, as previously discussed.

One factor that may be associated with anti-gay/lesbian violence is AIDS. Two-thirds of the groups reporting anti-gay/lesbian episodes to NGLTF in 1988 believed that AIDS had contributed to the violence in their communities (NGLTF, 1989). Fifteen percent of the anti-lesbian/gay incidents reported to NGLTF in 1989 were classified as AIDS-related (NGLTF, 1990), similar to the 17% in 1988 (NGLTF, 1989), 15% in 1987 (NGLTF, 1988), 14% in 1986 (NGLTF, 1987), and 8% in 1985 (NGLTF, 1986). It is likely that these percentages underrepresent the actual percentage of AIDS-related anti-gay/lesbian violence, since most of the local groups reporting to NGLTF do not specifically solicit such information from respondents (Berrill, 1990). Although the incidence of anti-gay/lesbian violence appears to have risen during the years that AIDS has become more publicized, violence and harassment of gay men and lesbians has a long history that predates the disease. AIDS activism and media coverage of AIDS have, however, probably contributed to anti-lesbian/gay victimization by dramatically increasing the visibility of lesbian and gay people. The fact that relatively few incidents of bias-related crimes against members of other groups at high risk for AIDS (e.g., hemophiliacs and intravenous drug users) have been documented suggests that AIDS-related anti-gay/lesbian violence reflects, at least in part, preexisting anti-gay/lesbian sentiment (Berrill, 1990). Herek and Glunt (1988) argue that AIDS is probably more of a justification for anti-gay violence than a cause of it.

Despite the fact that gay-bashing is prevalent, there has been only one published experiment that investigated the influence of a gay label on aggression (SanMiguel & Millham, 1976). In this study the investigators manipulated the perceived sexual orientation of a male confederate, outcome of a prior interaction between participants and a confederate (positive outcome, negative outcome, or no prior interaction), and attitudinal similarity of the participant to the confederate (very similar or very dissimilar). Participants' previously assessed attitudes toward homosexuality (very intolerant or neutral) served as a fourth independent variable. Following completion of the experimental task, each participant rated the confederate on his performance. Aggression was operationalized indirectly as a negative evaluation of the confederate, which would lead to a loss of money. Among the sample of heterosexual college men, a main effect of sexual orientation of the target person was obtained: More negative evaluations were given to gay targets than to unlabeled targets. An interaction between sexual orientation of the target and similarity of the target and participant revealed that participants who were induced to believe that they were similar to a heterosexual target were less aggressive toward him than were participants who believed that he was dissimilar; however, participants who were led to believe that they were similar to a gay target were more aggressive toward him than were participants who perceived the target as dissimilar. This effect was exaggerated among participants who expressed more negative attitudes toward homosexuality. Although participants who strongly advocated the repression of homosexuality were less aggressive toward heterosexual targets with whom they had experienced a positive outcome on a prior cooperative task than toward heterosexual targets with whom they had had a negative outcome experience, participants holding anti-gay attitudes were equally aggressive toward gay targets, regardless of the outcome of a previous interaction. These findings suggest that perceiving another man as gay is a powerful mediator of aggression for heterosexual college men, especially if the gay man is perceived as possessing attitudes similar to their own and if the repression of gay men is advocated.

In addition to providing information about the victims of anti-lesbian/gay violence, surveys of lesbians and gay men (conducted mostly by anti-violence projects) also provide most of the available data about the perpetrators of anti-lesbian/gay violence. In a national survey of lesbians and gay men conducted by Comstock (1991), 66% of those who had been victimized reported that their perpetrators were unknown to them. Following "unknown persons," the next most frequent perpetrators were fellow students (13%) and police (8%). Men were the perpetrators in 94% of the incidents reported by Comstock (1991), and in 87% of the incidents reported in 1989 to the Community United Against Violence, a San Francisco-based victim assistance organization (see Berrill, 1990). Comstock's (1991) survey indicated that regardless of the gender or race of the victim, most anti-gay/lesbian perpetrators are White (67%). This finding is similar to the national statistics for all crimes of violence released by the Bureau of Justice statistics in 1984 (69% White, 26% Black, and 4% Hispanic) (Comstock, 1991). Perpetrators from ethnic minority groups are more likely to commit an anti-lesbian/gay assault on another minority group member, but minority victims are more often assaulted by a White male (Comstock, 1991).

Among the Comstock (1991) sample, lesbians were victimized by men who were either alone or in groups 83% of the time, by women who were alone or in groups 7% of the time, and by a mixed-gender group 10% of the time; gay men were victimized by men who were alone or in a group 99% of the time, by a mixed-gender group 1% of the time, and never by only women. Fifty-eight percent of the sample studied by the Community United Against Violence (see Berrill, 1990), and 46% of the Comstock (1991) sample, reported that their attackers were 21 years old or younger. Approximately half of all victims were assaulted by persons close to them in age, while the remaining lesbian victims were usually attacked by older perpetrators, and the remaining gay male victims by younger perpetrators. In approximately half of all anti-gay/lesbian incidents of violence, there was more than one assailant. Lesbians were attacked more often when they were in pairs than when they were alone or in larger groups (44% of the time), whereas gay men were most often attacked when they were alone (66% of the time) (Comstock, 1991).

A comparison of the data from the Comstock (1991) survey with national crime statistics indicate that gay men and lesbians are more often attacked by strangers (66% of reported incidents) than are victims of all personal violent crime (56% of incidents). This is especially true when lesbians are the victims. Sixty-six percent of lesbian victims, compared to 43% of all female victims of violent crimes, are attacked by strangers. Comparing data from his sample with Bureau of Justice Statistics data on all personal violent crime, Comstock (1991) concluded that anti-gay/lesbian perpetrators are more likely to be 21 years old or less (46% vs. 29%). In addition, compared to perpetrators of all personal violent crime, perpetrators of anti-gay/lesbian violence are slightly more likely to be male (94% vs. 87%), are more likely to attack more than one victim at a time (47% vs. 13%), and are more likely to attack in pairs or groups (48% vs. 27%). Anti-gay/lesbian perpetrators attack in groups of four or more 20% of the time, compared to only 5% of the time among perpetrators of all personal violence. From these data, Comstock (1991) concluded that being an adolescent male, and being in the company of other adolescent males, are the two factors that best predict involvement in incidents of anti-gay/lesbian violence.

Other researchers (Berk, 1990; Berrill, 1990; Bohn, 1984; Harry, 1990) have also identified a general profile of "gay-bashers" as adolescent men, often acting with other adolescent men, who commit their crimes against strangers or distant acquaintances. As Comstock (1991) is careful to note, this does not imply that all young men in groups are perpetrators of anti-gay/lesbian violence; rather, it suggests that acceptable social behavior for young men, unlike that for any other demographic group, includes victimizing gay men and lesbians. Comstock (1991) has noted a number of anti-gay incidents reported in the mass media in which psychiatric and law enforcement professionals, as well as community members, describe the young male perpetrators as "average boys exhibiting typical behavior" (p. 93). Indeed, many of the offenders had not been involved in other serious criminal behavior and were described by correctional officers as atypical of other youthful violent offenders. Any account, then, of anti-gay/lesbian violence requires an analysis of group-specific behaviors rather than a psychological explanation of individual motivation (Comstock, 1991).

Violent acts targeting lesbians and gay men because of their perceived sexual orientation are classified as hate crimes. Berk (1990), however, is wary of explaining anti-lesbian/gay violence as a consequence of "homophobia." Attributing this violence to a culturally embedded constellation of negative attitudes and beliefs about lesbians and gay men does not account for the fact that most anti-gay/lesbian incidents are perpetrated by a specific age–gender group. Berk contends that "gay-bashing" is closer to being part of the definition of "homophobia" than a consequence of it. The inadequacy of anti-gay/lesbian hatred as an explanation for anti-gay/lesbian violence is illustrated by comments made by six young perpetrators during interviews conducted by Eric Weissman and published in the gay magazine *Christopher Street* in 1978 (cited in Comstock, 1991). All but one of the perpetrators expressed mild or no personal feelings of hostility toward gays and lesbians. Although they felt homosexuality was wrong, the attitudes of all but one were characterized by a "live-and-let-live" tolerance of homosexuals. Rather than attributing their offenses to personal feelings of hatred for homosexuals, they explained that the incidents were "fun" or "exciting," or were perpetrated to alleviate boredom. "Gay-bashing" may thus serve a "recreational" function for some adolescent men, and it may be the social acceptability of anti-gay/lesbian attitudes, beliefs, and behaviors rather than personal attitudes that encourages anti-gay/lesbian aggression (Comstock, 1991). There is considerable evidence that prejudicial attitudes and stereotypical beliefs may be independent of discriminatory behavior and are learned and maintained by different variables or sets of conditions.

THE RELATIONSHIP AMONG ATTITUDES, BELIEFS, AND BEHAVIORAL RESPONSES TO LESBIANS AND GAY MEN

The finding that anti-gay/lesbian attitudes are not good predictors of specific behaviors is consistent with the general social-psychological literature on attitude–behavior relationships. It has been well documented that global attitudes toward a class of objects are insufficient to predict specific behaviors toward particular members of that class (Ajzen & Fishbein, 1973, 1977, 1978, 1980), but that attitude–behavior consistency improves when the specificity of the attitudinal predictor matches the specificity of the behavioral criteria. In other words, attitudes toward performing a particular *action* (in response to a specific target at a specific time in a particular context) will more accurately predict behavior than will global attitudes toward an *object* or *class of objects*. It may be expected, then, that aggression against lesbians and gay men will be better predicted by the attitudes the actor has toward committing a specific aggressive act against a particular gay man or lesbian in a particular situation than by the actors global attitudes toward gay men and lesbians.

Although greater specificity in the measurement of attitudes may increase consistency between attitudes and behavior, "to some extent this approach embraces behavioral specificity and obviates the need for a general attitude concept" (Lord, Lepper, & Mackie, 1984, p. 5). Lord et al. have suggested that attitude–behavior consistency can be improved, while at the same time maintaining the concept of global attitudes, by a more precise specification of the attitude object rather than the attitude itself. They maintain that when people respond to global attitude measures, they are responding to a "cognitive prototype," or an image of a person or object that incorporates the characteristics perceived to be the most salient and essential features of that class of persons or objects. Specific behavioral responses to actual persons or objects, then, should correspond to global attitudes only to the degree that the actual target is consistent with the actor's prototype of the person or object. Support for this hypothesis was obtained in an experiment in which Lord and his colleagues manipulated the degree to which a fictitious stimulus person was consistent (very consistent vs. somewhat consistent) with each participant's prototype of a "homosexual." Participants' ratings of the likability of, and their willingness to associate with, a hypothetical gay man were significantly more consistent with their ratings of the likability of, and their willingness to associate with, "homosexuals" generally, when the target person was very typical (as opposed to only somewhat typical) of the participants' prototype of gay men. Because of the widely shared stereotype in U.S. culture that gay men and lesbians are gender deviants, Harry's (1982) findings that gay men who described themselves as "very feminine" or a "little feminine" were twice as likely as other gay men to have been "gay-bashed" suggests that incidents of anti-gay aggression may be partially a function of how similar the victim is to the perpetrator's prototype of gay men and lesbians.

Other cognitive factors that may be expected to influence anti-gay/lesbian aggression are the perceived consequences to the actor of aggressive acts, and the importance of those consequences. Ajzen and Fishbein (1973, 1980) have demonstrated that "behavioral intention," or what an individual verbally claims he or she is likely to do, is influenced by subjective norms—that is, by what an individual believes important others think he or she should or should not do. According to this formulation of attitude–behavior relations, it may be expected that specific acts of anti-gay aggression will be partially determined by an individual's perception of the consequences of anti-gay aggression, and by his or her perception of whether important others condone participation in it. The greater rates of anti-gay/lesbian aggression among adolescent boys and young men, then, may well be related to the usual lack of negative consequences for such behavior. Individual differences in anti-lesbian/gay aggression among young men may reflect individual differences in the perceived consequences of, and subjective norms with respect to, anti-gay/lesbian aggression.

HETEROSEXISM AND SEXISM

In addition to creating and maintaining heterosexual privilege, heterosexist practices, institutional rules, attitudes, and beliefs also reflect and contribute to sexism, or the privileging of men over women. It may even be that reinforcement of the sexist status quo is the primary function of heterosexism in a sexist society. The power of heterosexism to maintain a gender hierarchy is great enough that Pharr (1988) identified "homophobia" (along with economics and violence) as one of the three primary weapons of sexism. The interrelatedness of heterosexism and sexism is supported by evidence discussed earlier in this chapter; specifically, that the best predictor of heterosexist attitudes is adherence to traditional gender role beliefs; that the most widely shared and culturally validated stereotype of lesbians and gay men is that they are cross-gendered; and that men are more willing than women to endorse restrictions on the social roles of gays, are more likely than women to adhere to traditional gender ideology, and are advantaged over women in a sexist society.

Many feminists (e.g., Radicalesbians, 1973; Kitzinger, 1987) have noted the relationship between anti-lesbianism and the social control of all women, regardless of their sexual orientation. Women understand that to be called a lesbian is to be accused of being "unfeminine," of stepping out of the subordinate or passive roles prescribed by society.

> Lesbianism is the word, the label, the condition that holds women in line. When a woman hears this word tossed her way, she knows she is stepping out of line. . . . Lesbian is a label invented by the Man to throw at any woman who dares to be his equal, who dares to challenge his prerogatives (including that of all women as part of the exchange medium among men), who dares to assert the primacy of her own needs. . . . (Radicalesbians, 1973, pp. 241–242)

Accusing feminists particularly of being lesbians illustrates the way in which lesbian-baiting is employed to discourage women from challenging their subordinate status. Faderman (1980, cited in Kitzinger, 1987) cites the success of the characterization of feminists as lesbians as one cause of the demise of first wave feminism. Early in the second wave of feminism, the Radicalesbians (1973) identified this recurring strategy for discounting feminism:

> . . . To have the label applied to people active in women's liberation is just the most recent instance of a long history; older women will recall that not so long ago, any woman who was successful, independent, not orienting her whole life around a man, would hear this word. (p. 242)

Anti-lesbian violence is a less subtle means of punishing women who violate prescribed gender roles. On January 7, 1993, Ana Maria Rosales exited a gay bar in Washington, D.C., arm in arm with another woman (NGLTF, 1994). According to witnesses, a man confronted Rosales demanding to know why she wouldn't have sex with him, and, in vulgar terms, telling her that he was going to force her to have sex with him. He then drew a gun and shot Rosales, pointblank in the face. She died in minutes. It seems likely from the comments of the perpetrator that Rosales was targeted because of her apparent lack of accessibility to men.

In another incident, recounted in *The Village Voice* (Minkowitz, 1994), a chromosomal female legally named Teena Brandon, who self-identified as a man and "passed" using the name Brandon Teena, and who dated women, was shot to death along with a housemate and a houseguest on New Year's Eve 1993. The chain of events leading to the murder was precipitated when police in Richardson county, Nebraska arrested him and revealed his biological sex in the press in mid-December of 1993. On Christmas Eve, two men publicly stripped him to prove he was biologically female, drove him out of town, and raped him. Although Teena reported the crime to local police, they did not arrest the men. One of the men accused of raping him on Christmas Eve was arrested for the murders (NGLTF, 1994, p. 18). Because Teena rejected the label lesbian, preferring to identify himself as a man (Minkowitz, 1994), his murder would be better classified as transsexist than heterosexist. However, because the murderer was a former boyfriend of Teena's girlfriend who was enraged that his former girlfriend was dating a chromosomal female, it seems probable that heterosexism was at least a partially motivating factor. However classified, Teena's murder illustrates the interconnectedness of heterosexism and gender role enforcement. The fact that NGLTF documented the incident as anti-lesbian, and repeatedly referred to Teena as she, suggests how readily cross-gendered behavior/identity is presumed to be lesbian/gay.

Gay men are also widely presumed to be gender inverts. The strength of this stereotype is illustrated by Mohr's (1992) discussion of American Sign Language (ASL) for sexuality and sexual orientation. ASL signs for sexual acts are pictographs that vividly image the acts referred to. For example, the infinitive "to fuck" is indicated by repeatedly passing the index finger of one hand through a circle formed by touching the index finger and thumb of the other hand. Regional slang ASL expressions for gay men, however, are not pictographs, but instead suggest exaggerated femininity. One sign for "faggot," for example, is dry-licking a fingertip and then quickly stroking an eyebrow, as though painting it. As Mohr (1992) points out, this and other slang signs for gay men do not image the actions that presumably define men as gay (as would, e.g., touching both index fingers together). Rather, they

> simply presuppose that gay men as a class are worthy of derision inde-
> pendent of the acts that define an individual as a [gay man], and they
> contribute to the derision by enhancing stereotypes—of flightiness, mis-

placed femininity, and exaggeration. The general conventions of ASL clearly suggest that gay men are despised in virtue of some perceived group status that gays have rather than in virtue of the acts they perform. (p. 244)

The perceived group status that gay men presumably share is femininity, and it is femininity in men that is devalued. The interchangeability of gayness and femininity is further illustrated by the denigration of women and anything "feminine" often employed by coaches of male athletes. Nelson (1994) cites numerous examples of coaches calling athletes who have performed poorly "cunts," or depositing tampons and bras in their lockers. Calling a player a "faggot" is another common derogation, which does not refer to his sexuality per se, but to his weakness, timidity, or cowardice—in other words, his femininity. Because of the close association of male homosexuality with femininity, gay men are perceived as a threat to male dominance. According to Pharr (1988), misogyny gets transferred to gay men because they are perceived as breaking ranks with traditional male roles, which exclude male bonding and affection outside of sports and war.

Several authors (Bohn, 1984; Harry, 1990; Herek, 1990) suggest that the primary function of anti-gay violence is enforcement of the male sex role. According to Harry (1990) "gay-bashing" is an ideal means of asserting maleness, in that it is both sexual (it affirms one's commitment to exclusive heterosexuality) and violent—the two primary means through which male adolescents may express their commitment to masculinity. Harry (1990), in fact, concludes that the current mainstream construction of gender, in which any departure, especially a sexual departure, is defined as aberrant, is a necessary component of anti-gay/lesbian violence.

In the fight for legal and social equality, many gay men and lesbians have argued for greater tolerance on the grounds that they are just like heterosexuals, want the same things, and so forth. To the extent that such arguments attempt to deconstruct the stereotypes that gay men and lesbians are mentally ill, are dangerous child molesters, and desire to be members of the other gender, I agree. That is, I don't think that gays and lesbians and heterosexuals are essentially different types of people. However, lesbians and gay men, by their very existence, challenge the sexist status quo. Because sexist ideology depends on exaggerating the differences between women and men, and explaining gender differences as natural and immutable, gay men and lesbians threaten the foundation of sexism, whether consciously or not. They are living evidence that all social behavior, including sexual behavior, is learned and not predetermined by sex.

The stereotypes surrounding gender inversion function to shape and reinforce still powerful gender roles in society. If as this stereotype presumes and condemns, one is free to choose one's social roles independently of one's biological sex, then many guiding social divisions—domestic, commercial, political, military, and religious—might be threatened. The socially gender linked distinctions would blur . . . (Mohr, 1992, pp. 254–255)

As Kitzinger (1987) has noted, a radical feminist interpretation of lesbianism recognizes the threat to patriarchy that lesbianism indeed is, and reasserts the political implications of that choice.

IMPLICATIONS FOR PUBLIC POLICY
AND FUTURE RESEARCH

Since the early 1970s there has been a sizeable body of literature focused on documenting the prevalence and correlates of heterosexist prejudice and, to a lesser extent, stereotypes. This literature has been important both in identifying the dimensions of anti-lesbian/gay affect and cognitions, and in helping to depathologize lesbian and gay identities and experiences. I agree with Herek (1987) that we must also avoid the temptation to pathologize the "homophobe" or heterosexist and, instead, attempt to understand how anti-gay/lesbian attitudes and beliefs function to benefit the individual heterosexist and to maintain institutionalized heterosexual privilege and male dominance. Although attitudes about the morality of homosexuality have remained fairly constant over the past 20 years, attitudes about equal rights for lesbians and gay men have grown considerably more tolerant. This is reason to be hopeful, and suggests that strategies to reduce anti-gay attitudes appeal to the U.S. ideals of equality, freedom, and the dignity and rights of the individual.

While studying prejudice and stereotypes is important, it is also important to study discrimination. The work of documenting instances of heterosexist discrimination, and incidents of anti-gay/lesbian harassment and violence in the "real world" begun by victims' assistance organizations and NGLTF should continue. In addition, since we know that attitudes and beliefs are not good predictors of the way heterosexuals behave in face-to-face interactions with lesbians and gay men, we must also identify the variables that relate to increasing or decreasing discriminatory behavior. In order to do so, we need to find creative ways of operationalizing discrimination so that they reflect discrimination in the "real world." This would best be accomplished by taking lesbians' and gay men's experiences as the starting place for our research. Because anti-gay/lesbian discrimination results from lesbians' and gay men's marginalized social status, strategies for reducing discrimination must focus on improving the status of gay men and lesbians, including legislation that would guarantee gays' and lesbians' civil rights, and allow them full participation as citizens, including the rights to marry and to serve in the military.

Finally, because interpersonal heterosexist attitudes, beliefs, and behaviors, coupled with institutional heterosexist rules and practices, reflect, create, and maintain male dominance as well as heterosexual privilege, any strategies aimed at reducing or eliminating heterosexism must also must also be concerned with reducing or eliminating sexism.

ACKNOWLEDGMENTS

For helping me clarify and organize my thoughts, I would like to gratefully acknowledge my editor, major professor, and friend, Bernice Lott. Thanks also to Diane Maluso, and to Barbara Watkins, Marie Sprayberry, and Jodi Creditor at Guilford for their thoughtful and careful editing. Finally, my appreciation to Heather Bullock for her insightful comments on earlier drafts of this chapter.

REFERENCES

Aguero, J. E., Bloch, L., & Byrne, D. (1984). The relationships among sexual beliefs, attitudes, experience, and homophobia. *Journal of Homosexuality, 10*, 95–107.

Ajzen, I., & Fishbein, M. (1973). Attitudinal and normative variables as predictors of specific behaviors. *Journal of Personality and Social Psychology, 27*(1), 41–57.

Ajzen, I., & Fishbein, M. (1977). Attitude prototypes as determinants of attitude–behavior consistency. *Journal of Personality and Social Psychology, 46*(6), 1254–1266.

Ajzen, I., & Fishbein, M. (1980). *Understanding attitudes and predicting behavior.* Englewood Cliffs, NJ: Prentice-Hall.

Allport, G. W. (1954). *The nature of prejudice.* Reading, MA: Addison-Wesley.

Alston, J. P. (1974). Attitudes toward extramarital and homosexual relations. *Journal for the Scientific Study of Religion, 13*, 479–481.

Amir, Y. (1966). Contact hypothesis in ethnic relations. *Psychological Bulletin, 71*(5), 319–342.

Aurand, S. K., Adessa, R., & Bush, C. (1985). *Violence and discrimination against Philadelphia lesbian and gay people.* (Available from Philadelphia Lesbian and Gay Task Force, 1500 Cherry Street, Philadelphia, PA 19102)

Berk, R. A. (1990). Thinking about hate-motivated crimes. *Journal of Interpersonal Violence, 5*(3), 334–349.

Berrill, K. T. (1990). Anti-gay violence and victimization in the United States: An overview. *Journal of Interpersonal Violence, 5*(3), 274–294.

Berrill, K. T., & Herek, G. M. (1990). Violence against lesbians and gay men: An introduction. *Journal of Interpersonal Violence, 5*(3), 269–273.

Billiter, B., & Crouch, G. (1993, January 10). Man beaten in Laguna in possible hate crime. *Los Angeles Times* (Orange County Ed.)

Black, K. N., & Stevenson, M. R. (1984). The relationship of self-reported sex role characteristics and attitudes toward homosexuality. *Journal of Homosexuality, 10*, 83–93.

Bohn, T. R. (1984). Homophobic violence: Implications for social work practice. *Journal of Social Work and Human Sexuality, 2*(2–3), 91–112.

Bowman, R. (1979). Public attitudes toward homosexuality in New Zealand. *International Review of Modern Sociology, 9*, 229–238.

Brown, M., & Amoroso, D. (1975). Attitudes toward homosexuality among West Indian male and female college students. *Journal of Social Psychology, 97*, 163–168.

Bureau of Justice Statistics. (1991). *Criminal victimization in the U.S.: 1990.* Washington, DC: U.S. Department of Justice.

Cameron, P., & Ross, K. P. (1981). Social psychological aspects of the Judeo-Christian stance toward homosexuality. *Journal of Psychology and Theology, 9*(1), 40–57.

Churchill, W. (1967). *Homosexual behaviors among males: A cross-cultural and cross-species investigation.* New York: Hawthorn.

Collins, M. (1989). *1987–88 bias incident investigation analysis: End of year report.* New York: New York City Police Department.

Comstock, G. D. (1989). Victims of anti-gay/lesbian violence. *Journal of Interpersonal Violence, 4*, 101–106.

Comstock, G. D. (1991). *Violence against lesbians and gay men.* New York: Columbia University Press.

Cuenot, R. G., & Fugita, S. S. (1982). Perceived homosexuality: Measuring heterosexual attitudinal and nonverbal reactions. *Personality and Social Psychology Bulletin, 8*(1), 100–106.

D'Augelli, A. R. (1989). Lesbians' and gay men's experiences of discrimination and harassment in a university community. *American Journal of Community Psychology, 17*(3), 317–321.

D'Augelli, A. R., & Rose, M. L. (1990). Homophobia in a university community: Attitudes and experiences of heterosexual freshmen. *Journal of College Student Development, 31*, 484–491.

Dejowski, E. F. (1992). Public endorsement of restrictions on three aspects of free expression by homosexuals: Socio-demographic trends analysis 1973–1988. *Journal of Homosexuality, 23*(4), 1–18.

Douglas, C. J., Kalman, C. M., & Kalman, T. P. (1985). Homophobia among physicians and nurses. *Hospital and Community Psychiatry, 36*(12), 1309–1311.

Dunbar, J., Brown, M., & Amoroso, D. M. (1973). Some correlates of attitudes toward homosexuality. *Journal of Social Psychology, 89*, 271–279.

Dunbar, J., Brown, M., & Vuorinen, S. (1973). Attitudes toward homosexuality among Brazilian and Canadian college students. *Journal of Social Psychology, 90*, 173–183.

Eliason, M., Donelan, C., & Randall, C. (1992). Lesbian stereotypes. *Health Care for Women International, 13*, 131–144.

Ernulf, K. E., & Innala, S. M. (1987). The relationship between affective and cognitive components of homophobic reaction. *Archives of Sexual Behavior, 16*(6), 501–509.

Ernulf, K. E., Innala, S. M., & Whitam, F. L. (1989). Biological explanation, psychological explanation, and tolerance of homosexuals: A cross-national analysis of beliefs and attitudes. *Psychological Reports, 65*, 1003–1010.

Fazzino, J., & Bostrum, L. (Artists). (1993, October 9–October 30). *Documents of discrimination* [Art Exhibit]. Wakefield, RI: Hera Gallery.

Ficarrotto, T. J. (1990). Racism, sexism, and erotophobia: Attitudes of heterosexuals toward homosexuals. *Journal of Homosexuality, 19*(1), 111–116.

Finn, R., & McNeil, T. (1987). *The response of the criminal justice system to bias crime: An exploratory review*. (Available from Abt Associates, Inc., 55 Wheeler Street, Cambridge, MA 02138-1168)

Forstein, M. (1988). Homophobia: An overview. *Psychiatric Annals, 18*(1), 33–36.

Fyfe, B. (1983). "Homophobia" or homosexual bias reconsidered. *Archives of Sexual Behavior, 12*(6), 549–553.

Garcia, J. E., & Wright, S. W. (1991, August 18). Houston gay-bashing death sparks fury. *Austin American-Statesman*.

Gentry, C. S. (1987). Social distance regarding male and female homosexuals. *Journal of Social Psychology, 127*(2), 199–208.

Glassner, B., & Owen, C. (1976). Variations in attitudes toward homosexuality. *Cornell Journal of Social Relations, 11*(2), 161–176.

Glenn, N. D., & Weaver, C. N. (1979). Attitudes toward premarital, extramarital, and homosexual relations in the U.S. in the 1970s. *Journal of Sex Research, 15*(2), 108–118.

Gray, C., Russell, P., & Blockley, S. (1991). The effect upon helping behavior of wearing pro-gay identification. *British Journal of Social Psychology, 30*, 171–178.

Gross, L., Aurand, S. K., & Adessa, R. (1988). *Violence and discrimination against lesbian and gay people in Philadelphia and the Commonwealth of Philadelphia*. (Available from Philadelphia Lesbian and Gay Task Force, 1500 Cherry Street, Philadelphia, PA 19102)

Gross, A. E., Green, S. K., Storck, J. T., & Vanyur, J. M. (1980). Disclosure of sexual orientation and impressions of male and female homosexuals. *Personality and Social Psychology Bulletin, 6*(2), 307–314.

Gurwitz, S. B., & Marcus, M. (1978). Effects of anticipated interaction, sex, and homosexual stereotypes on first impressions. *Journal of Applied Social Psychology, 8*(1), 47–56.

Haaga, D. A. (1991). Homophobia? *Journal of Social Behavior and Personality, 6*(1), 171–174.

Hansen, G. L. (1982). Androgyny, sex-role orientation, and homosexism. *Journal of Psychology, 112*, 39–45.

Harry, J. (1982). Derivative deviance: The cases of extortion, fag-bashing and the shakedown of gay men. *Criminology, 19*, 546–564.

Harry, J. (1990). Conceptualizing anti-gay violence. *Journal of Interpersonal Violence, 5*(3), 350–358.

Henley, N. M., & Pincus, F. (1978). Interrelationship of sexist, racist, and anti-homosexual attitudes. *Psychological Reports, 42*, 83–90.

Herek, G. M. (1984). Beyond "homophobia": A social psychological perspective on attitudes toward lesbian and gay men. *Journal of Homosexuality, 10*, 1–21.

Herek, G. M. (1986a). The social psychology of homophobia: Toward a practical theory. *Review of Law and Social Change, 14*, 923–934.

Herek, G. M. (1986b). On heterosexual masculinity: Some psychical consequences of the social construction of gender and sexuality. *American Behavioral Scientist,* 29(5), 563–577.

Herek, G. M. (1986c). *Sexual orientation and prejudice at Yale: A report on the experiences of lesbian, gay and bisexual members of the Yale community.* Unpublished manuscript.

Herek, G. M. (1988). Heterosexuals' attitudes toward lesbians and gay men: Correlates and gender differences. *Journal of Sex Research, 25*(4), 451–477.

Herek, G. M. (1989). Hate crimes against lesbians and gay men: Issues for research and social policy. *American Psychologist, 44,* 948–955.

Herek, G. M. (1990). The context of anti-gay violence. *Journal of Interpersonal Violence,* 5(3), 316–333.

Herek, G. M., & Berrill, K. T. (1990). Documenting the victimization of lesbians and gay men. *Journal of Interpersonal Violence, 5*(3), 301–315.

Herek, G. M., & Glunt, E. K. (1988). An epidemic of stigma: Public reactions to AIDS. *American Psychologist, 43,* 886–891.

Hood, R. W. Jr. (1973). Dogmatism and opinions about mental illness. *Psychological Reports, 32,* 1283–1290.

Hudson, W. W., & Ricketts, W. A. (1980). A strategy for the measurement of homophobia. *Journal of Homosexuality, 5*(4), 357–372.

Hunter, J. (1990). Violence against lesbian and gay male youth. *Journal of Interpersonal Violence, 5*(3), 295–300.

Irwin, P., & Thompson, N. L. (1977). Acceptance of the rights of homosexuals: A social profile. *Journal of Homosexuality, 3*(2), 107–121.

Jenks, R. J. (1988). Nongays' perceptions of gays. *Annals of Sex Research, 1,* 139–150.

Karr, R. G. (1978). Homosexual labeling and the male role. *Journal of Social Issues, 34,* 73–83.

Kite, M. E. (1984). Sex differences in attitudes toward homosexuals: A meta-analytic review. *Journal of Homosexuality, 10,* 69–81.

Kite, M. E., & Deaux, K. (1986). Attitudes toward homosexuality: Assessment and behavioral consequences. *Basic and Applied Social Psychology, 7*(2), 137–162.

Kitzinger, C. (1987). *The social construction of lesbianism.* London: Sage.

Krulewitz, J. E., & Nash, J. E. (1980). Effects of sex-role attitudes and similarity on men's rejection of male homosexuals. *Journal of Personality and Social Psychology, 38*(1), 67–74.

Kurdek, L. A. (1988). Correlates of negative attitudes toward homosexuals in heterosexual college students. *Sex Roles, 18*(11–12), 727–738.

Laner, M. R., & Laner, R. H. (1979). Personal style or sexual preference? Why gay men are disliked. *International Review of Modern Sociology, 9,* 215–228.

Laner, M. R., & Laner, R. H. (1980). Sexual preference or personal style? Why lesbians are disliked. *Journal of Homosexuality, 5*(4), 339–356.

Larsen, K. S., Reed, M., & Hoffman, S. (1980). Attitudes of heterosexuals toward homosexuality: A Likert-type scale and construct validity. *Journal of Sex Research, 16*(3), 245–257.

Lehne, G. (1976). Homophobia among men. In D. S. David & R. Brannon (Eds.), *The forty-nine percent majority: The male sex role* (pp. 66–88). Reading, MA: Addison-Wesley.

Levitt, E., & Klassen, A. D. (1974). Public attitudes toward homosexuality: Part of the 1970 national survey by the Institute for Sex Research. *Journal of Homosexuality, 1*(1), 29–43.

Lieblich, A., & Friedman, G. (1985). Attitudes toward male and female homosexuality and sex-role stereotypes in Israeli and American students. *Sex Roles, 12*(5–6), 561–570.

Lord, C. G., Lepper, M. R., & Mackie, D. (1984). Attitude Prototypes as determinants of attitude-behavior consistency. *Journal of Personality and Social Psychology, 46*(6), 1254–1266.

Lott, B. (1987). Sexist discrimination as distancing behavior: I. A laboratory demonstration. *Psychology of Women Quarterly, 11*, 47–58.

Lott, B. (1993). Sexual harassment: Consequences and remedies. *Thought and Action, 8*(2), 89–103.

Lott, B., & Lott, A. J. (1985). Learning theory in contemporary social psychology. In G. Lindzey & E. Aronson (Eds.), *Handbook of social psychology* (3rd ed., Vol. 1, pp. 109–135). New York: Random House.

MacDonald, A. P. Jr. (1974). The importance of sex-role to gay liberation. *Homosexual Counseling Journal, 1*(4), 169–180.

MacDonald, A. P. Jr. (1976). Homophobia: Its roots and meanings. *Homosexual Counseling Journal, 3*(1), 23–33.

MacDonald, A. P. Jr., & Games, R. G. (1974). Some characteristics of those who hold positive and negative attitudes toward homosexuals. *Journal of Homosexuality, 4*(1), 9–27.

MacDonald, A. P. Jr., Huggins, J., Young, S., & Swanson, R. A. (1973). Attitudes toward homosexuality: Preservations of sex morality or the double standard. *Journal of Consulting and Clinical Psychology, 40*(1), 161.

Marsiglio, W. (1993). Attitudes toward homosexual activity and gays as friends: A national survey of heterosexual 15- to 19-year-old males. *Journal of Sex Research, 30*(1), 12–17.

McDermott, D., & Stadler, H. A. (1988). Attitudes of counseling students in the United States toward minority clients. *International Journal for the Advancement of Counseling, 11*, 61–69.

Millham, J., SanMiguel, C. L., & Kellogg, R. (1976). A factor-analytic conceptualization of attitudes toward male and female homosexuals. *Journal of Homosexuality, 2*(1), 3–10.

Millham, J., & Weinberger, L. E. (1977). Sexual preference, sex role appropriateness, and restriction of social access. *Journal of Homosexuality, 2*(4), 343–357.

Minkowitz, D. (1994, April 19). Love hurts. *Village Voice*, pp. 24–30.

Minnigerode, F. A. (1976). Attitudes toward homosexuality: Feminist attitudes and sexual conservatism. *Sex Roles, 2*(4), 347–352.

Mohr, R. D. (1992). *Gay ideas.* Boston: Beacon Press.

Morin, S. F., & Garfinkle, E. M. (1978). Male homophobia. *Journal of Social Issues, 34*(1), 29–47.

Myrdal, G. (1944). *An American dilemma: The Negro problem and modern society.* New York: Harper.

National Gay Task Force (NGTF). (1984). *Anti-gay/lesbian victimization: A study by* the National Gay Task Force in cooperation with gay and lesbian organizations in eight U.S. cities. (Available from NGLTF,1517 U Street N.W., Washington, DC 20009)

National Gay and Lesbian Task Force (NGLTF). (1986). *Anti-gay violence and victimization in 1985.* (Available from NGLTF at the address above)

National Gay and Lesbian Task Force (NGLTF). (1987). *Anti-gay violence, victimization and defamation in 1986.* (Available from NGLTF)

National Gay and Lesbian Task Force (NGLTF). (1988). *Anti-gay violence, victimization and defamation in 1987.* (Available from NGLTF)

National Gay and Lesbian Task Force (NGLTF). (1989). *Anti-gay violence, victimization and defamation in 1988.* (Available from NGLTF)

National Gay and Lesbian Task Force (NGLTF). (1990). *Anti-gay violence, victimization and defamation in 1989.* (Available from NGLTF)

National Gay and Lesbian Task Force (NGLTF). (1993). *Anti-gay violence, victimization and defamation in 1992.* (Available from NGLTF)

National Gay and Lesbian Task Force (NGLTF). (1994). *Anti-gay violence, victimization and defamation in 1993.* (Available from NGLTF)

Neisen, J. H. (1990). Heterosexism: Redefining homophobia for the 1990s. *Journal of Gay and Lesbian Psychotherapy, 1*(3), 21–35.

Nelson, M. B. (1994, July). How men's sports hurt women. *Glamour,* pp. 136–137, 170–173.

Newman, B. S. (1989). The relative importance of gender role attitudes to male and female attitudes toward lesbian. *Sex Roles, 21*(7–8), 451–465.

Nungesser, L. (1983). *Homosexual acts, actors, and identities.* New York: Praeger.

Nyberg, K. L., & Alston, J. P. (1976–1977). Analysis of public attitudes toward homosexual behavior. *Journal of Homosexuality, 2*(2), 99–107.

Page, S., & Yee, M. (1985). Conception of male and female homosexual stereotypes among university undergraduates. *Journal of Homosexuality, 12*(1), 109–118.

Pharr, S. (1988). *Homophobia: A weapon of sexism.* Little Rock, AR: Chardon Press.

Plasek, J. W., & Allard, J. (1984). Misconceptions of homophobia. *Journal of Homosexuality, 10,* 23–37.

Pooley, E. (1991, April 8). With extreme prejudice. *New York,* pp. 36–43.

Radicalesbians. (1973). The woman identified woman. In A. Koedt, E. Levine, & A. Rapone (Eds.), *The woman identified woman* (pp. 240–245). New York: Quadrangle Books.

Rayside, D., & Bowler, S. (1988). Public opinion and gay rights. *Canadian Review of Sociology and Anthropology, 25*(4), 649–660.

Rooney, E. A., & Gibbons, D. C. (1966). Societal reactions to crimes without victims. *Social Problems, 13,* 400–410.

Salholz, E., with McCormick, J., McKillop, P., & Hill, M. (1993, February 1). A grisly murder mystery: Was Alan Schindler killed because he was gay? *Newsweek,* p. 57.

SanMiguel, C. L., & Millham, J. (1976). The role of cognitive and situational variables in aggression toward homosexuals. *Journal of Homosexuality, 2,* 11–27.

Senzel, C. (1990). *1988–89 bias incident investigation analysis: End of year report.* New York: New York City Police Department.

Shaffer, D. R., & Wallace, A. (1990). Belief congruence and evaluator homophobia

as determinants of the attractiveness of component homosexual and heterosexual males. *Journal of Psychology and Human Sexuality, 3*(1), 67–87.

Sherif, M., Harvey, L. J., White, B. J., Hood, W. R., & Sherif, C. W. (1988). *The robbers'
cave experiment: Intergroup conflict and cooperation.* Middletown, CT: Wesleyan
University Press.

Simmons, J. L. (1965). Public stereotypes of deviants. *Social Problems, 13,* 223–232.

Smith, A. D., Resick, P. A., & Kilpatrick, D. G. (1980). Relationship among gender,
sex-role attitudes, thoughts, and behaviors. *Psychological Reports, 46,* 359–367.

Smith, K. T. (1971). Homophobia: A tentative personality profile. *Psychological
Reports, 29,* 1091–1094.

Smith, T. W. (1990). The polls—a report: The sexual revolution? *Public Opinion
Quarterly, 54,* 415–435.

Staats, G. R. (1978). Stereotype content and social distance: Changing views of
homosexuality. *Journal of Homosexuality, 4,* 15–28.

Stark, L. P. (1991). Traditional gender role beliefs and individual outcomes: An
exploratory analysis. *Sex Roles, 24*(9–10), 639–650.

Steffensmeier, D., & Steffensmeier, R. (1974). Sex differences in reactions to homosexuals: Research continuities and further developments. *Journal of Sex Research, 10,* 52–67.

Stephan, G. E. (1985). Intergroup relations. In G. Lindzey & E. Aronson (Eds.),
Handbook of social psychology (3rd ed., Vol. 2, pp. 599–658). New York: Random
House.

Stephan, G. E., & McMullin, D. R. (1982). Tolerance of sexual nonconformity: City
size as a situational and early learning determinant. *American Sociological
Review, 47,* 411–415.

Storms, M. D. (1978). Attitude toward homosexuality and femininity in men. *Journal
of Homosexuality, 3*(3), 257–263.

Taylor, A. (1983). Conceptions of masculinity and femininity as a basis for stereotypes of male and female homosexuals. *Journal of Homosexuality, 9,* 37–53.

Thompson, E. H., Grisanti, C., & Pleck, J. H. (1985). Attitudes toward the male role
and their correlates. *Sex Roles, 13*(7–8), 413–427.

VanderStoep, S., & Green, C. (1988). Religiosity and homonegativism: A path
analytic study. *Basic and Applied Social Psychology, 9*(2), 135–147.

Weinberg, G. (1972). *Society and the healthy homosexual.* New York: St. Martin's Press.

Weinberger, L. E., & Millham, J. (1979). Attitudinal homophobia and support of
traditional sex roles. *Journal of Homosexuality, 4*(3), 237–245.

Weiner, B. (1986). *An attributional theory of motivation and emotion.* New York: Springer.

Weiner, B., Perry, R. P., & Magnusson, J. (1988). An attributional analysis of reactions
to stigmas. *Journal of Personality and Social Psychology, 55,* 738–748.

Weis, C. B. Jr., & Dain, R. N. (1979). Ego development and sex attitudes in heterosexual and homosexual men and women. *Archives of Sexual Behavior, 8*(4),
341–356.

Weissbach, T. A., & Zagon, G. (1975). The effects of deviant group membership upon
impressions of personality. *Journal of Social Psychology, 95,* 263–266.

Whitley, B. E. (1987). The relationship of sex-role orientation to homosexuals'
attitudes toward homosexuals. *Sex Roles, 17*(1–2), 103–113.

Whitley, B. E. (1988). Sex differences in heterosexual's attitudes toward homosexuals: It depends upon what you ask. *Journal of Sex Research, 24,* 287–291.

Whitley, B. E. (1990). The relationship of heterosexuals attributions for the cause of homosexuality to attitudes toward lesbians and gay men. *Personality and Social Psychology Bulletin, 16*(2), 369–377.

Wilder, D. A. (1986). Social categorization: Implications for creation and reduction of intergroup bias. In L. Berkowitz (Ed.), *Advances in experimental social psychology* (Vol. 19, pp. 291–355). New York: Academic Press.

Yeskel, F. (1985). *The consequences of being gay: A report on the quality of life for lesbian, gay and bisexual students at the University of Massachusetts at Amherst.* (Available from the Office of Lesbian/Gay/Bisexual Concerns, 117 Cance House, University of Massachusetts, Amherst, MA 01003)

5

Class Acts
Middle-Class Responses
to the Poor

HEATHER E. BULLOCK

"Rebuilding Standards of Behavior Is Essential to Any Poverty Cure"
—SCOTT, *Providence Journal Bulletin*, March 2, 1994

"The War on Welfare Mothers: Reform May Put Them to Work, but Will It Discourage Illegitimacy?"
—*Time*, June 20, 1994

"Clinton Report: Homelessness Serious"
—*Providence Journal-Bulletin*,
February 17, 1994

Despite the strongly held belief that the United States is a "classless" nation, headlines such as these remind us that it is in fact stratified by social class. The richest 10% of U.S. citizens own 72% of the wealth in the country, while the remaining 90% own only 28% of the wealth (Joint Economic Committee of the U.S. Congress, 1986). Winnick (1989) argues that the incredible share of wealth and power held by so few belies claims of democracy. Despite the facts of income inequality and the skewed distribution of wealth, many Americans dislike talking about social class, preferring to emphasize egalitarianism when considering life in the United States (Mantsios, 1992). The myth of classlessness appears to be a central ideological tenet (Ehrenreich, 1990).

In the United States, higher incomes are associated with high status, high power, and unrestricted access to resources, whereas lower incomes are associated with low status, low power, and limited access to resources. Because the working class, the working poor, and poor people hold less status and power in U.S. society than the middle and upper classes, they are the most likely targets of classist discrimination. Like sexism, racism, ageism, and heterosexism, classism occurs at both the institutional and the interpersonal levels. As noted by Langston (1992, p. 112), "When we experience classism, it will be because of our lack of money (i.e., choices and power in this society) and because of the way we talk, think, act, move—because of our culture." To borrow from Young's (1992) definition of sexism, "classism" can be defined as the oppression of the poor through a network of everyday practices, attitudes, assumptions, behaviors, and institutional rules. And by analogy with Lott's (1987; see also Chapter 2, this volume) analysis of interpersonal sexism, it is proposed that interpersonal classism is composed of the related but independent dimensions of prejudice, stereotypes, and discrimination. Within this social-psychological framework, classist prejudice consists of negative attitudes toward the poor; classist stereotypes are widely shared and socially sanctioned beliefs about the poor, and classist discrimination includes face-to-face overt behaviors that distance, avoid, and/or exclude the poor.

As the economic disparity between the rich and the poor grows, and as the number of people living in poverty continues to rise, it is increasingly difficult to ignore inequity in U.S. life (although many seem to work hard to do so); and, once again, poverty is being "rediscovered" as a significant social issue in the United States (Katz, 1989). During the past 10 years, psychologists have shown considerable interest in homelessness (one facet of poverty)—both its causes and its remedies. Especially noteworthy are special issues of the *Journal of Social Issues* (Shinn & Weitzman, 1990) and the *American Psychologist* (Jones, Levine, & Rosenberg, 1991), as well as the National Institute of Mental Health's (1992) *Outcasts on Main Street*, all of which are entirely devoted to homelessness. Although poverty is repeatedly cited as a predictor of homelessness (Kiesler, 1991; Milburn & D'Ercole, 1991), psychologists have paid little attention to many other issues relating to poverty. Social psychologists have been criticized for overlooking issues surrounding social class and for asking research questions that pathologize and stigmatize the poor (Harper, 1991). For example, studies seldom investigate positive experiences in the lives of poor people or the processes by which poor people can facilitate social change (see Wagner & Cohen, 1991).

Even when poor people are included in research investigations, their experiences are seldom discussed in their own voices (Edin, 1991). Clinicians and therapists have been criticized for employing treatments laden with ethnocentric and classist assumptions that further stigmatize poor clients (Saba & Rodgers, 1989). Finally, when psychologists do study social class issues, the focus is generally on middle-class attitudes and stereotypes about the poor, particularly welfare recipients, and middle class attributions for poverty. Little psychological research has examined discriminatory behavior against poor people, particularly in the interpersonal realm.

This chapter focuses on classist behavior, but since most social-psychological research pertaining to social class has dealt with classist attitudes, beliefs, and attributions for poverty, and since attitudes and beliefs are components of classism, I also review research on the latter issues. Although the working class and the working poor are targets of classist discrimination, I have chosen to focus on classist responses to welfare recipients, because they can be considered the poorest of the poor. The United States is the geographical context for this review, but some international findings from other industrialized countries (e.g., Great Britain) are also discussed.

DEFINING SOCIAL CLASS AND POVERTY

Social scientists have not reached a consensus concerning the measurement and construction of social stratification. For example, researchers have debated whether class differentiation is a discrete or continuous variable, and have questioned the adequacy of the indicators typically used to assess class standing (Haug, 1972). The current consensus among researchers is that multiple indicators of class standing are superior to single indicators, and social class is typically operationalized in terms of some combination of educational attainment, income, occupation, neighborhood, and residence (Hollingshead & Redlich, 1958; Centers, 1961; Warner, 1972). In addition to these objective measures, "subjective" indicators of class standing are also commonly used. For example, individuals are sometimes asked to identify the social class to which they feel they belong (Bott, 1972); when they are, the majority of respondents in the United States describe themselves as members of the middle class (Gallup & Newport, 1990).

More informal indicators of class standing are typically used by people during interpersonal interactions. For example, when trying to assess an individual's class standing, others may examine the style and quality of the person's clothing, the restaurants dined in, the type of car driven, the stores shopped in, or recreational activities (Barber, 1957). Higher socioeconomic groups are generally reported to consume a greater range and variety of foods that meet current nutritional standards than lower socioeconomic groups (Merrel, 1992). Personal characteristics such as language, speech patterns, and walking style may also be used as symbolic indicators of social class (Barber, 1957; Langston, 1992). The use of these symbolic indicators remind us that social class is socially constructed or created rather than natural or inherent.

Measures of social class generally result in the assignment of individuals to one of four social class categories: (1) the upper class, which includes the traditional owners of capital; (2) the middle class, which includes managers, professionals, and small-business owners; (3) the working class, which includes skilled, semiskilled, and unskilled laborers, in both the industrial and service sectors of the economy; and (4) the lower class, which includes the working poor, the poor, the homeless, and people on public assistance (Szymanski, 1983). Classification systems can be made even more detailed by designating "upper" and "lower" groupings, such as the "upper" middle class or the "lower" middle class (Warner, 1972).

In part, discussions of class status are problematic because they require sweeping generalizations about large groups of people, the way they live, and how they earn their money (Ehrenreich, 1990). Describing such difficulties, Ehrenreich (1990) states, "Class is a notion that is inherently fuzzy at the edges" (p. 13). This "fuzziness" is especially evident when discussing the so-called middle class, because it is a group so frequently referred to but so loosely defined. Refining class terminology, Ehrenreich (1990) prefers "professional–managerial class" or "professional middle class" over "middle class" because of their greater specificity. She describes the professional middle class as made up of those people whose economic and social status is based on education rather than ownership of property or capital, and she estimates its size at no more than 20% of the population. Ehrenreich (1990) includes within the professional middle class administrative professionals, white-collar managers (whose positions require at least a college degree), engineers, government bureaucrats, therapists, financial managers, scientists, corporate executives (at least through middle levels of management), professors, schoolteachers, and anchorpersons. Throughout this chapter, the term "middle class" is used to refer to this select group.

The relative nature of classism is apparent when we consider the skewed distribution of wealth in the United States. Compared to the truly rich, even the middle class could be perceived as part of the "lower class." Clearly, the middle class holds less power than the truly rich—the corporate elite, the small minority of people who own the majority of the wealth in the United States. Nevertheless, the middle class holds considerable power in relation to the working class, the working poor, and the poor. Commenting on the privileged status of the middle class, Ehrenreich (1990) states, "In our culture, the professional, and largely white, middle class is taken as a social norm—a bland and neutral mainstream—from which every other group or class is ultimately a kind of deviation" (p. 3). Thus the working class, the working poor, and poor people hold less status and power in U.S. society than the middle and upper classes, and are accordingly the most likely targets of classist discrimination.

In 1993, for the fourth consecutive year, the number of poor people in the United States increased. The Census Bureau's annual poverty report found that 39.3 million people, or 15.1% of the population, had fallen below pverty thresholds in 1993. This estimate of persons living below the Social Security Administration's official poverty line is the highest since 1961 when 39.6 million Americans were judged to be poor (Schmid, 1994). Estimates of poverty would vastly increase if those people hovering precariously just above the official poverty thresholds were also included in government calculations. For example, the Bureau of the Census reported that in 1989 31.5 million or 12.5% of persons in the United States were living in poverty, but critics argued that during 1989, 56 million or 22.8% of the population resided in households with incomes that could not realistically provide for basic necessities (Schwartz & Volgy, 1992).

The classification of being poor in the United States is determined by one's relation to the "poverty line." The first official poverty line was developed in the 1960s, following results from the Department of Agriculture's 1955 Food Consumption Survey, which established an "economy food budget" (the cost of a minimally adequate diet). The survey indicated that a typical family spent about a third of its budget on food. Subsequently, poverty thresholds were calculated by multiplying by three the cost of the economy food plan for each family size (Wise, 1992). Although slight revisions have been made, and the threshold is adjusted each year according to the Consumer Price Index, the initial formula remains unchanged and has been heavily criticized by advocates for the poor. Many argue that the poverty line must be revised to reflect how consumer patterns have changed since 1955. When poverty thresholds are set low, calculations of the number of Americans living in poverty underestimate the true number of persons who are poor. Ruggles (1990) estimates that if the poverty thresholds were modestly increased, calculations of the number of people living in poverty would double.

Even according to the official Social Security Administration's poverty thresholds, the number living in poverty is alarming, as is the rate at which women and children have entered the ranks of the poor. Analyses of census data indicate that single mothers and "displaced homemakers" are four times more likely to live in poverty than the population as a whole ("Single Women and Poverty Strongly Linked," 1994). Although women's poverty is certainly not a new phenomenon, sociologist Diana Pearce (1978) coined the term "the feminization of poverty" to describe a phenomenon observed between 1950 and 1980, during which time women's poverty rates increased relative to men's across all age groups and among African-Americans as well as European-Americans (McClanahan, Sorenson, & Watson, 1989; Sidel, 1992; Miller, 1992). It is estimated that one-third of all families in the United States headed by women live below the poverty line and such inequality is multiplied when ethnicity is considered (U.S. Bureau of the Census, 1993). For example, almost half of all female-led African-American households live in poverty (U.S. Bureau of the Census, 1993). The increase in the number of poor families headed by a woman accounted for 84% of the net increase in poor families between 1989 and 1990 (U.S. Bureau of the Census, 1991). Furthermore, whereas women constituted only 3% of the homeless in the 1950s and 1960s, it is currently estimated that female-headed households are the fastest-growing segment of the U.S. homeless population (Women's Action Coalition, 1993).

CLASSIST ATTITUDES AND BELIEFS

Stereotype Acquisition and Awareness of Social Class

Little is known about the precise age at which children learn social class stereotypes, but children as young as second-graders tend to agree that becoming wealthy is difficult and that becoming poor is easy (Karniol, 1985). Children as young as 5 have been found to believe that the harder one works the richer one gets, and that the poor do not work hard enough or do not work at all (Danzinger, 1958). It appears that sometime between childhood and adolescence there is a shift among middle-class children from describing the poor in terms of observable, physical characteristics (e.g., messy clothing) to referring to personal characteristics such as laziness (Leahy, 1981). In a study of children ranging in age from 5 to 18, Leahy (1981) found that with increasing age there was a growing tendency to perceive the rich and poor not only as differing in terms of physical characteristics, but also as being different kinds of people. With increasing age, descriptions involving lack of effort, lack of ability, and other negative personality traits became more common. Leahy (1981) also found that upper-middle-class children were more likely to describe the poor as possessing negative traits, whereas poor children were more likely to describe poor people as worrying about having very little money. In a later study, Leahy (1983) found that upper-middle-class children and middle-class children were more likely than others to deny the possibility of status change for the poor.

By adolescence, negative character traits are readily ascribed to the poor. In a study of 638 adolescents, poor strangers were judged to steal more often, to feel worse about themselves, and to make friends less easily than either neutral or wealthy strangers (Skafte, 1988). Wealthy strangers were judged to be more intelligent, to make better grades, to be more likely to succeed in the future, to be healthier, and to be happier than neutral or poor strangers.

Middle-Class Stereotypes about the Poor and about Welfare Recipients

Because people in the United States are evaluated in terms of their monetary worth, it is not surprising that poor people are negatively evaluated by the nonpoor. People who receive public assistance are the poorest of the poor, and most research concerning social class has focused on the attitudes and beliefs of the nonpoor toward welfare recipients. Historical and political analyses of poverty in the United States indicate that contemporary middle-class attitudes and stereotypes about poor people have very old roots (Piven & Cloward, 1987a, 1993; Katz, 1986, 1989, 1993). Even before the 16th century, the magistrates of Basel had identified 25 categories of beggars and created appropriate punishments for each (Piven & Cloward, 1993). Before the 20th century, communities in the United States assisted poor permanent residents from their own neighborhoods; the distinction between neighbors and strangers was clear. However, as people became more mobile, it became increasingly difficult to establish the community to which someone belonged. During the 19th century, it was popular to separate the poor into two classes: the truly needy (impotent, deserving) "poor" versus the able-bodied (undeserving) "paupers" (Katz, 1989). The distinction between the poor and paupers hardened into moral categories, and the destitution of paupers was attributed to intemperance and vice. The transmutation of pauperism into a moral category affected all poor people; despite efforts to distinguish these categories, poverty was more and more perceived as the result of willful vice (Katz, 1989). Although we seldom hear poor people referred to as "paupers" today, the moral judgment of the poor persists in stereotypes about them.

Contemporary stereotypes about poor people are embedded in, and reinforced by, the popular and pervasive "culture of poverty" hypothesis. Essentially, this hypothesis proposes that the poor are destitute because they share and transmit to their children a set of defective behaviors, values, and personality traits (Ehrenreich, 1987; Sullivan, 1989). Such supposed traits include laziness, inability to defer gratification, lack of respect for or interest in education, unwillingness to work, dishonesty, and sexual promiscuity as well as apathy or ignorance about birth control (Sharff, 1981; Piven & Cloward, 1987b; Ehrenreich, 1987, 1990; Duncan, Hill, & Hoffman, 1988). It is therefore expected that individuals who receive public assistance will become dependent on the government for support, will exhibit any or all of the previously mentioned traits, and will transmit these deficiencies to their children. The "culture of poverty" hypothesis is a "flawed character" explanation. Rather than regarding the poor as lacking sufficient opportunities for advancement, the poor are perceived as failing to seize opportunities because they lack diligence and initiative. The "culture of poverty" explanation resides in the undesirable personality traits and behaviors of the poor, which are said to be transmitted from one generation to another (Sullivan, 1989).

Among middle-class persons, perceptions of welfare recipients and the welfare system are overwhelmingly negative. Poor people and welfare recipients are typically characterized as dishonest, dependent, lazy, uninterested in education, and promiscuous. In the United States (Feagin, 1975; Alston & Dean, 1972; Desmond, Price, & Eoff, 1989), Great Britain (Furnham, 1982, 1983), and Australia (Feather, 1974), welfare recipients have been consistently stereotyped as dishonest. In one U.S. nationwide survey, 84% of middle-class respondents were found to believe that welfare recipients are dishonest about their needs (Feagin, 1975). Negative attitudes toward the welfare system and welfare recipients are frequently voiced in letters sent in response to newspaper and magazines articles about welfare (see McCrary, 1993; Crooke, 1993; Minnis, 1993). Yet, ironically, middle-class and wealthy Americans also receive public assistance from programs referred to by some as "welfare for the well-off" (Goodgame, 1993). For example, nonpoor Americans can receive Social Security subsidies, health care subsidies, housing subsidies, and benefits from tax shelters. These forms of assistance are rarely thought of as "welfare" and carry no stigma.

The very word "welfare" seems to conjure up negative images. Welfare has been labeled as wasteful, excessive, and unproductive (Schlitz, cited in Smith, 1987). Investigating how wording affects support for public assistance, Smith (1987) compared different versions of spending-priority scales to determine whether support varied as a function of reference to "welfare," to "the poor," to the "unemployed," or to "food stamps." On the average, support for assistance to the poor was 39 percentage points higher than support for welfare. Support for the unemployed exceeded support for welfare by 12 percentage points. Only support for food stamps was rated as low as or lower than support for welfare. Smith (1987) asserts that the greater support found for the poor and the unemployed illustrates the association of wastefulness, fraud, and bureaucracy with welfare. Welfare recipients are also perceived as having more influence on U.S. life and politics than they deserve (Smith, 1987). It has been suggested that "welfare" is devalued because of its association with minorities (Smith, 1987; Wright, 1977; Ehrenreich, 1991). Although the majority of welfare recipients are European-American, it is falsely believed that most recipients are minorities (Axelson & Hendrickson, 1985). Thus, negative perceptions of welfare recipients may partially reflect racism.

Women on welfare are often stereotyped as promiscuous, as devaluing two-parent families, and as having large families in order to receive increased welfare benefits. Although it has been shown that welfare benefits do not significantly affect the incidence of out-of-wedlock births, and have only a minimal impact on divorce and separation rates among single African-American and European-American women (Ellwood & Summers, 1986; Wilson & Neckerman, 1986), almost 60% of a sample of 192 nurses in one study (Desmond et al., 1989) were found to believe that women become pregnant to collect welfare. In self-report interviews with recipients of Aid to Families with Dependent Children (AFDC), women do not report becoming pregnant to receive increased benefits. In fact, the average AFDC family has only two children at home (Sidel, 1992).

Poor people are typically characterized as being lazy, and welfare is said to serve as a disincentive that encourages recipients to shun work and enjoy a "free ride" (Kaus, 1991; Mead, 1991; Murray, 1991; Magnet, 1991). These beliefs are also not supported by studies examining the effects of AFDC benefits on work incentive (Zinn & Sarri, 1984; Ellwood & Summers, 1986), or by ethnographic studies of poor communities (Sullivan, 1989; Bourgois, 1989; Sharff, 1981). Furthermore, many poor people do work. In 1992, approximately 40% of poor persons over 15 years of age worked part-time, and 9% worked full-time the year round (U.S. Bureau of the Census, 1993). It is estimated that one-quarter of all the homeless work, but that their wages are too low to afford permanent housing.

The poor are further stereotyped as uneducated and as devaluing educational attainment. Although the number of years of school completed is not a guarantee against poverty, it does influence the likelihood of being poor. Poverty rates do decrease dramatically as years of schooling increase. But information collected on the educational attainment of the poor in 1991 indicated that 53% of family householders 25 years and older were high school graduates, 18% had completed one or more years of college, and only 12.5% had not completed seventh grade (U.S. Bureau of the Census, 1992). The desire to learn new skills and pursue self-improvement through education is frequently heard in the frustrated complaints of AFDC recipients, who will lose their aid if they pursue a bachelor's degree (Popkin, 1990). Ethnographic research indicates that poor parents and their children value education (Sullivan, 1989); considering the ravaged condition of many poor, inner-city schools, the continued attendance of children is in and of itself a testament to the desire to learn (Kozol, 1991).

Poor people are often perceived as being passive or dependent (see Ehrenreich, 1987). In a survey of 1,250 U.S. respondents, 37% of the sample said they believed that the poor prefer to stay on welfare, and 64% believed that welfare makes people dependent (Colasanto, 1989). Empirical data do not support the belief that public assistance causes dependence on government "handouts." A recent analysis of poverty and poverty escape rates in nine industrialized countries conducted by Duncan, Hauser, Schmauss, Messinger, Muffels, Nolan and Ray (cited in Mortimer, 1994) found that a greater percentage of people moved out of poverty in countries granting more generous benefits (e.g., Finland and France) than in countries granting smaller benefits (e.g., the United States and Ireland). Despite research indicating that the majority of those on welfare remain on it for only 2 years (Zinn & Sarri, 1984; Corcoran, Duncan, & Hill, 1984; Gottschalk, McClanahan, & Sandefur, 1994), it is typically believed that once individuals receive welfare they will need assistance permanently (Kaus, 1991).

Health care providers, who may be expected to be unbiased and to treat all patients equally, have been found to have negative attitudes and beliefs that may act as a barrier to those seeking care. For example, Desmond et al. (1989) found that 43% of their sample of 192 nurses believed that poor people prefer to stay on welfare, and 35% believed that people on welfare live well. Although year-to-year changes in the number of persons in poverty are in general relatively small, the poverty population is actually much more dynamic than is commonly believed. Many more people change poverty status from one year to the next than is indicated by simply looking at the net change in the poverty rate (U.S. Bureau of the Census, 1993). Finally, the cross-generational transmission of welfare dependency has not received strong empirical support. Following daughters of welfare-dependent families over 19 years, Duncan et al. (1988) found that 64% of these women never received AFDC assistance. Such statistics clearly contradict the stereotypical assumption that poverty and welfare dependency are necessarily transmitted to the children of dependent families.

Images of Class Status in the Mass Media

For the most part, television situation comedies and films ignore class issues by portraying a world in which middle-class status is the norm. Television characters who are homeless or receiving public assistance are generally invisible unless they are part of a "Christmas miracle" story. Mantsios (1992) has identified three characteristics of story lines about the poor: First, they tend to create and reinforce negative class stereotypes; second, they tend to portray instances of upward mobility or class fluidity; finally, they depict cross-class love stories, which ultimately show that people are really the same "inside," regardless of class status.

Working-class characters are more commonly depicted in television situation comedies than are poorer characters. Ehrenreich (1990) asserts that the mass media have created two overlapping images of the working class: On television, the blue-collar man is portrayed as a buffoon; and in the movies, the blue-collar man is presented as dangerous. The patriarchal, racist Archie Bunker from *All in the Family* was perhaps the quintessential image of the blue-collar male "buffoon." Michael Douglas personifies the dangerous working-class man in *Falling Down*, a film about a missile plant worker who goes on a violence spree after losing his job. Presently, working-class women rather than men seem to be the focus of media attention. Two TV series, *Roseanne* and *Grace under Fire*, center around strong working-class women struggling to provide for themselves and their families. Although the character Roseanne is certainly more brash than traditional images of middle-class women, she is also intelligent, committed to her family, and responsible. Images of class do not appear to be the sole basis of Roseanne's humor, however, and most episodes center around issues other than class status.

Stereotypical depictions of the working class continue to flourish. *Someone like Me*, for example, is a situation comedy revolving around two junior high school friends (a middle-class girl and a working-class girl) and the difficult relationship between their mothers. In the premiere episode, the working-class girl is too embarrassed to hold a birthday party in her own home because it is filthy (garbage covers the floor, dirty dishes line the shelf area, and mountains of dirty laundry dominate the corners of rooms), so the middle-class girl offers to hold the party in her impeccably neat home. A stark contrast is created between the two mothers. The divorced working-class mother, who sells cosmetics for a living, is relatively plain in dress and appearance, chain-smokes, and has little time to spend with her two children; the middle-class mother, the wife of an optometrist, is physically attractive, leads an organized life, and punctually attends all of her daughter's swim meets. Pitying the working-class girl, the middle-class mother prepares an elaborate party with a beautiful cake. The working-class mother, late to her own daughter's party, arrives with a frozen cake, a bottle of Cold Duck for the kids, and slasher films for entertainment. Needless to say, the night ends in disaster and humiliation.

Analyzing media images of women, Sidel (1990) asserts that working-class women are frequently stereotyped as being less attractive than their middle-class counterparts. For example, Roxanne, the secretary on *L.A. Law*, was considerably less attractive than the female attorneys at the firm. On *Cheers*, Diane (Shelley Long) and Rebecca (Kirstie Alley) were both more attractive than working-class Carla (Rhea Perlman) (Sidel, 1990). Because women's physical attractiveness is so highly valued in our society, it is rather predicable that members of undervalued groups, such as poor women, would be stereotyped as unattractive.

Class-based story lines also tend to emphasize mobility by highlighting the ascent from "rags to riches," typically through magic, luck, or marriage. "Rags to riches" messages saturate the airwaves and their omnipresence is evident in the elated expressions of Publishers Clearinghouse sweepstakes winners and in prime-time programs such as *The Fresh Prince of Bel-Air* and *Models, Inc.* Nowhere is the dream of upward mobility more clearly articulated than in the Publishers Clearinghouse jingle which urges us to, "Think about your daydreams and what you would do if you won millions from out of the blue. Miracles can happen, happen to you. Publishers Clearinghouse, the house where dreams come true."

"Wrong side of the track" romances (i.e., "poor boy, rich girl" stories or the opposite) frequently illustrate that class lines can be easily transcended. Illustrating both the ascent from rags to riches and the belief that love conquers all, the film *Pretty Woman* centers around a poor but beautiful prostitute (Julia Roberts) who ends up in a committed relationship with a wealthy "john" (Richard Gere). Daytime dramas also thrive on cross-class love stories. For example, on *General Hospital*, the wealthy and sophisticated Ned Ashton is in love with the flamboyant and often tacky working-class Lois. Similarly, on *All My Children*, two of the richest men in town are married to women from working-class origins. Discussing the underlying messages of story lines such as these, DeMott (1990) states, "The message is unvarying: the surface of things may look structured, and some members of society may talk themselves into believing that escape from fixed levels is impossible, but actually where we place ourselves is up to us; whenever we wish to, we can upend the folks on the hill" (p. 66).

Stories about poverty and welfare recipients in television news programs are also relatively scarce. In an analysis of news programming from 1981 to 1986, Iyengar (1991) found that the major networks aired more than 300 stories on both unemployment and racial inequality, but fewer than 200 stories on poverty. Subsequently, Iyengar (1991) estimated that during that time period, viewers of any one particular national newscast watched an average of less than one story a month on poverty, and between one and two stories a month on both unemployment and racial inequality. Furthermore, Iyengar found that stories about poverty were predominantly episodic, whereas stories about unemployment were typically thematic. In other words, stories about poverty typically focused on poverty as an individual issue by showing a particular instance of a poor person. On the other hand, stories about unemployment usually portrayed unemployment as a general issue by including information about current unemployment statistics and interviewing public officials and economists about the potential impact of unemployment on economic activity.

Intrigued by the possibility that the framing of news stories influences our perception of social issues, Iyengar (1991) asked participants to view an episodic or a thematic videotaped story about poverty. Overall, episodic viewers were significantly more likely than thematic viewers to explain poverty in terms of individual factors (i.e., to stress the role of personal responsibility in creating poverty), whereas thematic viewers were significantly more likely to explain the causes of poverty in social terms (i.e., to stress societal causes such as low wages). Specifically, participants viewing thematic stories were found to be twice as likely as episodic viewers to make social causal attributions. Although thematic framing conditions triggered the highest proportion of societal treatment responses, participants in both the episodic and the thematic groups tended to assign responsibility for treating poverty to society rather than to poor people. Further investigations by Iyengar (1991) indicated that framing effects were influenced in part by the type of poor person being depicted. For example, single teenage and adult mothers, particularly Black mothers, were found to elicit more individualistic causal and treatment responses than were White mothers, elderly widows, children, and unemployed men. Iyengar's (1991) findings powerfully illustrate the necessity of examining how media images and the framing of news stories contribute to our understanding of social issues. To further examine the role of attributions for poverty, I now turn specifically to this area.

Attributions for Class Status

Stereotypes about poor people are imbedded in, and influence, the ways in which poverty is explained. Understanding the types of attributions middle-class persons use to explain poverty is important, because attributions may serve to justify classist behaviors.

Three types of explanations for poverty have emerged consistently in the research literature: individualistic, structural, and fatalistic (Tomaskovic-Dewey, 1988). "Individualistic" explanations stress the role of individuals in creating their own poverty. The poor are perceived as having deficient characteristics that have led to their less privileged status, such as lack of thrift and proper money management, promiscuity, drunkenness, lack of effort/laziness, and lack of interest in self-improvement (Feather, 1974; Feagin, 1975; Furnham, 1982a). The philosophy underlying individualistic explanations is illustrated by the following statement: "All men [sic] can better themselves: the circumstances of American life do not imprison men in their class or station—if there is such a prison, the iron bars are within each man" (Lane, cited in Kinder & Sears, 1985, p. 674). "Structural" explanations focus on how economic and social conditions are responsible for poverty. These explanations generally stress low wages in business and industry, failure of society to provide good schools, prejudice and discrimination, being taken advantage of by the rich, failure of industry to provide enough jobs, and inefficient trade unions (Feather, 1974; Feagin, 1975; Furnham, 1982a). The third type of explanation for poverty, "fatalistic," emphasizes bad luck, illness, and unfortunate circumstances (Feather, 1974; Feagin, 1975; Furnham, 1982a).

Feagin (1975) found that in the United States individualistic reasons were believed to be significantly more important than structural or fatalistic explanations. About half of his sample rated lack of thrift, laziness, and loose morals, all individualistic factors, as very important reasons for poverty. Individualistic explanations were found to be endorsed primarily by European-American Protestants and Catholics, people over 50, the middle-income group, and the moderately educated. Structural reasons were most frequently given by African-American Protestants, Jews, people under 30, and people without high school diplomas. When Feagin's data are compared with those from a more recent sample (Kluegel & Smith, 1986), there appears to be remarkable stability in attributions for poverty. The continued perception of poverty as an individual problem is high-lighted by a Gallup poll survey (Gallup, 1992) in which participants were asked to identify the most important problems facing the United States. Somewhat expectedly, the majority of respondents identified "economic problems" (e.g., unemployment and the economy) as the country's most pressing concerns. Although these results are interesting, it is the way the results are presented that is particularly striking. Poverty and homelessness are listed as "noneconomic problems" along with education, crime, ethics, AIDS, the environment, health care, and drug abuse. Why is unemployment regarded as an "economic problem" while poverty is not?

Attributions for wealth in the United States have also been found to focus more often on individualistic explanations, such as personal drive, willingness to take risks, and hard work or initiative. Such factors are more frequently and strongly endorsed than structural explanations, such as having political influence (Klugel & Smith, 1985). In a 1990 national survey, 50% of 1,255 respondents attributed wealth to strong effort (Gallup & Newport, 1990). Attributions for wealth appear to be related to political affiliation. For example, in Great Britain, Furnham (1983b) found that Conservatives were more likely to endorse individualistic attributions for wealth, whereas Labour Party voters were more likely to explain wealth in structural terms.

Explanations for poverty and wealth have obvious implications for how class inequality should be addressed. Beliefs about public assistance have been found to be related to attributions for poverty and to the extent to which the causes are perceived as modifiable (Furnham, 1982a). It is not surprising that people who make individualistic attributions are also more likely to believe that too much money is being spent on welfare (Feagin, 1975; Alston & Dean, 1972). If the poor are believed to be unmotivated and as failing to seize opportunities, responsibility is seen as residing within an individual, and the poor are perceived as undeserving. Legislation providing funding or services to the poor is then more likely to be met with resistance. Conversely, people who make structural attributions are more likely to believe that not enough money is being spent on welfare (Feagin, 1975; Alston & Dean, 1972). If the poor are believed to be victims of low wages or economic factors, they are likely to be perceived as deserving of assistance, and welfare spending is not opposed.

Although it is tempting to infer a direct relationship between causal attributions for poverty and support for welfare spending, the complexity of people's values and of the variables influencing their behaviors cannot be overlooked. Attributions for poverty are not the only variables influencing the stand taken on social policy. For example, a middle class individual may blame poor people for their lower status, but may also be concerned about the well-being of poor children, and therefore may still vote to support increased public assistance spending (Feather, 1974). Some subgroups of the poor (e.g., single mothers and middle-aged women) may be perceived as being particularly undeserving of financial support, while other subgroups (e.g., children) may be seen as especially deserving of public support (Butler & Weatherly, 1992; Iyengar, 1990, 1991). Other factors, such as whether an individual is actively seeking employment, may also influence perceived deservingness (Will, 1993). And just as individualistic attributions may not necessarily lead to anti-welfare beliefs and voting behavior, structural attributions may not guarantee respect for the poor.

Attributions for poverty do not help us predict whether an individual will engage in classist behaviors under particular circumstances, but several background factors and beliefs have been found to be correlated with attributions. Preference for one explanation over another has been found to be significantly correlated with education, political affiliation, belief in a just world, and belief in the Protestant work ethic.

Although higher education is usually associated with more liberal views, a simple linear relationship does not hold true for attitudes toward welfare spending and explanations of poverty. For example, Alston and Dean (1972) found that almost 40% of respondents who had finished high school or had gone to college attributed poverty to lack of effort. The general pattern of results is that the less educated (those who have completed sixth grade or less) make the most structural attributions; the moderately educated (those who have completed some high school and graduates of trade or high school) make the most individualistic attributions; and the more educated (those who have gone to college and beyond) are somewhat less inclined to make individualistic attributions than the moderately educated (Furnham, 1983; Feather, 1974; Feagin, 1975, p. 99). Even this generalization is not always supported for the college-educated. Although people with less education consistently seem to make more structural attributions than high school graduates or those with some college education, the findings are not as clear-cut in regard to the attributions of college graduates. Longitudinal analyses in one investigation (Guimond &

Palmer, 1990) showed that over 4 years of college, the causal attributions of students changed significantly as a function of their field of study. Specifically, social science students were found to endorse structural explanations for poverty significantly more than commerce or engineering students.

Political affiliation appears to be correlated with attributions for poverty. In the United States (Feagin, 1975; AuClaire, 1984; Colasanto, 1989), Great Britain (Furnham, 1982a, 1983, 1985a; Wagstaff, 1983), Australia (Feather, 1985), and India (Pandey, Sinha, Prakash, & Tripathi, 1982), conservative political affiliation is more strongly associated with individualistic attributions than structural explanations. In the United States, for example, Democrats, have been found to make more structural attributions for poverty than Republicans. A survey of 1,255 respondents revealed that 46% of Republicans compared to 27% of Democrats identified lack of effort as the cause of poverty (Gallup & Newport, 1990). Similar findings are revealed by another U.S. nationwide survey of 1,255 respondents, in which 50% of Republicans compared to 32% of Democrats endorsed lack of effort as the primary cause of poverty (Colasanto, 1989). Political affiliation also appears to be strongly related to attitudes toward welfare spending, with Democrats generally less opposed than Republicans (AuClaire, 1984).

Central to ideology in the United States, the beliefs of the Protestant work ethic include the following: (1) Each individual should work hard and try to succeed in competition with others; (2) those who work hard should be rewarded with success (wealth, property, and prestige); (3) because of widespread equal opportunity, those who work hard will in fact be rewarded with success; and (4) economic failure is the individual's own fault and reveals lack of effort (Axelson & Hendrickson, 1985). The aphorism "God helps those who help themselves" underlies this ideology. In the context of the work ethic, the poor are perceived as "dependent" takers rather than "achieving" givers (Judd, 1986). It is not surprising that strong believers in the work ethic have been found to make significantly more individualistic attributions for poverty than weaker believers and to hold anti-welfare beliefs, whereas low believers in the work ethic have been found to favor welfare benefits and to feel sympathy for recipients (Furnham, 1982b, 1984; Wagstaff, 1983).

It is premature, however, to conclude that belief in the work ethic clearly determines how poverty is explained. Investigating the attitudes of 202 middle-class professionals (public defenders, social workers, and computer scientists), Axelson and Hendrickson (1985) found that 90% of their sample believed in the work ethic, but that only 16% accepted individualistic explanations for poverty and 56% endorsed structural explanations. Axelson and Hendrickson (1985) noted, however, that their sample may have been atypical in two respects: Participants were well educated (98% held at least a bachelor's degree), and almost three-quarters of the sample were social workers and public defenders with a professional commitment to helping the poor. Yet even in this sample, those with greater commitment to the work ethic had the least knowledge about the poor, and only half of the participants knew that the majority of welfare recipients are White. Almost half (46%) did not believe that the poor had a desire to work or earn their own way.

Associated with the work ethic is the belief that the world is a "just" place. According to the just-world hypothesis, "Individuals have a need to believe that they live in a world where people generally get what they deserve. The belief that the world is just enables the individual to confront his [sic] physical and social environment as though they were stable and orderly" (Lerner & Miller, 1978, p. 1030). Believers in the just-world hypothesis tend to have negative attitudes toward the poor and underprivileged, and to believe in the work ethic (Rubin & Peplau, cited in Furnham, 1985b; Harper, Wagstaff, Newton, & Harnson, 1990).

Self-Perceptions of the Poor

How do the poor perceive themselves? Do the poor think of themselves as possessing deficient characteristics? Luft (1951) investigated these questions by having a sample of college students complete a personality inventory as though they were either a poor or a rich man. The results indicated that the hypothetical poor man was evaluated as being less self-reliant, as having less personal worth, as being more nervous, as possessing poorer social skills, and as being more antisocial than the hypothetical rich man. In contrast, the rich man was evaluated as relatively healthy, happy, and well adjusted. When Luft asked an actual sample of poor men to complete the same personality inventory, however, the poor men rated themselves just as positively in terms of social skills, self-reliance, and personal adjustment as the college students had rated the hypothetical rich man. These data strongly suggest that the poor do not perceive themselves as possessing the negative characteristics they are believed to possess by the middle class.

When asked to explain unemployment, employed people are more likely to give individualistic explanations, whereas unemployed people are more likely to give structural explanations (Furnham, 1982c). High school students have been found to blame unemployment more on such internal factors as lack of motivation than the unemployed do (Feather, 1985). These findings illustrate the well-known "fundamental attribution error": Whereas actors tend to explain their own behavior in terms of situational variables, observers tend to make dispositional attributions—that is, to explain the actors' behavior in terms of personality or character variables (Kelley & Mischela, 1980). The tendency of the nonpoor (observers) to explain poverty in terms of personal characteristics such as laziness even when societal factors are equally salient is an example of this attributional error.

CLASSIST BEHAVIORS

Institutional Discrimination

I now turn to an examination of the behavioral component of classism—namely, to discrimination in the form of exclusion, distancing, and avoidance. Research on this component is sparse, particularly with respect to face-to-face situations. Although classist discrimination occurs on an individual as well as an institutional level, significantly more attention has been given to the latter. Institutional classist discrimination refers to the everyday exclusion of poor people from social institutions, such as inadequate access to high-quality health care and well-equipped schools, as well as limited employment opportunities. Institutional discrimination directed against welfare recipients and the homeless is particularly obvious. For example, cities such as Atlanta, Chicago, Seattle, Minneapolis, San Francisco, and Honolulu have passed various forms of anti-vagrancy legislation to keep homeless people off the streets, and in New York the police commissioner has pledged to crack down on "quality of life" offenses by fining panhandlers (Kaplan, Brant, Katel, Holmes, & Gordon, 1994).

Less obvious are the discriminatory assumptions and guidelines governing the welfare system itself. Some states are implementing welfare reform programs that make benefits contingent on "responsible" behavior by recipients; such programs have been called "the new paternalism" (Detweiler & Boehm, 1992). In other states, welfare reform programs focus more on behavior modification (Moynihan, 1992; Nathan, 1992). For example, New Jersey's new laws stipulate that recipients whose youngest child is 2 years of age or older must participate in some form of educational or vocational training to receive benefits (Florio, 1992). Furthermore, parents who have additional children while receiving AFDC will not be granted additional benefits.

Discussing New Jersey's plan, Bryant, the Democratic majority leader of the New Jersey State Assembly states,

> A middle class wage earner does not go to his boss to say, "I'm having another child, so I'm entitled to a raise." The wage earner works extra hours, gets a part-time job, or adjusts the family budget to compensate for the new arrival. There is nothing wrong with instilling this responsible, work-ethic value in poor people as they become better educated, better skilled, and self-sufficient. (Florio & Bryant, 1992, p. 10)

It can be inferred from Florio's words that welfare recipients are considered to be less responsible and less interested in work than middle-class workers. Furthermore, whereas middle-class mothers are encouraged to stay home with their young children, the "new paternalism" will penalize welfare mothers for similar behavior. States such as California, Wisconsin, and Michigan have proposed similar programs (Detweiler & Boehm, 1992). Welfare reform measures currently in the forefront of the U.S. domestic agenda (DeParle, 1994) can be considered discriminatory, because they limit the options of poor people and hold people accountable to different standards of behavior on the basis of social class.

Although the classist assumptions underlying welfare reform are seldom recognized or discussed in the mass media, other forms of discrimination are sometimes reported in the press. For example, the common banking practice of underlending in poor communities, and the violation of fair lending laws, have been examined (Foust & Holland, 1993). Environmental discrimination has also received public attention (Satchell, 1992; "Greenery and Poverty," 1993). Residents of poor neighborhoods and minority groups suffer disproportionately from noxious industries and facilities (e.g., toxic waste incinerators) located in their neighborhoods. An investigation of this issue by the Environmental Protection Agency, begun in 1990 by an ethnically representative 30-member task force, concluded that minority communities do experience "greater than average" exposure to certain pollutants (Satchell, 1992). Poverty, low property values, and lack of political power were identified as major contributing correlates of pollutant-exposed communities.

The Clinton administration's proposal to provide the United States with universal health care brought attention to the current situation of unequal access to health care—another form of class discrimination. Although the Medicaid program offers treatment to the poorest citizens (most often in emergency situations), many of the poor and working poor are uninsured. The consequences of unequal access to health care and the health effects of living in poverty are clear: Poor children are eight times more likely to die of disease and are 30 times more likely to have a low birth weight than middle-class children are (Ladner & Gourdine, 1984; Currie & Cole, 1993). One study in Washington, D.C., found that 50% of African-American men living in public housing suffered from hypertension, as compared with 20% of all African-American men in the city (Gorman, 1991).

As the cost of medical treatment continues to skyrocket and as the number of people able to afford hospital care dwindles, medical professionals are debating the merit of rationing medical service, particularly costly treatments such as intensive care. For example, Engelhardt and Rie (1986) propose that those who can afford intensive health care treatment should be permitted to purchase it and receive full care. For those who have lost the "social lottery" (i.e., the poor), they suggest a rationing system by which intensive care could be denied if the cost is deemed disproportionately high or the "quality of life" is deemed disproportionately low. Justifying a medical rationing based on patients' ability to pay, Engelhardt and Rie (1986) explain, "If losing at the natural and social lotteries does not per se vest any individual with a claim on innocent others for care, and if the goods sought are privately owned then the fact that individuals in need do not find resources for treatment may be an unfortunate circumstance, not an unfair circumstance" (p. 1160). Such a rationing system appears to be based on the classist assumption that the lives of those who cannot afford treatment are less valuable than the lives of those who can afford treatment. Who has the right to decide whether another person's "quality of life" is low? Meissner (1986) warns that the elderly and disabled poor are especially likely to be the targets of such rationing strategies, and urges both medical and legal professionals to fight against the implementation of medical rationing.

The damaging consequences of poverty for health are exacerbated by subtle forms of discrimination by those who work in institutions committed to "helping" the poor. Investigating nurses' perceptions of the poor, Desmond et al. (1989) found that 36% of the 192 nurses questioned attributed poverty to lack of effort and that 27% attributed poverty to squandered opportunities. To some extent, all of the nurses sampled believed that the poor are dishonest, and 40% of the nurses reported that the poor take advantage of the health care system. However, 36% believed that poor patients do not receive care equivalent to that of other patients, and 43% agreed that transferring poor patients from one hospital to another was common. Poor clients may receive medical attention that is less individualized and inferior in quality, compared to the treatment given to their nonpoor counterparts. Contraceptive testing, involuntary sterilization, and coercive treatment during pregnancy all occur more often among poor women than among other women (Kolder, Gallagher, & Parsons, 1987).

Classist discrimination in health care may also take the form of omission, which is most apparent in the treatment of ethnic minorities. For example, African-Americans hospitalized for pneumonia have been found to receive less intensive care treatment than European-Americans (Gorman, 1991). It can be argued that part of the reason why health care providers may provide inadequate care to African-Americans is that they are assumed to be poor. Although a disproportionate number of poor minority women are HIV-positive, this population has not been targeted for education and prevention campaigns. Shayne and Kaplan (1991) argue that these women are "double victims" by virtue of their poverty and their HIV-positive status. Because women's health issues receive significantly less attention than men's, HIV-positive poor women may be considered "triple victims" if gender is also considered (Mahowald, 1993).

Discrimination against the poor has been documented among mental health professionals. Battered women's shelters disproportionately house working-class and poor women, whereas most shelter staff members are from the middle class. Davidson and Jenkins (1989) propose that classism may permeate battered women's shelters and impair the ability of staff members to work effectively and sympathetically with residents. Middle-class staff members may hold lower expectations for poor and working-class residents, and may spend less time assisting these residents in planning for their futures—a possibility that merits investigation. A study comparing the attitudes of psychiatric residents and graduate social work students participating in an interdisciplinary community mental health program found that at the end of the 1-year training period, social work students held more favorable attitudes toward working with poor clients than psychiatric residents did (Moffic, Brochstein, Blattstein, & Adams, 1983). Specifically, psychiatric residents were found to hold less democratic values, to express less commitment to egalitarian treatment of clients, to respond less favorably toward community-based services, and to express less support for the interdisciplinary functioning of mental health workers than social work students. Although Moffic et al. (1983) concluded that the residents' less favorable attitudes toward working in public health care settings did not constitute a "major problem," it could be argued that negative attitudes such as these influence the treatment poor clients receive.

Class bias in mental illness diagnoses has been well documented. For example, the poor are more likely to be diagnosed as psychotic and given chemical interventions, whereas middle-class patients are more likely to be diagnosed as neurotic and treated with psychotherapy (Judd, 1986). Extreme diagnoses are given disproportionately to poor persons. Following a longitudinal study of 313 poor urban mental patients, Lurigio and Lewis (1989) suggested that decent housing, employment, and improved family relations would be more effective interventions than medication and psychiatric diagnoses.

A study of social workers by Reeser and Epstein (1987) revealed a fascinating paradox. Although more social workers subscribed to structural explanations for poverty in 1984 than in 1968 (81% compared with 61%), only 37% in 1984 and 53% in 1968 believed that one of the professional goals of social workers was to promote societal change. Likewise, while 51% favored devoting social workers' resources to the problems of the poor in 1968, only 23% did so in 1984. So, despite their more structural conception of the causes of poverty, 1984 social workers appeared to be less committed to activist goals than their 1968 predecessors and were less supportive of working with the poor. Over the past two decades, the social work profession's interest in poverty issues and in work with poor families and individuals has decreased (Hagen, 1992). The number of social workers who actually work with the poor, as well as the number of social workers who prefer to work with the poor, has decreased (Reeser & Epstein, 1987; Stewart, 1981). Approximately 40% of the 140,000 members of the National Association of Social Workers (NASW) are now engaged in private practice (counseling or psychotherapy) for some part of their work, and two-thirds of the legislative priorities of NASW state chapters involve licensure or third-party payments (Specht & Courtney, 1994). The Council of Social Work Education's current standards for accrediting schools in the field do not include requirements for courses dealing with the poor, dependent children, or publicly supported social services (Specht & Courtney, 1994). Hagen (1992) attributes this declining interest in working with the poor to the following factors: the withdrawal of training and education monies for social workers; the requirement that public welfare separate income maintenance functions from social services; the perceived failure of social work to reduce AFDC caseloads; and the low status and lack of professional enhancement associated with working with poor people. Whatever the reasons, social workers are spending less time with poor populations, and this distancing and exclusion can be regarded as a form of discrimination.

Quality of education also appears to be influenced by class status (Mitchell, 1991). Channel One, a 12-minute classroom television news program that includes 2 minutes of commercials, is one indication of the lack of resources and the substandard curriculum offered in poor schools (Walsh, 1993). Supposedly designed to improve students' knowledge of current events, Channel One has been criticized for its billing as a "partnership between education and business" and for the lack of research demonstrating its effectiveness (Rudinow, 1990). In a study of over 17,000 schools, it was found that schools with a high concentration of poor students were almost twice as likely to use Channel One than schools with a low concentration of poor students (Morgan, cited in Walsh, 1993). Participating Channel One schools are loaned free video equipment in exchange for requiring students to watch the daily program, and it seems likely that these schools are motivated more by the "free" video equipment than by the educational value of the programming. Working-class and poor parents appear to be concerned about the quality of education being given to their children and to realize that middle-class schools have greater resources. Interviewing 35 working-class parents whose children attended "poor" neighborhood schools, Brantlinger (1985) found that 77% of the participants were aware of the low status associated with their neighborhood schools and believed that their schools were inferior to other schools in the district. Furthermore, 70% of the working-class respondents felt that middle-class parents in other districts would not want their own children to attend the schools attended by working-class children.

Poor and "underclass" workers may experience discrimination in employment and hiring practices. Gray (1975) has argued that working-class European-Americans are excluded from the field of psychology and face virtually the same discrimination in higher education and professional employment as ethnic minorities. He requested that the American Psychological Association's Board of Social and Ethical Responsibility in Psychology consider working-class people as affirmative action candidates, and proposed that their interests be represented by an advocate with membership on the Committee on Equal Opportunity in Psychology. Deciding that discrimination against working-class Whites is "extremely complex," the board did not take action (Conger, 1975).

The increasingly used term "underclass" is defined inconsistently in the sociological and psychological literature, but is typically used to describe chronically poor African-Americans and Hispanics who reside in the inner city. Both Gans (1992) and Katz (1993) convincingly argue that the term "underclass" is classist and disguises anti-Black and anti-Hispanic attitudes and beliefs. Because members of the "underclass" (i.e., poor minority inner-city populations) are popularly associated with crime, illiteracy, drug use, welfare dependency, and a poor work ethic, employers may be reluctant to hire or work with those they perceive to be members of this group. To avoid hiring "underclass" workers, employers may look for indicators of class and neighborhood. A study of 185 White middle-class employers in the Chicago area by Neckerman and Kirchenman (1991) found that recruitment and interviewing strategies were biased against poor inner-city African-Americans. When targeting neighborhoods or institutions for recruitment, employers avoided inner-city populations. Selective recruiting strategies were more common among employers located in poor African-American neighborhoods than among those located elsewhere, and students attending suburban or Catholic high schools were more heavily recruited than were students from primarily African-American and public schools. The majority of the employers studied did not recruit employees through state employment agencies or through welfare programs. Negative perceptions of inner-city African-American workers appeared to underlie much of the selective recruiting. For example, almost half of the employers commented on the lack of work ethic among these workers; 32% mentioned their lack of dependability; and 38% described bad attitudes (i.e., apathy and ignorance). Residents from poor neighborhoods or the city's housing projects were typically described as coming from a "different world" with "different rules." Employers also reported using a variety of subjective strategies during interviews to determine potential employees' productivity and character, such as their perceived straightforwardness when answering questions.

The interaction of class and ethnicity is also reflected in differential incarceration rates. In Pinellas County, Florida, for example, poor pregnant women, particularly African-American women, are prosecuted more frequently than European-American middle-class women for drug use, even though drug use during pregnancy is equally prevalent in both groups (Mantsios, 1992). When ethnicity is held constant, it appears that poor women are reported for drug use significantly more often than middle-class women are. In the Pinellas County sample, 60% of the 133 women reported for drug use had annual incomes of less than $12,000, whereas only 8% had incomes of more than $25,000 a year.

Furthermore, class status is significantly related to the treatment of offenders within the legal system. Because poor minority juvenile offenders, particularly those involved in drug offenses, may be perceived as a threat to White middle-class populations, Sampson and Laub (1993) hypothesized that counties characterized by ethnic inequality and a large concentration of "underclass" neighborhoods (i.e., areas characterized by a high percentage of minorities, poverty, female-headed households, and households on welfare) would impose more severe forms of social control on juvenile offenders than other counties would. They tested this hypothesis by examining 1985 data from the National Juvenile Court Data Archives for more than 200 counties, and approximately 538,000 individual juvenile case records. "Underclass" poverty was found to be significantly related to the detention of petitioned drug offenders and to the out-of-home placement of drug and personal crime offenders. Regardless of other county characteristics, the concentration of "underclass" poverty increased the out-of- home placement rates of African-Americans for both personal and drug violations. Out-of-home placement is the most intrusive intervention possible in the juvenile system. Sampson and Laub (1993) believe their findings demonstrate that "underclass" African-American males are viewed as a threat to the European-American middle class, and are therefore subjected to increased social control by the juvenile justice system.

Given the more severe treatment of poor people and poor minorities within U.S. law enforcement and justice systems, it is important to assess social class bias among practicing attorneys. Gordon and Bauer (1985) asked 50 attorneys in private practice to read a transcript of an interview between an attorney and a middle-class or a working-class defendant accused of assault and battery. The working-class defendant was described as a service station attendant with a $10,000 income and as having completed 3 years of high school. The middle-class defendant was depicted as an insurance salesman with a bachelor's degree and an annual income of $32,000. Both men were described as married with three children. After reading the transcript, each attorney was asked to rate the defendant's credibility, sincerity, common sense, psychological sophistication, stability of personality, and likelihood of committing a crime. The working-class defendant was evaluated more negatively than the middle-class defendant, but this difference was not a statistically significant one, suggesting that social class bias may be less pronounced among attorneys than is often assumed.

Interpersonal Discrimination

Although the previously cited research documents the existence of classist discrimination at the institutional level, empirical research examining face-to-face discrimination in the everyday lives of poor people is virtually nonexistent, despite the frequency with which it is reported anecdotally and in conversations with the poor. To learn about the everyday experiences of poor women, I visited two shelters for poor women in Providence, Rhode Island; I also attended several meetings of Parents for Progress, an advocacy group for people on public assistance, primarily attended by women receiving AFDC. I asked the women I met in both contexts to describe their own experiences of interpersonal classism. Although the women were comfortable with me, several individuals asked not to be identified by name, because they did not want to be publicly linked to AFDC when they were no longer receiving assistance. For this reason, in describing my findings, I only use the names of women who wished to be identified.

Evidence of various sorts, including interviews with women on welfare, suggests that poor people commonly experience face-to-face classist discrimination in their daily activities. Describing life on welfare, one woman stated, "It's painful when people discriminate against you because you're on welfare. I feel less than . . . lower class. Other people pity you" ("Students Speak Out,"1994, p. 1). Another woman explained, "When you look for housing, you're suspect when they find out you're on welfare. They think you're wild, you'll tear their house apart or you're on drugs" ("Students Speak Out," 1994, p. 1). Discussing the "culture" of the welfare agency and her interactions with social workers, one woman explained, "They could sit down and talk to you as a human being. They could explain to you what's what, and what's going to happen [but they don't]" (Hagen & Davis, 1994, p. 36). Discrimination and the intersection of race and class are illustrated by the recent class action suit filed against the Denny's restaurant chain. Treated with mistrust, African-Americans and other customers of color were kept waiting longer than European-American customers and were required to pay at the time of service rather than after finishing their meal (Labaton, 1994). It appears that Denny's management assumed that African-American customers were poor and therefore could not be trusted to pay for their meals. I have noted similar suspicion in some of the small neighborhood stores located in poor neighborhoods in the Providence area. On any given school morning, a long single row of children lines the sidewalk, but only one or two children at a time are permitted to enter the store. Evidently shop owners are concerned with stealing, and only allow a small number of children in the store at a time so they can be carefully observed. It is difficult to imagine children being treated with such suspicion in middle-class or affluent neighborhoods.

People on welfare often talk about the humiliation associated with receiving public assistance, particularly their experiences with food stamps (Funiciello, 1993). For example, one woman reported that if she bought chocolate milk with food stamps, she was looked upon by fellow shoppers as though she had purchased "strawberries and Cadillacs" (quoted in Popkin, 1990, p. 72). Despite the record high set in March 1993, at which time 27.4 million or approximately 10% of Americans were receiving food stamps (Clarke, 1993), the stigma attached to food stamps remains strong. Most of the women I spoke with mentioned how embarrassed they are when using food stamps, how other shoppers scrutinize their purchases, and how customers "huff and puff" or tap their fingernails impatiently when they see food stamps. Gina, a Latina woman, described an incident in which a woman two carts ahead of her paid for her purchases using food stamps. After the woman left, the cashier complained for several minutes to the next customer (who was paying with cash) that "they really should get jobs." Gina, who also was using food stamps, confronted the cashier when making her purchase. The cashier explained that her comments were not directed at Gina, but at "other" people on welfare. Rarely studied systematically, incidents such as these constitute the "hidden injuries of class" (Piven & Cloward, 1971, 1993). The stigma attached to receiving welfare reminds recipients that they have less power and fewer options in our society than others, and are thus perceived as being of less value.

Harassment by bus drivers appeared to be a relatively common experience among the women I met. In Rhode Island, AFDC recipients may be granted bus passes allowing them to ride the bus free of charge during designated hours. Although the AFDC pass is supposed to be sufficient identification, several women described being humiliated by bus drivers who asked for multiple forms of identification. One African-American woman described receiving snide comments frequently from bus drivers when she uses her AFDC pass, such as "Here's another one."

Several women described going to one bank to cash their welfare checks and to another bank to cash their part-time pay checks. When I asked Cheryl, an African-American woman, why it was necessary to use different banks, she explained that if she cashed her welfare check at the same bank she cashed her pay check, she would lose the respect of the tellers. She stated, "I go where the majority of the AFDC parents go so that I don't stand out. Being a Black woman, I have two or three strikes against me—I'm a woman, I'm Black, and I'm on AFDC, so you've got to be more than the other person. You have to prove yourself to be more."

Both the subtlety and the power of interpersonal classism are highlighted by this incident. Cheryl and most of the other women I spoke with could not recall an incident in which tellers were blatantly rude when cashing welfare checks. Instead, most women discussed being met with a condescending attitude, as though they had a "disease," or with smirks of disgust. Describing how she is treated by nonpoor, classist people, Cheryl stated, "They look down on you, it's their attitude, it's their look. They don't do things in a friendly way—it's like a 'look down' attitude. You can tell they have a smirk on their face." Despite the subtlety of such cues, they are powerful enough to alter the behavior of some poor women, sending them on time-consuming trips to different banks to avoid possible humiliation.

Of course, interpersonal classism is not always subtle. For example, Gina recounted how she was treated while trying to cash her first AFDC check. Unaware that she needed to have both a driver's license and an AFDC identification card to cash her check, Gina tried to cash her check with only her license. Gina explains, "In an unusually loud voice, the teller asked me for my AFDC identification, so that everyone around me could hear that I was on welfare. I didn't even have an AFDC card. The teller lectured me, saying, 'How dare you try to cash your check without your AFDC I.D.' I just left, totally humiliated." Too embarrassed to cash her AFDC checks in person after this incident, Gina used automatic teller machines after banking hours so that she would not have to interact with tellers.

As I spoke with women on welfare, it became clear that their experiences of interpersonal classism take place primarily in situations in which they are identified as welfare recipients. AFDC checks, food stamps, and AFDC identification cards serve as obvious indicators that someone is poor, and it makes sense that welfare recipients experience classism in situations in which these indicators are present. I also asked women about their personal relationships and whether they were excluded or distanced by friends or family members. Diane, a European-American woman, reported that her ex-husband's family (to whom she had been close for over a decade) cut off all contact with her when she started receiving public assistance. However, for the most part, women did not report discrimination from classmates, coworkers, or family members. In part, this may be attributable to the fact that the majority of women I spoke with explained that they "don't advertise" they are on AFDC and do not tell other people they receive assistance until they are sure these people will be accepting.

However, some working-class and poor students describe encountering classist discrimination in lectures, dorm rooms, and university offices, as well as from classmates (Ouellette, 1993). Working-class and poor students frequently report feeling disoriented and alienated in classrooms in which professors assume that all students are from middle-class backgrounds (Ryan & Sackray, 1992). Work schedules and cash shortages can also create uncomfortable barriers between working-class students and their middle-class peers, and single mothers attending college describe concealing that they receive welfare because they fear being ostracized by their peers and treated with disrespect by financial aid officers (Ouellette, 1993).

In a unique investigation of social integration, Rosenbaum, Popkin, Kaufman, and Rusin (1991) examined the experiences of low-income African-American families who, supported by a program that assists families in securing better housing, moved into different types of neighborhoods. It was found that the low-income African-American families experienced more social isolation (i.e., fewer friendships and interactions with neighbors) when they moved into predominantly European-American middle-class suburban areas than when they moved into predominantly African-American city neighborhoods. The suburban movers reported twice as much harassment as the city movers during their first year in their new residence, but by the second year this difference had disappeared. When the individual attributes of the new suburban residents were controlled for (i.e., years of education, AFDC use, and number of children), multiple-regression analysis revealed that AFDC use was negatively correlated with total number of friends. In other words, families that were using AFDC had fewer friends than those that were not. Such findings strikingly illustrate the ways in which middle-class persons distance themselves from the poor.

Choosing not to help someone is another example of interpersonal discrimination. Some unobtrusive studies of discriminatory racist behavior have offered White participants an opportunity to aid Black and White experimental confederates, and found that more aid was given to the latter (Crosby, Bromley, & Saxe, 1980). A similar technique, manipulating symbolic indicators of social class, has been used to study interpersonal classism. In an investigation by Juhnke et al. (1987), well or poorly dressed White confederates requested directions from randomly selected White shoppers either to an exclusive tennis club in the vicinity or to a thrift shop located at a well-known intersection in a less desirable community. The length of time respondents spent giving directions served as the dependent measure. A significant interaction effect between style of dress and direction request indicated that respondents spent significantly more time giving directions to poorly dressed confederates who asked directions to the thrift shop than to those who asked directions to the tennis club. When the confederates were well dressed, respondents did not differ reliably in time spent giving directions to the thrift shop and the tennis club. That the increased time spent with poorly dressed confederates who asked for directions to the thrift shop may have reflected an assumption about their lesser intelligence is suggested by the report of one confederate that when he was in the poorly dressed condition, respondents explained directions clearly and slowly, whereas when he was in the well-dressed condition, directions were given more quickly.

RECONSIDERING THE AMERICAN DREAM, OR HOW CLASSISM REWARDS THE NONPOOR

Classist attitudes, beliefs, and behaviors contribute to maintaining the privilege and status of nonpoor individuals, and may therefore be very difficult to change. On a broad, societal level, classism reinforces capitalism as the primary political–economic system in the United States and maintains individualism as America's dominant ideological focus. Free enterprise, a market economy, competition in the market place, the centrality of private ownership, and self-regulation are key components of capitalism (Peterson, Albaum, & Kozmetsky, 1990). As Piven and Cloward (1993, p. 4) explain, "Capitalism . . . relies primarily upon the mechanisms of a market—the promise of financial rewards or penalties—to motivate men and women to work and to hold them in their occupational tasks." Under such a system, some people control wealth by owning or operating the means of production, while many others work to produce goods but do not share in the profits. Put simply, capitalism in the United States depends on inequality (Bonacich, 1992). Most Americans perceive capitalism favorably. For example, the majority of a sample of 1,556 middle-class persons were found in one study to believe that a free society can exist under capitalistic systems; that capitalism encourages individual freedom of thought, choice, and behavior; and that under capitalism every individual has the opportunity to develop his or her own special abilities (Peterson et al., 1990). Capitalism is thus associated with freedom and a high standard of living.

The social dimensions of capitalism contribute to its popularity in the United States. Belief in the Protestant work ethic and a just world, social Darwinism (economic "survival of the fittest"), and individualism justify capitalism and in turn are reinforced by it. The shared premise underlying such beliefs is that through hard work anyone can improve his or her status, and perhaps even achieve upper-class standing; it is this hope that is at the heart of the "American dream." Summarizing the possibilities represented by this "dream," Bremner (1956) stated, "The promise of America was not affluence, but independence; not ease, but a chance to work for oneself, to be self supporting, and to win esteem through hard and honest labor" (p. 16). The success of modern-day Horatio Alger films such as *Working Girl*, in which a working-class secretary moves her way up the corporate ladder through her ingenuity and hard work, reflect continued belief in upward mobility.

Classism and beliefs about upward mobility also prevent middle-class persons from questioning the unequal distribution of wealth in the United States. As noted earlier, in relation to the rich or the corporate elite, even the middle class is part of the "lower class" (Ehrenreich, 1990). By focusing on how the poor allegedly drain taxpayers' monies and resources, many middle-class persons lose sight of where the real power in U.S. society lies, and ultimately it is the corporate elite that most benefits from this. By creating and maintaining distance between the middle class and the working class, the working poor, and the poor, classism prevents these groups from presenting a unified challenge to the corporate elite.

On an individual or personal level, attitudes, beliefs, and behaviors reinforce middle- and upper-class people in their belief that the world is a just place, and that people (including themselves) get what they deserve. Classism contributes to the sense that social class standing is "natural." The belief in the "naturalness" of class standing allows nonpoor people to believe that their higher status is earned and reflects their own "natural" superiority (Langston, 1992). Thus, most persons in the United States perceive the distribution of wealth to be fair. For example, 85% of a sample of approximately 1,500 middle-class respondents were found to believe that incomes cannot be made more equal, since people's abilities and talents are unequal (Kluegel & Smith, 1986). The majority of this sample also believed that incomes cannot be made more equal because it is human nature to want to have more than others have. Furthermore, policies that propose to redistribute capital away from the rich by limiting incomes, limiting inheritances, and instituting government ownership are unpopular in the United States (Kluegel & Smith, 1986). Such findings indicate that class status is regarded as natural, the result of hard work and talent, and should not be interfered with. Such beliefs may keep working poor, poor, and homeless people employed in low-wage jobs in the hope that they too will rise through ability and talent, and may thus discourage poor people from challenging the prevailing system.

Classism encourages the nonpoor to feel that they deserve their class status, and enhances feelings of security and personal control. Thus, there are both economic and psychological benefits to those who are classist. Classism is manifested in distancing from the poor and in perceiving working-class, working poor, poor, and homeless people as "other." Typically, it is only during times of economic recession that some middle-class persons join the ranks of the poor, and classist assumptions and behaviors begin to be questioned. An example, as of this writing, is the "discovery" by the Clinton administration of the size and seriousness of the problem of homelessness. A report written by an interagency group "argues that poverty, racism, and past budget cuts are pushing many families into the ranks of the dispossessed" ("Clinton Report: Homelessness Serious," 1994, p. A2).

DIRECTIONS FOR FUTURE RESEARCH

The United States is not a classless society, and, as the previously discussed research documents, classist attitudes, beliefs, and behaviors are commonplace. Yet there has been little systematic study of classism, particularly interpersonal classist behaviors. Because poor people participate (to various degrees) in social service organizations, it makes sense that much of what we do know about classism is on the institutional level. It is also likely that the "myth of classlessness" contributes in part to the lack of empirical studies of classism.

Most research on classism focuses on middle-class stereotypes about the poor and attributions for poverty. Because attributions for poverty have been found to be correlated with political affiliation and support for welfare funding, they may also serve to justify classist behaviors. The predictive validity of explanations for poverty in relation to both interpersonal classist behaviors and public policy decisions warrants further investigation. Furthermore, research analyzing the types of attributions made by the poor and the extent to which poor people themselves internalize class stereotypes is necessary.

Although the comprehensive study of classist attitudes and beliefs is important, it is critical that we also focus our attention on classist behaviors. Since attitudes and attributions are not reliable predictors of the way nonpoor people behave in face-to-face interactions with poor people, psychologists must identify the variables that contribute to discriminatory behavior. Specifically, we must determine under what conditions classist behaviors are most and least likely to occur. To achieve this goal, a research agenda with the everyday experiences of poor people as its starting point is necessary. For example, although poor women often describe being humiliated when they use food stamps, the treatment of food stamp users has not been empirically studied. Field studies examining interpersonal classism should be conducted in places where the lives of middle-class and poor people intersect, such as the supermarket or the bank.

The research agenda I am proposing requires that social psychologists move beyond convenient college student samples and examine how taxpaying, middle-class citizens behave toward poor people. Of particular importance is determining how the poor are treated by the people upon whom they depend for services, such as social workers, medical professionals, lawyers, police officers, and teachers. Furthermore, because some of the interpersonal discrimination experienced by poor people is relatively subtle, measures sophisticated enough to detect covert discrimination must be developed. Discrimination against the working poor and the working class, as well as classist responses to welfare recipients, must be investigated. It is in this way that the "hidden injuries" of class can be exposed.

SOCIAL POLICY IMPLICATIONS

Despite the pervasiveness of classist attitudes, beliefs, and behaviors in the United States, class status, let alone classism, is rarely discussed. Most U.S. residents will at some time be exposed to news stories or programs pertaining to sexism, racism, and heterosexism, and to information that labels some behaviors as sexist, racist, or heterosexist. But classism and class issues are not part of public dialogue. Since classist behaviors are seldom labeled and publicly identified as such, one of the most basic but critical changes in social policy must be to expand the public dialogue about class hierarchy in the United States. For example, central to the "American dream" is the belief that people can transcend their class status if they work hard enough or if they obtain a "good" education. The majority of the poor do not live in poverty permanently, but how much mobility is possible? Although the majority of top political leaders originate from middle-class backgrounds (Dye, 1990), Makinson's (1992) review of U.S. congressional spending indicates that only the wealthiest or most well connected can wage competitive campaigns. For example, on average, Senate winners spent $3.9 million to win their seats in 1990 (Makinson, 1992). Clearly, this indicates that those of upper-class and middle-class status are afforded opportunities that most working-class and poor citizens are not. How does class status influence opportunities, power, and access to resources? This is a question that must be given serious consideration in the public forum. Smith ("Wealth in America," 1986–1987), in commenting on findings from his study of wealth in the United States, noted that "using one's wealth to 'buy the best' whether it is the best of legal representation, political lobbying, or even first rate medical care or education, can mean gaining an advantage over those who cannot afford the same quality of representation or services. There may even be consequences for democratic processes . . . threatening the equal distribution of polical power intended by the founders of our nation" (p. 3).

Beyond simply acknowledging that the United States is a class-stratified society, the language of public discourse concerning poverty issues must also be considered. As Katz (1989) explains,

> American political discourse has redefined issues of power and distribution as questions of identity, morality, and patronage. This is what happened to poverty, which slipped easily, unreflectively, into a language of

family, race, and culture rather than inequality, power, and exploitation. The silence is therefore no anomaly; rather, it is the expected outcome of the way American political discussion has ignored, deflected, or framed issues of political economy for a very long time. (p. 8)

Newspaper and news magazine articles about welfare focus almost exclusively on single motherhood, low self-esteem, and the "underclass." The continuing emphasis on these aspects of poverty illustrate that the shift in language (and in thinking) that Katz (1989) calls for will involve considerable effort.

Because the vocabulary of poverty and class individualizes these issues, it is not surprising that U.S. policies concerning poverty stress individualism and personal responsibility, rather than social and economic factors such as deindustrialization, diminished union power, and the increasing income gap between the very wealthy and all other Americans. Rather than addressing these structural factors, popular welfare reform proposals currently concentrate on regulating the behavior of welfare recipients. For example, some states, such as New Jersey, have implemented a "family cap" rule that prohibits women from receiving increased AFDC allotments if they have a child while on assistance; other states, such as Wisconsin, have made the receipt of AFDC benefits contingent on children's school attendance. On the national level, the Clinton administration proposes that welfare recipients only be allowed to receive AFDC benefits for 2 years, at which time they will be required to find work in the private sector or accept a government-subsidized job.

Several questions about these reform proposals are immediately apparent. First, is it ethical to attempt to limit the number of children that poor women have? Surely the government would never try to place such limitations on the birth of middle-class children, and it is doubtful that anyone would propose that restrictions be placed on the tax benefits middle-class parents receive for having larger families. The "family cap" plan clearly illustrates the low value placed on poor women and their children in U.S. society. Furthermore, women on welfare have an average of only two children, and very few women become pregnant so that they can receive increased benefits (which are on average, a mere $64 each month per child). In light of these facts, we must question the purpose of policies designed to curb the number of children poor women have. Similarly, most people leave the welfare rolls within 2 years; therefore, what will be gained by programs aimed at 2-year recipients? Policies that provide special subsidies and support for single mothers, increased opportunities for women in the workplace, assistance with childcare, and higher wages for women's work would have more long-run benefits.

It appears that many welfare policies and reform proposals are driven by classist stereotypes rather than by the actual lives and experiences of poor people. Public policy must address the broader structural causes of poverty, instead of simply focusing on individual behavior. For example, rather than focusing on perceived lack of motivation among the poor, a more constructive policy approach would be to examine the structure of the U.S. economy, particularly the impact of minimum-wage jobs. Contingent on the number of dependents, an individual could work full-time and still live below the poverty line ($15,141 for a family of four, in 1994) (Pear, 1995). We must demand and develop policies that create universal health care, affordable housing, subsidized day care, better-paying jobs for women and people of color, and a minimum wage that allows people to live securely. Countries with more generous, successful social welfare programs, such as Sweden, could serve as models as the United States refines its own policies.

Policy makers must also reassess how poverty thresholds are calculated, as well the amount of money allotted to welfare recipients. Setting low poverty thresholds leads to underestimates of the number of people living in poverty, which in turn minimize the extent to which poverty is perceived as a significant issue and further marginalize the poor. New poverty threshold formulas that accurately assess the amount of money people need must be developed (see Ruggles, 1990; Pear, 1995). In accord with these adjusments, welfare monies must be increased so that recipients can live above official poverty thresholds. The possibility of increasing welfare benefits or providing guaranteed annual incomes is rarely discussed, because it is popularly believed that increased benefits would be a disincentive to work and to family life (Piven & Cloward, 1987b). The disincentive rationale appears to be deeply rooted in the desire to maintain existing power relations and in the classist assumption that the motives of the poor can be reduced to money. Unfortunately, thoughtless acceptance of the disincentive rationale prohibits public discussion of increasing welfare benefits and maintains punitive welfare policies.

Because classism occurs on both the institutional and the interpersonal levels, it is important that policies address both of these dimensions. Much of what we know about classism is on the institutional level; thus, institutional policy suggestions are relatively straightforward. But how are we to address interpersonal classism? Service providers to the poor—physicians, lawyers, teachers, social workers, and police officers, as well as employers and landlords—need to be educated about classism, and laws against classism must be developed and enforced. Because people's worth is strongly associated in U.S. society with their material wealth, reducing classism will be difficult; however, if institutional policies respecting the poor are implemented, it is possible that the treatment of poor individuals by the nonpoor may also improve. Describing a society free of classism,

152 THE SOCIAL PSYCHOLOGY OF INTERPERSONAL DISCRIMINATION

Ehrenreich (1990) states, "As the dream unfolds into the future, class ceases to be a meaningful dimension of human variety. The steep gradients of wealth and poverty, power and helplessness, are abolished, and genuine democracy can take root, at last, in level ground" (p. 256). Within this vision lies the promise of a more egalitarian society.

ACKNOWLEDGMENT

This chapter is dedicated to the women who shared their experiences on public assistance with me. I wish to thank them for their willingness to tell their stories.

REFERENCES

Alston, J. P., & Dean, K. I. (1972). Socioeconomic factors associated with attitudes toward welfare recipients and the causes of poverty. *Social Service Review, 46,* 13–22.

AuClaire, P. A. (1984). Public attitudes toward social welfare expenditures. *Social Work, 29,* 139–144.

Axelson, L. J., & Hendrickson, R. M. (1985). Notes on policy and practice: Middle-class attitudes toward the poor; Are they changing? *Social Service Review, 59,* 296–304.

Barber, B. (1957). *Social stratification: A comparative analysis of structure and process.* New York: Harcourt, Brace & World.

Bonacich, E. (1992). Inequality in America: The failure of the American system for people of color. In M. L. Anderson & P. H. Collins (Eds.), *Race, class, and gender: An anthology* (pp. 96–110). Belmont, CA: Wadsworth.

Bott, E. (1972). The concept of class as a reference group. In G. W. Thielbar & S. D. Feldman (Eds.), *Issues in social inequality* (pp. 47–69). Boston: Little, Brown.

Bourgois, P. (1989, November 12). Just another night on crack street. *New York Times Magazine,* pp. 53–65.

Brantlinger, E. (1985). What low-income parents want from schools: A different view of aspirations. *Interchange, 16*(4), 14–28.

Bremner, R. H. (1956). *From the depths: The discovery of poverty in the United States.* New York: New York University Press.

Butler, S. S., & Weatherly, R. A. (1992). Poor women at midlife and categories of neglect. *Social Work, 37,* 510–515.

Centers, R. (1961). *The Psychology of social classes: A study of class consciousness.* New York: Russell & Russell.

Clarke, K. (1993, November–December). Growing hunger. *Utne Reader, 60,* 63–68.

Clinton report: Homelessness serious. (1994, February 17). *Providence Journal-Bulletin,* p. A2.

Colasanto, D. (1989). Bush presidency tarnished by growing concern about poverty. *Gallup Poll Monthly, 287,* 2–6.

Conger, J. J. (1975). Proceedings of the American Psychological Association, Incorporated, for the year of 1974: Minutes of the annual meeting of the Council of Representatives. *American Psychologist, 30,* 620–651.

Corcoran, M., Duncan, G. J., & Hill, M. S. (1984). The economic fortunes of women and children: Lessons from the panel study of income dynamics. *Signs: Journal of Women in Culture and Society, 10,* 232–248.

Crooke, S. (1993, December 27). Disagreeing about dependency [Letter to the editor]. *Newsweek,* p. 7.

Crosby, F., Bromley, S., & Saxe, L. (1980). Recent unobtrusive studies of Black and White discrimination and prejudice: A literature review. *Psychological Bulletin, 87*(3), 546–563.

Currie, J., & Cole, N. (1993). Welfare and child health: The link between AFDC participation and birth weight. *American Economic Review, 83,* 971–985.

Danzinger, K. (1958). Children's earliest conception of economic relationships (Australia). *Journal of Social Psychology, 47,* 231–240.

Davidson, B. P., & Jenkins, P. J. (1989). Class diversity in shelter life. *Social Work, 34,* 491–495.

DeMott, B. (1990). *The imperial middle: Why Americans can't think straight about class.* New York: William Morrow.

DeParle, J. (1994, January 30). Change in welfare likely to need big jobs program. *New York Times,* pp. 1, 22.

Desmond, S. M., Price, J. H., & Eoff, T. A. (1989). Nurses' perceptions regarding health care and the poor. *Psychological Reports, 65,* 1043–1052.

Detweiler, B., & Boehm, S. (Eds.). (1992). The new paternalism: Will states be able to change client behavior? [Special issue]. *Public Welfare, 50.*

Duncan, G., Hill, M. S., & Hoffman, S. D. (1988). Welfare dependence across the generations. *Science, 239,* 467–471.

Dye, T. R. (1990). *Who's running America: The Bush era* (5th ed.). Englewood Cliffs, NJ: Prentice-Hall.

Edin, K. (1991). Surviving the welfare system: How AFDC recipients make ends meet in Chicago. *Social Problems, 38,* 462–474.

Ehrenreich, B. (1987). The new right attack on social welfare. In F. Block, R. A. Cloward, B. Ehrenreich, & F. F. Piven, *The mean season: The attack on the welfare state* (pp. 161–195). New York: Pantheon Books.

Ehrenreich, B. (1990). *Fear of falling: The inner life of the middle class.* New York: Harper Perennial.

Ehrenreich, B. (1991, December 26). Welfare: A White secret. *Time,* p. 86.

Ellwood, D. T., & Summers, L. H. (1986). Poverty in America: Is welfare the answer or the problem? In S. H. Danzinger & D. H. Weinberg (Eds.), *Fighting poverty: What works and what doesn't* (pp. 78–105). Cambridge, MA: Harvard University Press.

Engelhardt, H. T., & Rie, M. (1986). Intensive care units, scarce resources, and conflicting principles of justice. *Journal of the American Medical Association, 255,* 1159–1164.

Feagin, J. (1975). *Subordinating the poor: Welfare and American beliefs.* Englewood Cliffs, NJ: Prentice-Hall.

Feather, N. T. (1974). Explanations of poverty in Australian and American samples: The person, society, or fate? *Australian Journal of Psychology, 26,* 199–216.

Feather, N. T. (1985). Attitudes, values, and attributions: Explanations of unemployment. *Journal of Personality and Social Psychology, 48,* 876–889.

Florio, J. J., & Bryant, W. R. (1992). New Jersey's different approach: Its package goes farthest, fastest. *Public Welfare, 50,* 7–10.

Foust, D., & Holland, K. (1993, April 19). Taking a sharper look at bank examiners. *Business Week,* pp. 99–100.

Funiciello, T. (1992). The poverty industry. In P. S. Rothenberg (Ed.), *Race, class, and gender in the United States: An integrated study* (2nd ed., pp. 120–128). New York: St. Martin's Press.

Funiciello, T. (1993). *Tyranny of kindness: Dismantling the welfare system to end poverty in America.* New York: Atlantic Monthly Press.

Furnham, A. (1982a). Why are the poor always with us? Explanations for poverty in Great Britain. *British Journal of Social Psychology, 21,* 311–322.

Furnham, A. (1982b). The Protestant work ethic and attitudes towards unemployment. *Journal of Occupational Psychology, 55,* 277–286.

Furnham, A. (1982c). Explanations for unemployment in Britain. *European Journal of Social Psychology, 12,* 335–352.

Furnham, A. (1983a). Attitudes toward the unemployed receiving Social Security benefits. *Human Relations, 36,* 135–150.

Furnham, A. (1983b). Attributions for affluence. *Personality and Individual Differences, 4,* 31–40.

Furnham, A. (1984). The Protestant work ethic: A review of the psychological literature. *European Journal of Social Psychology, 14,* 87–104.

Furnham, A. (1985a). The determinants of attitudes towards Social Security recipients. *British Journal of Social Psychology, 24,* 19–27.

Furnham, A. (1985b). Just world beliefs in an unjust society: A cross cultural comparison. *European Journal of Social Psychology, 15,* 363–366.

Gallup, G. (1992). Most important problem/Republican and Democratic parties. *The Gallup Poll: Public opinion 1992* (p. 57). Wilmington, DE: Scholarly Resources.

Gallup, G., & Newport, F. (1990). Americans widely disagree on what constitutes rich. *Gallup Poll Monthly, 298,* 28–36.

Gans, H. (1992). Deconstructing the underclass. In P. S. Rothenberg (Ed.), *Race, class, and gender in the United States: An integrated study* (pp. 358–364). New York: St. Martin's Press.

Guimond, S., & Palmer, D. L. (1990). Type of academic training and causal attributions for social problems. *European Journal of Social Psychology, 20,* 61–75.

Goodgame, D. (1993, February 22). Welfare for the well-off. *Time,* pp. 36–38.

Gordon, R. H., & Bauer, G. (1985). Social class bias of practicing attorneys. *Psychological Reports, 57,* 931–935.

Gorman, C. (1991, September 16). Why do blacks die young? *Time,* pp. 50–52.

Gottschalk, P., McClanahan, S., & Sandefeur, G. D. (1994). The dynamics and intergenerational transmission of poverty and welfare participation. In S. Danzinger, G. Sandefur, & D. Weinberg (Eds.), *Confronting poverty: Prescriptions for change* (pp. 85–108). New York: Russell Sage Foundation.

Gray, D. M. (1975). Affirmative action for working class whites. *American Psychologist, 31,* 94.

Greenery and poverty. (1993, September 18). *The Economist,* p. 80.

Hagen, J. L. (1992). Women, work, and welfare: Is there a role for social work? *Social Work, 37,* 9–14.

Hagen, J. L., & Davis, L. V. (1994). Women on welfare talk about reform: Clients in focus groups discuss teen pregnancy, child support, and time limits. *Public Welfare, 52,* 30–40.

Harper, D. (1991). The role of psychology in the analysis of poverty: Some suggestions. *Psychology and Developing Countries, 3,* 193–201.

Haug, M. (1972). An assessment of inequality measures. In G. W. Thielbar & S. D. Feldman (Eds.), *Issues in social inequality* (pp. 429–444). Boston: Little, Brown.

Hollingshead, A. B., & Redlich, F. C. (1958). *Social class and mental illness: A community study.* New York: Wiley.

Iyengar, S. (1990). Framing responsibility for political issues: The case of poverty. *Political Behavior, 12,* 19–40.

Iyengar, S. (1991). *Is anyone responsible: How television frames political issues.* Chicago: University of Chicago Press.

Joint Economic Committee of the U.S. Congress. (1986). *The concentration of wealth in the United States.* Washington, DC: Author.

Jones, J. M., Levine, I. S., & Rosenberg, A. A. (Eds.). (1991). Homelessness [Special issue]. *American Psychologist, 46.*

Judd, P. (1986). The mentally ill poor in America. *Journal of Applied Social Science, 10,* 40–50.

Juhnke, R., Barmann, B., Cunningham, M., Smith, E., Vickery, K., Hohl, J., & Quinones, J. (1987). Effect of attractiveness and nature of request on helping behavior. *Journal of Social Psychology, 127,* 317–322.

Kaplan, D. A., Brant, M., Katel, P., Holmes, S., & Gordon, J. (1994, January 17). These guys do windows. *Newsweek,* p. 48.

Karniol, R. (1985). Children's causal scripts and derogation of the poor: An attributional analysis. *Journal of Personality and Social Psychology, 48,* 791–798.

Katz, M. B. (1986). *In the shadow of the poorhouse: A social history of welfare in America.* New York: Basic Books.

Katz, M. B. (1989). *The undeserving poor: From the war on poverty to the war on welfare.* New York: Pantheon Books.

Katz, M. B. (Ed.). (1993). *The "underclass" debate: Views from history.* Princeton, NJ: Princeton University Press.

Kaus, M. (1991). The work ethic state. In T. A. Mehuron (Ed.), *Points of light: New approaches to ending welfare dependency* (pp. 19–36). Washington, DC: Ethics and Public Policy Center.

Kelley, H. H., & Mischela, J. L. (1980). Attribution theory and research. *Annual Review of Psychology, 31,* 457–501.

Kiesler, C. A. (1991). Homelessness and public policy priorities. *American Psychologist, 46,* 1245–1252.

Kinder, D. R., & Sears, D. O. (1985). Public opinion and political action. In G. Lindzey & E. Aronson (Eds.), *Handbook of social psychology* (3rd ed., Vol. 2, pp. 659–741). New York: Random House.

Kluegel, J. R., & Smith, E. R. (1986). *Beliefs about inequality: Americans' views of what is and what ought to be.* New York: Aldine/De Gruyter.

Kolder, V., Gallagher, J., & Parsons, M. (1987). Court-ordered obstetrical interventions. *New England Journal of Medicine, 316,* 1192–1196.

Kozol, J. (1991). *Savage inequalities.* New York: Harper Perennial.

Labaton, S. (1994, May 29). Denny's gets a bill for the side orders of bigotry. *New York Times,* p. 4.

Ladner, J. A., & Gourdine, R. M. (1984). Intergenerational teenage motherhood. *Sage, 1,* 22–24.

Langston, D. (1992). Tired of playing monopoly? In M. L. Anderson & P. H. Collins (Eds.), *Race, class, and gender: An anthology* (pp. 110–120). Belmont, CA: Wadsworth.

Leahy, R. L. (1981). The development of the conception of economic inequality: I. Descriptions and comparisons of rich and poor people. *Child Development, 52,* 523–532.

Leahy, R. L. (1983). Development of the conception of economic inequality: II. Explanations, justifications, and concepts of mobility and change. *Developmental Psychology, 19,* 111–125.

Lott, B. (1987). Sexist discrimination as distancing behavior: I. A laboratory demonstration. *Psychology of Women Quarterly, 11,* 47–58.

Luft, J. (1957). Monetary value and the perception of persons. *Journal of Social Psychology, 46,* 245–251.

Lurigio, A. J., & Lewis, D. A. (1989). Worlds that fail: A longitudinal study of urban mental patients. *Journal of Social Issues, 45,* 79–90.

Magnet, M. (1991). The underclass: What can be done? In T. A. Mehuron (Ed.), *Points of light: New approaches to ending welfare dependency* (pp. 99–112). Washington, DC: Ethics and Public Policy Center.

Mahowald, M. B. (1993). *Women and children in health care: An unequal majority.* New York: Oxford University Press.

Makison, L. (1992). *Open secrets: The encyclopedia of congressional money and politics* (2nd ed.). Washington, DC: Center for Responsive Politics.

Mantsios, G. (1992). Rewards and opportunities: The politics and economics of class in the U.S. In P. S. Rothenberg (Ed.), *Race, class, and gender in the United States: An integrated study* (2nd ed., pp. 96–109). New York: St. Martin's Press.

McClanahan, S. S., Sorenson, A., & Watson, D. (1989). Sex differences in poverty, 1950–1980. *Signs, 15,* 102–122.

McCrary, T. (1993, December 6). My turn: Getting off the welfare carousel. *Newsweek,* p. 11.

Minnis, D. (1993, December 27). Disagreeing about dependency [Letter to the editor]. *Newsweek,* p. 7.

Mead, L. (1991). The work obligation. In T. A. Mehuron (Ed.), *Points of light: New approaches to ending welfare dependency* (pp. 57–72). Washington, DC: Ethics and Public Policy Center.

Meissner, J. (1986). Legal services and medical treatment of poor people: A need for advocacy. *Issues in Law and Medicine, 2,* 3–13.

Merrel, S. (1992). Patterns of food consumption. *Current Sociology, 40*(2), 54–60.

Milburn, N., & D'Ercole, A. (1991). Homeless women: Moving towards a comprehensive model. *American Psychologist, 46*, 1161–1169.

Miller, D. C. (1992). *Women and welfare: A feminist analysis.* New York: Praeger.

Mitchell, E. (1991, December 14). Do the poor deserve bad schools? *Time,* pp. 60–61.

Moffic, H. S., Brochstein, J., Blattstein, A., & Adams, G. L. (1983). Attitudes in the provision of public sector health and mental health care. *Social Work in Health Care, 8,* 17–27.

Mortimer, J. (1994, May). Welfare can fuel upward mobility. *Institute for Social Research Newsletter,* p. 6.

Moynihan, D. P. (1992). Welfare is back in the news. *Public Welfare, 50,* 6.

Murray, C. (1991). How social policy shapes behavior. In T. A. Mehuron (Ed.), *Points of light: New approaches to ending welfare dependency* (pp. 73–84). Washington, DC: Ethics and Public Policy Center.

Nathan, R. P. (1992). New Jersey's mix of carrots and sticks: The problem is with the sticks. *Public Welfare, 50,* 11.

National Institute of Mental Health. (1992). *Outcasts on Main Street: Report of the Federal Task Force on Homelessness and Severe Mental Illness.* Washington, DC: Interagency Council on the Homeless.

Neckerman, K. M., & Kirchenman, J. (1991). Hiring strategies, racial bias, and innercity workers. *Social Problems, 38,* 433–445.

Ouellette, L. (1993). Class bias on campus. *Utne Reader, 59,* 19–24.

Pandey, J., Sinha, Y., Prakash, A., & Tripathi, R. (1982). Right–left political ideologies and attribution of the causes of poverty. *European Journal of Social Psychology, 12,* 327–331.

Pear, R. (1995, April 30). A revised definition of poverty may raise number of U.S. poor. *New York Times,* pp. 1, 21.

Pearce, D. (1978). The feminization of poverty: Women, work, and welfare. *Urban and Social Change Review, 3,* 1–4.

Peterson, R. A., Albaum, G., & Kometsky, G. (1990). *Modern American capitalism: Understanding public attitudes and perceptions.* New York: Quorum Books.

Piven, F. F., & Cloward, R. A. (1971). *Regulating the poor: The functions of public welfare* (1st ed.). New York: Random House.

Piven, F. F., & Cloward, R. A. (1987a). The historical sources of the contemporary relief debate. In F. Block, R. A. Cloward, B. Ehrenreich, & F. F. Piven, *The mean season: The attack on the welfare state* (pp. 3–44). New York: Pantheon Books.

Piven, F. F., & Cloward, R. A. (1987b). The contemporary relief debate. In F. Block, R. A. Cloward, B. Ehrenreich, & F. F. Piven, *The mean season: The attack on the welfare state* (pp. 45–108). New York: Pantheon Books.

Piven, F. F., & Cloward, R. A. (1993). *Regulating the poor: The functions of public welfare* (2nd ed.). New York: Vintage Books.

Popkin, S. J. (1990). Welfare: Views from the bottom. *Social Problems, 37,* 64–79.

Reeser, L. C., & Epstein, I. (1987). Social workers' attitudes toward poverty and social action: 1968–1984. *Social Service Review, 61,* 610–621.

Rosenbaum, J. E., Popkin, S. J., Kaufman, J. E., & Rusin, J. (1991). Social integration of low–income black adults in middle-class white suburbs. *Social Problems, 38,* 448–461.

Rudinow, J. (1990). Channel One whittles away at education. *Educational Leadership*, 47, 70–73.

Ruggles, P. (1990). *Drawing the line: Alternative poverty measures and their implications for public policy*. Washington, DC: Urban Institute Press.

Ryan, J., & Sackray, C. (1992). Bob Cole. In M. L. Anderson & P. H. Collins (Eds.), *Race, class, and gender: An anthology* (pp. 110–120). Belmont, CA: Wadsworth.

Saba, G. W., & Rodgers, D. V. (1989). Discrimination in urban family practice: Lessons from minority poor families. *Journal of Psychotherapy and the Family*, 177–207.

Sampson, R. J., & Laub, J. H. (1993). Structural variations in juvenile court processing: Inequality, the underclass, and social control. *Law and Society Review, 27*, 285–310.

Satchell, M. (1992, May 4). A whiff of discrimination? *U.S. News and World Report*, pp. 34–35.

Schmid, R. E. (1994, October 7). Poverty found to be on rise despite upturn: Widening rich–poor gap reported. *The Boston Globe*.

Schwartz, J. E., & Volgy, T. J. (1992). *The forgotten poor*. New York: Norton.

Scott, B. R. (1994, March 2). Rebuilding standards of behavior is essential to any poverty cure. *Providence Journal-Bulletin*, p. A11.

Sharff, J. W. (1981, March). Free enterprise and the ghetto family. *Psychology Today*, pp. 40–48.

Shayne, V. T., & Kaplan, B. (1991). Double victims: Poor women and AIDS. *Women and Health, 17*, 21–37.

Shinn, M., & Weitzman, B. C. (1990). Urban homelessness [Special issue]. *Journal of Social Issues, 46*.

Sidel, R. (1990). *On her own: Growing up in the shadow of the American dream*. New York: Penguin.

Sidel, R. (1992). *Women and children last: The plight of poor women in affluent America* New York: Penguin.

Single women and poverty strongly linked. (1994, February 20). *New York Times*, p. 35.

Skafte, D. (1988). The effects of perceived wealth and poverty on adolescents' character judgments. *Journal of Social Psychology, 129*, 93–99.

Smith, T. W. (1987). That which we call welfare by any other name would smell sweeter: An analysis of the impact of question wording on response. *Public Opinion Quarterly, 51*, 75–83.

Specht, H., & Courtney, M. E. (1994). *Unfaithful angels: How social work abandoned Its mission*. New York: Free Press.

Students speak out. (1994, March–April). *Happenings at Dorcas Place*, p. 1.

Sullivan, M. (1989). *Getting paid: Youth crime and work in the inner city.*. Ithaca, NY: Cornell University Press.

Szymanski, A. (1983). *Class structure*. New York: Praeger.

Tomaskovic-Dewey, D. (1988). Poverty and social welfare in the United States. In D. Tomaksovic-Dewey (Ed.), *Poverty and social welfare in the United States* (pp. 1–26). Boulder, CO: Westview Press.

U.S. Bureau of the Census. (1991). *Poverty in the United States: 1990* (Current

Population Reports, Series P-60, No. 175). Washington, DC: U.S. Government Printing Office.

U.S. Bureau of the Census. (1992). *Poverty in the United States: 1991* (Current Population Reports, Series P-60, No. 181). Washington, DC: U.S. Government Printing Office.

U.S. Bureau of the Census. (1993). *Poverty in the United States: 1992* (Current Population Reports, Series P-60, No. 185). Washington, DC: U.S. Government Printing Office.

Wagner, D., & Cohen, M. (1991). The power of the people: Homeless protesters in the aftermath of social movement participation. *Social Problems, 38*, 543–561.

Wagstaff, G. T. (1983). Attitudes to poverty, the Protestant ethic, and political affiliation: A preliminary investigation. *Social Behavior and Personality, 11*, 45–47.

Walsh, M. (1993, October 27). Channel One more often used in poorer schools, study finds. *Education Week*, p.5.

The war on welfare mothers: Reform may put them to work, but will it discourage illegitimacy? (1994, June 20). *Time*.

Warner, W. L. (1972). Social class: Description and measurement. In G. W. Thielbar & S. D. Feldman (Eds.), *Issues in social inequality* (pp. 6–25). Boston: Little, Brown.

Wealth in America. (Winter 1986–1987). *ISR Newsletter* [Institute for Social Research, University of Michigan], pp. 3–5.

Will, J. A. (1993). The dimensions of poverty: Public perceptions of the deserving poor. *Social Science Research, 22*, 312–332.

Wilson, W. J., & Neckerman, K. M. (1986). Poverty and family structure: The widening gap between evidence and public policy issues. In S. H. Danzinger & D. H. Weinberg (Eds.), *Fighting poverty: What works and what doesn't* (pp. 232–259). Cambridge, MA: Harvard University Press.

Winnick, A. J. (1989). *Toward two societies: The changing distributions of income and wealth in the U.S. since 1960*. New York: Praeger.

Wise, T. (1992). Being poor isn't enough. In P. S. Rothenberg (Ed.), *Race, class, and gender in the United States: An integrated study* (2nd ed., pp. 136–139). New York: St. Martin's Press.

Women's Action Coalition. (1993). *WAC stats: The facts about women*. New York: New York Press.

Wright, G. C. (1977). Racism and welfare policy in America. *Social Science Quarterly, 57*, 718–730.

Young, I. M. (1992). Five faces of oppression. In T. E. Wartenberg (Ed.), *Rethinking power* (pp. 174–195). Albany: State University of New York Press.

Zinn, D., & Sarri, R. (1984). Turning back the clock on public welfare. *Signs, 10*, 355–370.

6

Ageism in Interpersonal Settings

MONISHA PASUPATHI
LAURA L. CARSTENSEN
JEANNE L. TSAI

U nlike sexism and racism, ageism continues to go largely unacknowledged in day-to-day life in the United States. The current social climate allows people to voice reservations freely about older people, in a way that would be patently unacceptable in discussions about race or gender. Ageism is so firmly embedded within the social fabric of U.S. culture that few people even question the fact that age is considered a legitimate reason for limiting access to health care and productive employment. Ironically, older people represent the only stigmatized group that, barring premature death, we all eventually join. Thus, ageism holds considerable relevance for all people, regardless of their current age. However, despite the clear demonstration of ageism evidenced in retirement and hiring policies, insurance practices, and other age-biased laws and policies, empirical evidence for ageist behavior in interpersonal settings is more elusive.

This chapter focuses on ageism as studied by the social sciences. We emphasize interpersonal behavior, but we touch on other aspects of ageism as well. First, however, we paint a broad picture of the elderly population in an attempt to neutralize some common misperceptions about old age that our readers may share.

DEFINING OLD AGE AND AGEISM

The expression "old age is new" refers to the fact that only in recent history has it become normative to experience old age. Life expectancy at birth has increased by more than 30 years since the turn of the century, largely because improved sanitation and vaccination programs have reduced infant mortality. This has allowed most children born in industrialized countries to live out their entire life-span. As a result, the absolute and relative number of older people in developed countries has exploded during the 20th century, especially the "very old" group (see below). In 1900, 4% of the U.S. population was over the age of 65, but currently 12% of the population meets this age criterion; by the year 2020, 24% of the population will be over the age of 65 (Myers, 1990). Since the reduction in infant mortality has nearly reached its limit, the 21st century will not witness a continuation of this trend.

Who Are the Elderly?

Although it is beyond the scope of this chapter to provide a full description of the elderly population, one central feature should be noted: Older cohorts are more heterogeneous than any other age group, along virtually any dimension (Dannefer & Perlmutter, 1990). Whitborne (1987) refers to adult development as a process of differentiation; that is, people become increasingly individualized as they age. As a result, the elderly are a highly diverse group of people, including the wisest members of society as well as the most demented.

By convention, old age begins at age 65. The widespread use of this initially arbitrary age criterion has in some sense created its utility. That is, because most researchers use this cutoff, most studies of aging do describe people 65 years of age and older. Still, because aging is a gradual and cumulative process, the categorical term "old age" can be misleading. To address specific age groups more adequately, some scientists have come to refer to the "young-old" (65–75), the "old-old" (76–84) and the "very old" (over 85). However, individual variability is notable even within these smaller age categories.

The scientific study of aging has been largely a search for age-related decrement, from the slowing of mental processes to physical decline. In fact, one of the more subtle forms of ageism can be found in the way science has studied old age (Carstensen & Freund, 1994; Schaie, 1993). Given that the quest has been focused on problems, it follows that gerontological researchers have primarily documented the problems older people face. But even though the search has been focused on decrement, it has had its surprises. Despite some common problems, older people appear in general to be doing quite well. For example, with the exception of the dementias, the prevalence of all other psychological disorders is lower among older people. Moreover, although dementia is a disease of late life, it occurs far less frequently than many imagine: Only 5% of people over 65 suffer from some form of dementia (Jorm, 1987). Although this percentage increases with age, the majority of people never suffer from dementia. Similarly, the image of the prototypical old person as a frail nursing home resident is misleading. Only 5% of older people live in nursing homes at any point in time; the vast majority of older people live independently in the community (American Association of Homes for the Aging, 1991).

Ageism

"Ageism" is not a precisely defined concept in the psychological literature or in everyday usage. Broadly, it may be defined as discrimination based on chronological age. In the social-psychological literature, ageism has typically been understood as including negative beliefs, attitudes, and stereotypes about elderly persons. Although ageist attitudes are relatively easy to identify, it is unclear how these attitudes translate into actual behavior. Without evidence for negative behavior, it is difficult to speak of interpersonal ageism, even with ample evidence of ageism at the level of public policy and legislation. Our current focus is on behavioral ageism rather than on ageist attitudes or structural ageism.

For our purposes, we define "ageist behavior" as behavior that discriminates on the basis of chronological age. Such discrimination can involve overtly hostile behavior, but it also includes behaviors that may appear quite positive but that ultimately serve to prevent elderly people from attaining their goals. Ageist behavior, then, must be contingent upon chronological age and must produce some sort of harmful impact.

In this chapter, we first address evidence for negative attitudes toward, beliefs about, and stereotypes of elderly people. We then examine the evidence for ageist behavior, both related and unrelated to ageist attitudes. We use the term "age-differentiated" to refer to behavior that differs as a function of the age of the target, but may or may not reflect negative overgeneralizations based on chronological age. We do so because much of the existing research is fraught with uncertainties regarding the nature of the documented behaviors. For example, many observed behaviors are not clearly negative or hostile. In addition, whether or not the behaviors were driven by negative expectations of the elderly targets is often unknown.

Indeed, in some cases, behavior distinctions could reflect respect or accommodations to genuine limitations of the target person. Finally, it is often unclear whether the observed behaviors constrain elders' desired goals—an uncertainty that stems largely from a failure to adequately address the impact of the age-differentiated treatment.

AGEIST ATTITUDES, BELIEFS, AND STEREOTYPES

Behavior that is ageist is often presumed to be associated with underlying negative conceptions of the old. Therefore, in this section we discuss evidence for ageism based on research that examines attitudes toward and beliefs about the elderly. As we review below, age is a dimension by which people categorize other people, and conceptions of the elderly include both negative and positive elements. However, conceptions of the old appear to be more negative than positive.

Several studies have found that age is a highly salient dimension along which people are categorized (Kite, Deaux, & Miele, 1991; Brewer & Lui, 1989). In fact, Kite et al. (1991) find that age is a more salient social category than gender. Not only is age a salient dimension, but shared stereotypes about elderly people exist (Brewer, Dull, & Lui, 1981; Brewer & Lui, 1989; Hummert, 1990). These include the "elder statesperson," the "senior citizen," and the "golden ager" (Brewer et al., 1981; Brewer & Lui, 1989; Hummert, 1990). Both young and old people share stereotypes of the elderly, although there are some differences in their categories. Most notably, older people appear to have more subcategories within the broad category "old" than do younger adults. Interestingly, stereotypes of the elderly often represent polar opposites or extremes, such as "wise" and "demented," "kind" and "grouchy," and "experienced" and "incompetent."

Although stereotypes of the elderly are both positive and negative, people appear to hold more negative than positive beliefs about aging (see Rubin & Brown, 1975; Heckhausen, Dixon, & Baltes, 1989). In one study, Heckhausen et al. (1989) asked young, middle-aged, and elderly adults to review a list of adjectives such as "dignified," "fair-minded," "shrewd," and "powerful," among others. Respondents rated each adjective for the degree to which it *increased* over the lifespan, the desirability of that increase, and the ages at which the increase began and ended. Heckhausen et al. concluded that people of different age groups share similar beliefs about adult development. Moreover, these beliefs are not unidirectional; aging is apparently perceived as a process involving gains (increases in desirable attributes, decreases in undesirable ones) and losses (increases in undesirable attributes, decreases in desirable ones). Despite the existence of positive and negative beliefs, the ratio between gains and losses is thought to become more and more negative at older ages, as Figure 6.1 shows. For people in their early 80s, gains and losses are considered to be roughly equivalent, but the relative percentage of losses is thought to increase rapidly from that point on.

Just as beliefs and stereotypes about the elderly are ambivalent but tend to be negative, the attitude literature also reflects both negativity and ambiguity. Very early work by Tuckman and Lorge showed that a wide variety of people display negative attitudes toward the elderly (Tuckman & Lorge, 1952, 1958; Lorge, Tuckman, & Abrams, 1954). In fact, negative conceptions of the elderly can be documented as soon as children are able to discriminate age among adults (Looft, 1971). Despite these early findings, it is unclear just how negative people's attitudes toward the elderly

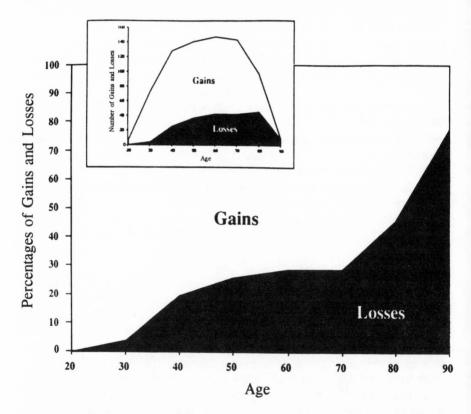

FIGURE 6.1. Quantitative relations of gains and losses across the adult lifespan: Percentages and absolute numbers (insert). From Heckhausen, Dixon, and Baltes (1989). Copyright 1989 by the American Psychological Association. Reprinted by permission.

are (Hummert, 1990; Brewer et al., 1981). For example, even though much of the literature shows that elderly people are viewed more negatively than the young, both groups are described on the positive side of neutral (Crockett & Hummert, 1987). In this sense, then, ageism may be relative rather than absolute.

Overall, more negatively than positively valenced stereotypes about the elderly exist; negative beliefs about aging exist; and elderly people are evaluated more negatively than young people. Therefore, we can conclude that there is reasonable evidence for ageism in attitudes and beliefs about the old. A recent meta-analysis (Kite & Johnson, 1988) also supports the notion that general conceptions of people grow increasingly negative as the target group gets older.

Furthermore, a recent study using measures that were relatively immune to social desirability constraints suggests that people hold negative representations of the elderly, whether or not they consciously subscribe to that representation (Perdue & Gurtman, 1990). Perdue and Gurtman (1990) reasoned that an existing negative representation of the elderly should influence learning. Using an incidental-memory paradigm, they presented participants with a list of adjectives that were unequivocally positive or negative. Participants were asked to read each word and to make one of four judgments about it: (1) whether it was a desirable trait, (2) whether it described them, (3) whether it described an old person, or (4) whether it described a young person. Those who had been asked whether the word was typical of an old person recalled negative words more easily. Those asked whether the word was more typical of a young person recalled positive words more easily. A subsequent priming task in the same study demonstrated that this bias was unconscious, that is, respondents were unaware of their ageist responses. In other words, despite laudable conscious efforts to be egalitarian, people are likely to hold negative representations of the elderly.

In short, views of the elderly are predominantly negative, whether these are measured in terms of stereotypes, beliefs, attitudes, or learning. Although our particular focus is on the harmful behaviors that may result from negative attitudes and beliefs, negative attitudes may be harmful in their own right. According to Deaux's (1984) expectancy model of the effects of prejudice, stereotypes about the elderly will lead the elderly to develop specific expectations about their performance on particular tasks. That is, negative attitudes and stereotypes can influence the elderly's self-efficacy beliefs about task performance—beliefs that affect their actual performance (cf. Bandura, 1986, 1989). If people perform as they expect to perform on a given task, they attribute that performance to stable and internal causes. Thus, stereotype-consistent performance leads people to believe in and accept the specific implications of stereotypes about them.

For example, elderly people who are aware of the stereotypes about aging and memory may expect to perform poorly on memory tasks. If they do perform poorly, they assume that it is because they are old, and make an attribution that reinforces their expectations. Recent work suggests that elderly people who do not share widely held negative beliefs about aging do not show performance decrements on memory tasks (Levy & Langer, 1994).

Unfortunately, the literature on attitudes, beliefs, and stereotypes about aging leaves us quite ignorant about how people behave toward the elderly in day-to-day situations. There are several reasons why this may be the case. First, questionnaire methods are open to the biases of self-report (e.g., self-presentation), and often ask for global evaluations of elderly targets rather than for predictions of behavior toward the targets. As Perdue and Gurtman (1990) have shown, negative representations of the elderly are easily documented when other measures are used. It is unlikely that respondents in questionnaire studies can predict precisely how they would behave in actual situations. There is good evidence that people are not good at predicting their own behavior without knowing the particular constraints of the situation. Thus, the relationship between attitudes and behavior is known to be tenuous at best (Ajzen & Fishbein, 1977). Consequently, even if a person holds unambiguously negative attitudes toward the elderly, it is not clear that in a specific situation those attitudes would result in negative behavior.

In the next section, we review work that documents age-differentiated behavior in interpersonal settings, rather than ageist attitudes, beliefs, or stereotypes. We adopt a relatively open conception of behavior that includes actions such as referrals for psychological services (Gatz & Pearson, 1988), microanalytic approaches to linguistic behavior (Greene, Adelman, Charon, & Hoffman, 1986; Greene, Adelman, Charon, & Friedmann, 1989), and social attention contingent on dependent behavior (Baltes, Burgess, & Stewart, 1980; Baltes & Reisenzein, 1986). As previously mentioned, little work on interpersonal interaction with the elderly exists. The studies that we cite here are representative of what is known about interpersonal behavior toward the elderly.

EVIDENCE FOR BEHAVIORAL AGEISM

In considering the evidence for behavioral ageism, we begin with the relatively specific contexts of medical and institutional settings, and then move to more global everyday contexts in the community. Medical and institutional settings provide numerous examples of behavior that appear clearly ageist. In community contexts, the picture is less clear.

Medical Settings

Treatment and Referrals

Gatz and Pearson (1988) suggest that even though medical practitioners may not hold negative attitudes toward the elderly, they may possess specific biases regarding their treatment. For example, clinicians are more likely to prescribe drug treatments to elderly depressed patients than to refer them to psychotherapists. These biases stem from the misconception that elders are "stuck in their ways" and are incapable of introspection. The misconception persists despite ample evidence that psychotherapy works just as well for the depressed elderly as for depressed young people (Carstensen, 1988; Gatz & Pearson, 1988).

Physician–Patient Communication

Physician–patient communication can be a problem, regardless of the age of the patient. Studies of informed consent procedures suggest that patients, whether young or old, understand and recall very little of what doctors tell them (Mann, 1994). Explanations for this phenomenon vary; some blame patients for their anxiety and lack of medical knowledge, whereas others blame physicians for failing to use comprehensible language or to be receptive to patient concerns (Siminoff, 1989).

Some research suggests that this phenomenon worsens when the patient is old. In a series of studies, physician–patient interchanges involving elderly and young patients were audiotaped during follow-up visits for earlier problems (Greene et al., 1986, 1989). Audiotapes were subsequently coded for topics raised, initiators of topic, reference to age, misattributions of symptoms to old age, compliments and social amenities, use of jargon, open-ended questions, doctor patience, doctor engagement, doctor egalitarianism, doctor responsiveness, patient assertiveness, patient tension, patient expressiveness, and patient friendliness. Physicians addressed elderly patients with less patience, engagement, and respect than they showed to young patients. Furthermore, young patients received more open-ended questions, more detailed information about their conditions, and more support from physicians (Greene et al., 1986)—factors that presumably contribute to better treatment. Although the elderly patients were sicker than the younger patients, all age effects remained significant even after illness severity was statistically controlled for. Finally Greene et al. (1989) examined the degree to which physicians and patients agreed about topics they discussed during office visits. There was less concordance between the reports of elderly patients and their physicians than between young patients and their physicians.

One possible explanation for this age-differentiated treatment is that the elderly are more passive consumers of health care, and therefore do not seek or desire the same kind of treatment from doctors as young patients. However, in this study elderly patients were no less assertive, expressive, or friendly than younger patients, nor were they more tense (Greene et al., 1986). Despite the fact that there were no age differences in patient behaviors, physicians were less likely to respond to a topic raised by an elderly patient than to one raised by a young patient. This was particularly true when issues were psychosocial in nature, such as problems with family members or partners; concerns about health; or questions about tests, treatments, or procedures. Clearly, these findings suggest a lack of communication or understanding by physicians, patients, or both.

All told, the research of Greene and colleagues presents substantial evidence that physicians treat the elderly differently from the young. Age-differentiated behavior in physician–patient settings is particularly significant, because elders spend far more time in physicians' offices and far more dollars on health care than any other segment of the population (Kane & Kane, 1990). Thus, the physician–patient relationship may be increasingly important in later life.

Institutional Settings

Babytalk to Elderly People

A glaring example of age-differentiated behavior in nursing homes is provided by the literature on "babytalk" directed to older adults (Caporeal, 1981; Caporeal & Culbertson, 1986; Caporeal, Lukaszewski, & Culbertson, 1983; Ryan, Giles, Bartolucci, & Henwood, 1986). "Babytalk" is characterized by high, variable pitch and simplified content (Ryan et al., 1986). It is typical of parent–infant interactions, but is also found when people are addressing older children and retarded adults (DePaulo & Coleman, 1986).

Babytalk is clearly present in nursing homes. Caporeal (1981) audiotaped nursing home staff members as they performed their jobs. Utterances directed at a range of care receivers, aged 60 to 90 years, were transcribed and coded as either babytalk or nonbabytalk. Raters judged 22% of these verbal utterances as babytalk. When content-filtered, these same statements were indistinguishable from mother–infant speech.

How do elders perceive this babytalk? Babytalk may be quite pleasant to hear—for example, infants prefer it to other types of speech (Fernald & Mazzie, 1991). In fact, a second set of raters (viz., students) judged elder-directed babytalk to be more pleasant than normal adult speech. However, raters did not know to whom the talk was addressed; therefore, it is possible that they would have rated the speech as less pleasant had they known that it was directed toward adults rather than children. Thus, babytalk may be perceived as pleasant when addressed to children, but as condescending when addressed to competent adults.

Caporeal et al. (1983) set out to document the impact of elder-directed babytalk on residents of nursing homes. They asked residents to indicate their preferences for content-filtered statements that were either normal speech directed at adults (not residents), normal speech directed at elderly care recipients, or babytalk directed at elderly care recipients. Caregiving staff members were also asked to make judgments about the speech samples. They were asked to choose the voice that would be most preferred by elderly residents, and the voice that would be most effective for interacting with the residents. In addition, caregivers were asked about their expectations for various care receivers.

Most elderly people preferred adult-type speech to babytalk. There was a subset of elderly care recipients who preferred babytalk over adult-type speech; however, they were relatively lower in functional ability than the rest of the sample. Caregivers who had generally low expectations of the elderly thought that babytalk would be preferred by elderly and be more effective in dealing with the elderly. These findings suggest that staff members' expectations of elders, rather than the elders' individual characteristics, predict staff members' use of babytalk (Caporeal, 1981; Caporeal et al., 1983). Although Caporeal et al. (1983) did not measure these staff members' actual use of babytalk, their findings have important implications for the use of babytalk. Elderly persons may perceive babytalk as communicating the speaker's low expectations for their abilities. For high-functioning elders, the discrepancy between these expectations and their own (as high-functioning adults) may have detrimental effects (see Deaux, 1984). Low-functioning elders, on the other hand, may prefer babytalk to adult-type speech because the use of babytalk communicates expectations that are more consistent with their own.

Nursing Homes and Dependency

In nursing homes, age-differentiated treatment exists in the reinforcement of specific behaviors that promote dependency. Although residence in a nursing home setting implies some degree of dependency, elderly residents can typically engage in a considerable amount of independent behavior. Doing so should improve their sense of efficacy in multiple domains (Rodin, 1986). However, in some cases, the cost of behaving independently may be the loss of social support. Over the years, Baltes and her colleagues have studied the ways in which nursing home staff members respond to self-care behaviors from residents. Baltes et al. (1980) developed a systematic coding system in which residents' self-care behaviors (e.g., brushing teeth, dressing) are coded as either independent (performed without assistance) or dependent (requiring assistance). Staff responses are coded as either dependence-supporting, independence-supporting, no response, or other response. Dependence-supporting behaviors include staff assistance in self-care behaviors, praise for the acceptance of help, or discouragement of independent self-care behavior. Independence-supporting behaviors include encouragement and praise for independent self-care behavior, and discouragement of requests for assistance. Baltes et al.'s findings showed reliably that when residents engaged in independent acts, staff members did not respond to them. In contrast, when dependent behaviors were displayed, the staff responded consistently and positively. Thus, a nursing home appears to be an environment where dependence is reinforced and independence is ignored.

To determine whether this phenomemon could be attributed to age or to institutional settings, Baltes and Reisenzein (1986) used a similar paradigm to compare the treatment of institutionalized children and institutionalized elderly people. They found that twice as much support was given to the elderly for dependent behaviors as for independent behaviors, whereas the reverse pattern was true for children. Thus, institutionalization per se is not the cause of the dependence-supporting environment observed in nursing homes. Although these two populations are not entirely comparable, it is at least clear that in institutional contexts, the elderly are treated very differently from children.

The above-cited studies demonstrate that elderly people are treated differently and rather negatively by health care professionals in a variety of settings. As we discuss below, although dependency may not be a completely negative outcome, and babytalk may communicate warmth as well as expectations of incompetence, all of the age-differentiated treatment we have listed thus far could be considered ageist. Of course, in all of the studies cited, this age-differentiated treatment occured in the context of pre-existing power imbalances (physicians and nursing home staffs hold a great deal of power in comparison to patients and residents, regardless of age) and with relatively frail elders. These studies do not adequately address how interpersonal ageism influences social interactions with healthy, community-dwelling elderly persons. In this population, age-differentiated behavior also exists; however, it is more difficult to determine whether such behavior is ageist.

Community Settings

Dependency in the Community

To examine the generalizability of their findings, Baltes and Wahl (1992) examined interactions between community-dwelling elderly and their social partners, and compared them with those between nursing home residents and staff members. Elders' behaviors were coded as sleeping, constructively engaged, destructively engaged, nonengaged, independent self-care behavior, or dependent self-care behavior. Social partners' responses were coded as dependence supporting, independence-supporting, engagement-supporting, nonengagement-supporting, nonresponse, or leaving. With regard to dependent behaviors, both the community elderly and nursing home residents were treated similarly by their social partners—that is, social partners responded to elders' dependent behaviors in a dependence-supporting manner. With respect to independent self-care behaviors, however, the two elderly groups differed. In the nursing home, as in previous work, independent behaviors were for the most part ignored by staff members. In the community, however, independent behaviors received a variety of responses. For one-third of the time, social partners responded in an independence-supporting way; for the remainder of the time, independent behaviors received dependence-supporting responses.

Thus, the work of Baltes and Wahl (1992) suggests that although there may be similarities between institutional and noninstitutional settings, there also may be differences. As they note, these differences may arise from the ambiguous nature of social interactions in noninstitutional settings. For example, in medical and institutional settings, social interactions entail clear goals regarding the treatment of patients. In contrast, the goals of social partners in more casual social settings are less clear. Consequently, ambivalent responses that reflect a complicated mixture of ageist attitudes, desires to assist elders, and goals of promoting their independence may result. In any case, these behaviors differ from those toward the young. What about interactions between the young and the old? We now turn to interpersonal communications in a variety of contexts.

Intergenerational Communication

The findings from studies on intergenerational communication are mixed; some suggest no or little age-differentiated behavior, whereas others document robust age-differentiated behavior. In one early study (Rubin & Brown, 1975), college students were asked to rate the competence of people of various ages across a variety of cognitive skills, some of which are stereotypically believed to decline in old age (e.g., memory), and others of which are believed to increase (e.g., wisdom). In general, students rated people's competence in these domains as curvilinear—increasing until middle adulthood, and then decreasing. They were then asked to explain a game to a hypothetical listener of a particular age. The listener was represented by an ink drawing that was suggestive of a particular age. Students spoke fewer words per utterance when speaking to children, adolescent, and elderly "listeners" than when speaking to young and middle-aged adult "listeners." The number of words per utterance was considered a rough index of the complexity of the explanation. Thus, the elderly received both simple explanations and lower competency ratings; in fact, they were treated like children and adolescents rather than like competent adults. Unfortunately, this study did not examine actual interpersonal interaction. It is possible that had Rubin and Brown employed real listeners rather than drawings in their design, the explanations given by the students would have differed. Real listeners give signals that indicate their comprehension and allow the speaker to move on, or signals indicating lack of comprehension and asking for further detail; in the absence of such signals, speakers have difficulty (Krauss, Garlock, Bricker, & McMahon, 1977).

Another project examined the behavior of children as they interacted with elderly people (Isaacs & Bearison, 1986). Children aged 4, 6, and 8 were first asked about their ageist attitudes. Four-year-olds did not demonstrate ageist attitudes, whereas 6- and 8-year-olds did. Each child was then brought into a room with a child-sized table, chairs, and two jigsaw puzzles. The experimenter and an adult confederate were in the room. Confederates were either elderly adults (approximately 75 years old) or young adults (approximately 35 years old). All confederates were healthy, were fashionably dressed, and had professional experience working with children. Each child was asked to work on the puzzle with the confederate. Behaviorally, the children were quite discriminating: They sat farther away from, made less eye contact with, spoke fewer words to, initiated less conversation with, and asked for less help from aged confederates. However, children's attitudes correlated with only some of their behaviors. Ageist attitudes were strongly correlated with the age of a child. Ageist behavior, on the other hand, was less related to a child's age. Thus, although 4-year-olds asked for assistance more often overall and sat closer to the elderly confederates than their older peers did, on all other measures children of all ages behaved similarly.

Other studies of intergenerational interaction include Montepare, Steinberg, and Rosenberg's (1992) examination of college students' speech to their grandparents and their parents. Speech directed at grandparents had a higher pitch and was more feminine, deferential, and unpleasant than speech directed toward parents, according to observers' ratings. Interestingly, it was not more simple than speech directed toward parents. The authors suggest that these characteristics reflected the greater deference and lesser intimacy college students felt toward their grandparents compared to their parents. In addition, they conclude that age-differentiated speech is not a reflection of negative attitudes, although their rationale is unclear.

Further evidence of age-differentiated behavior in intergenerational interactions is provided by a second study, conducted in a less naturalistic setting (Coupland, Coupland, Giles, Henwood, & Wiemann, 1988). Elderly adults and nonelderly adults were paired once with same-aged peers, and once with partners of a different age; in each case, partners were instructed to get to know each other. Sessions were videotaped, and conversations between partners were transcribed and coded for painful self-disclosure, operationalized as the discussion of loneliness, disengagement, and other troubles. Overall, elderly participants were found to engage in painful self-disclosure more often than younger participants. Moreover, young adults appeared to be influenced by their partners' age, whereas the elderly adults were not. Elderly adults disclosed to young and old social partners alike, whereas young adults were more likely to disclose to same-age peers.

In our laboratory, we examined intergenerational interaction in two groups: European-Americans and Chinese-Americans (Tsai & Carstensen, 1991). These groups were chosen because the ethnographic literature suggests that Chinese Americans may hold fewer ageist attitudes than do European-Americans (Chang, Chang, & Shen, 1984; Cheung, 1989; Lee, 1986). Studying both groups afforded a chance to look at attitude–behavior relationships, as well as to examine behavior in a group that is purportedly not ageist. Participants aged 18–21 years were paired with other women of the same ethnicity, who were either the same age or elderly. Pairs were instructed to come to agreement on a topic about which they held opposite opinions (as assessed by previously administered questionnaires). Topics ranged from "mothers' employment outside the home" to the "use of the military to combat drugs."

Raters gauged the respectfulness, politeness, patience, responsiveness, comfort, and directiveness of participants toward their partners. Both similarities and differences in the behavior of participants were identified as a function of their social partners' age. Participants were comparably patient, comfortable, and responsive toward both young and old social partners. However, compared to those interacting with young partners, those interacting with older social partners were more respectful, polite, and directive, and changed their opinions more *during* the interaction (but returned to their initial opinions after the interaction). In addition, participants paired with elderly partners moved their chairs closer to their partners (as measured by the distances between the partners' chairs). Thus, as in previous work, we found ample evidence for age-differentiated behavior on the part of young adults. Interestingly, no differences between the two ethnic groups were found: Despite different expressed attitudes towards the elderly, both European-Americans and Chinese-Americans behaved differently toward partners who were older.

Existing Research: Limitations

The existing research on ageist behavior spans a variety of settings and paradigms. Although most studies do show age-differentiated treatment of social partners, the interpretation of findings is hampered by various limitations.

One limitation involves apparent reliability of effects. For example, Isaacs and Bearison (1986) found that children sat further from elderly partners, whereas Tsai and Carstensen (1991) found that young adults sat closer to elderly partners. The inconsistency of these findings suggests that researchers should consider not only characteristics of the elderly targets of age-differentiated behavior, but also characteristics of their social partners. Although this point seems obvious, much of the existing literature has not varied the characteristics of social partners, such as their age, ethnicity, and/or gender. Moreover, most of the work we have reviewed examines strangers interacting. When familiar partners are examined, findings may be altered—for example, Montepare et al. (1992) found that speech to grandparents and parents was similar in complexity, whereas Rubin and Brown (1975) found that speech to elderly targets was simplified. Familiar or intimate others—people who constitute an elderly person's inner social network—may behave very differently toward the elderly individual than strangers may.

Clearly, the social context is important as well, and it rarely receives the attention it deserves. For example, behavior that is appropriate in one setting may be inappropriate in another; therefore, researchers attempting to document ageist, sexist, or racist behavior must consider the possibility that the social context both inhibits and alters the expression of behavior. For example, increased politeness of young adults toward elderly confederates may serve as a socially acceptable way of distancing from an elderly person. Alternatively, it may be an attempt to follow a rule of respect for elders. Similarly, disclosing painful events to elderly people may violate norms of "not burdening" the older persons with the insignificant troubles of youth. Because perceptions of the social context are often unaddressed, it is difficult to interpret findings of age-differentiated behavior.

Another limitation of the existing literature is its failure to address the interplay among factors such as sexism, racism, homophobia, and ageism. Sometimes referred to as "double jeopardy," "triple jeopardy,", or "multiple jeopardy," the intersection of old age with other stigmatized characteristics represents largely uncharted territory, particularly in the domain of interpersonal interaction. Because the majority of elderly people are women, sexism must be addressed. And because the combined proportion of minority elderly is expected to double by the next century, the intersection of ageism and ethnicity is clearly important to understand (National Academy on Aging, 1994).

SUMMARY AND CONCLUSIONS

The literature provides ample evidence that people treat the elderly differently from younger people in medical, institutional, and community settings. However, we caution against the automatic conclusions that age-differentiated behavior represents ageism. Recall that according to the definition of ageist behavior we have proposed earlier, ageist behavior must be based on chronological age and must have harmful effects. Harmful effects can derive from overtly hostile behavior or from behavior that blocks an elderly person's desired goals. Very little of the age-differentiated behavior we have detailed above can be clearly categorized as hostile or negative. Some of it may even be construed quite positively, such as increased politeness (Tsai & Carstensen, 1991). Perhaps one way we can identify whether such behavior is positive or negative is by incorporating the perspectives of the elderly in the work. Another way of better understanding such behavior is to examine its impact via other measures: For example, would elderly people negotiating with younger adults perform better or worse when sitting closer or farther away from their partners? Unfortunately, a central limitation of the existing literature is its failure to address harmful impact by either of these criteria.

Social science research on attitudes toward the elderly suggests that people hold ambivalent views of the elderly, believing that the elderly are wise as well as demented, grouchy as well as kind. The literature on behavior toward the elderly appears similar. It seems that old age encompasses both positive and negative stereotypes, and that the elderly are the recipients of differential treatment that is sometimes positive and sometimes negative. People treat the elderly with more respect, but are also more directive of a conversation with an elderly person (Tsai & Carstensen, 1991). In the community, people treat the independent behavior of the elderly with ambivalence—sometimes rewarding such behavior, sometimes discouraging it (Baltes & Wahl, 1992). This ambivalence makes it difficult to characterize ageist behavior.

Not only is age-differentiated behavior frequently ambivalent, but the problem of interpreting such behavior is exacerbated by the fact that aging is associated with genuine changes that may require accommodation by social partners. Unlike race and gender, aging is associated with some predictable deficits, most notably losses in sensory perception and in short-term memory functioning (Zarit & Zarit, 1987). Consider the following scenario: An elderly adult woman, in good health but with some hearing loss, is instructed to get acquainted with a young adult woman. The young adult, when talking to peers, tends to speak quite rapidly. However, as the young adult begins a conversation with the elderly adult, the young speaker slows her speech dramatically. Why? Is she ageist? Or is she accommodating to the needs of the listener? Perhaps the elderly listener was initially having difficulty hearing the young woman, and gave subtle cues to this effect. In fact, it could be argued that *failing* to respond to an elderly person's need for accommodation constitutes ageism.

Not all elderly adults have hearing deficits, of course. We expect that actual age-related changes do not account for all, or even most, of the age-differentiated treatment that we have documented. Rather, age-differentiated treatment is likely to stem from an overgeneralization of the homogeneity and magnitude of real age-related changes. Many elderly adults (about 28%) experience significant hearing loss (Zarit & Zarit, 1987), but not all elderly people have hearing difficulties. The young adult who overgeneralizes assumes *a priori* that all elderly adults, including her present social partner, are hard of hearing. The young adult may further assume that the magnitude of the hearing loss (often reasonably small) is large, requiring overaccommodation through shouting—a strategy that is ineffective even when the social partner does have hearing loss! We would argue that that scenario is clearly ageist.

There is substantial evidence for ageist behavior in medical and institutional settings. The treatment of elderly nursing home residents and of elderly patients is likely to produce poorer outcomes along multiple measures, ranging from satisfaction with the institution to physical health. In the community, the picture is less clear, but our intuition is that many of the age-differentiated behaviors we have reported do hold negative consequences for elderly persons, even when they appear to be superficially positive. Being held at a distance from others, even through excessive politeness—particularly at a time of life when emotional exchange may be placed at a premium (Carstensen, 1993)—may result in significant costs, despite the best intentions. These costs have not been documented in the current literature.

Further research on ageism is vitally important. We will all eventually become old, and we will also be the recipients of differential treatment based on our age. Whether we label this treatment "ageist" or "age-differentiated," it is crucial to understand its impact and potential for harm. As long as we treat the problem of ageism as "someone else's," we are guilty of making the elderly into "them" rather than "us." Such a dichotomy is false, and can only make our own aging an unneccessarily fearsome and arduous process. Speaking particularly of women, Barbara MacDonald (1991) notes the irony of our attitudes toward the elderly:

> We are the women we once saw as boring. We are the women we didn't want to look at. We are the women we expected should sit on the sidelines always loving and admiring us. And we are the women we were once told we must have "respect" for, this admonition to prevent our taunting, our jeers, our ignoring—to prevent our showing contempt for old women. (p. 58)

POLICY IMPLICATIONS OF AGEISM

Again, in everyday life, there is substantial evidence of ageism at the level of institutions. Some institutional policies and some behaviors toward the elderly are clearly ageist (i.e., they are based on chronological age rather than an individual's abilities, stem from hostile and negative feelings, and constrain the desired opportunities of elders). Most of these policies and behaviors occur in the workplace and in medical settings, and in these cases we strongly advocate policy reform. Ageist behavior in less formal settings, however, is more ambiguous; therefore, recommendations for reform are more difficult to suggest. We believe that in general, ageism exists because of gross misconceptions about the elderly—overgeneralizations of age-related changes and overestimations of their magnitude. Therefore, to combat ageism more broadly, we advocate policies intended to prevent ageism via education.

Work Settings

In work settings, ageist policies such as mandatory retirement laws abound. Mandatory retirement laws are based on the misconceptions that age is a good predictor of competence, and that competence invariably decreases in later life. In fact, age is a poor predictor of competence in most areas, including the workplace. Moreover, some people believe that without mandatory retirement laws, employees over 65 will continue to work past their capabilities. In fact, this may not be cause for concern. Even without mandatory laws, adults usually retire. For example, at the University of Wisconsin–Madison, there has not been a mandatory retirement age for 10 years; however, the average age of retirement has remained unchanged (Goodman, 1994). Of course, there are a number of possible explanations for the lack of change. Despite the dissolution of mandatory retirement laws, subtle pressures to retire at certain ages may still exist. Similarly, retirement at a certain age may be such a strong social norm that individuals voluntarily retire at the appropriate age. However, it is also possible that elders are deciding for themselves when to retire. Given the importance of self-efficacy for health and the fact that there is great variability in terms of when elders need to retire, we believe that it is important for elders themselves to make this choice. To combat the ageist policy of mandatory retirement, we recommend that competence assessed on the basis of actual job performance, rather than age, be the basis of retirement decisions.

Medical Settings

In medical settings, elderly people are frequently treated in ageist ways— sometimes as a matter of policy and sometimes not. For example, cancer-screening programs often ignore adults over 65, despite the increased cancer risk of those in this group (Derby, 1991). Furthermore, the withdrawal of food and hydration from terminally ill patients is sometimes based upon age (Uddo, 1986). Finally, physicians may "slow-code" elderly patients, resulting in treatment that is given too slowly or in dosages that are too low to be effective (Uddo, 1986). Such practices are based on the idea that elders' lives are not worth saving, since they are on the brink of death in any case. To combat such ageist beliefs, we recommend that clinical work with elders and education about treatment issues of the elderly be incorporated into standard medical training. In addition, students must be informed of the potential for and consequences of treating elderly patients differently from young patients.

Informal Settings

Ageism also exists in less formal settings, although it is much harder to demonstrate. Age-differentiated behaviors such as secondary babytalk and dependency-supporting behaviors may have a harmful impact by reducing an elderly person's sense of self-efficacy. However, in some cases they may be desired by elderly people. Because the impact of these behaviors is ambiguous, targeting such behavior with legislation is premature. Furthermore, policies that legislate the interpersonal behavior of citizens may be at odds with principles of freedom and personal privacy. Therefore, as suggested earlier, we argue for an educational policy that exposes children to people of all ages in positive ways. For example, having elderly tutors in the classroom (Cartensen, Mason, & Caldwell, 1982), and including elderly characters in teaching materials, might serve to improve intergenerational interaction by simply altering the notion that the elderly are different from most others.

Multiple Jeopardy

In addition to policies such as mandatory retirement, which are clearly ageist, there are policies that contribute to multiple jeopardy for elderly women and ethnic minority elderly. Women are less likely to receive retirement benefits, and their received benefits are generally lower than men's. Because of discriminatory Social Security laws (Carstensen & Pasupathi, 1993), the different career patterns of men and women result in lower benefits for women (Patterson, 1994). Of course, existing gender inequalities in pay for equal work also contribute to later-life disadvantage for women. Elderly people from other disadvantaged groups, who worked in lower-status jobs with no pension benefits, are similarly at high risk for poverty in late life. Clearly, policies that are generally ageist require consideration. But policies that exert disproportionate negative effects on certain groups of elderly people should also be revised.

A Final Caution

We have distinguished among work, medical, and informal settings, believing that in work and medical settings ageist policies should be reformed, whereas in informal settings more discretion should be used. We assume this stance for two reasons: (1) Ageism may be more ambiguous in informal settings than in work and medical contexts; and (2) policies that attempt to regulate the behavior of people in informal settings imply that the elderly cannot deal with unpleasant people as well as young people can—that is, that the elderly cannot adequately select social partners who do not discriminate against them. The evidence from studies of social partner choice among the elderly suggest that, if anything, the opposite is true (Cartensen, 1993). The elderly appear quite capable of handling their social worlds to their own satisfaction. In work and medical contexts, however, the elderly are comprised in their abilities both to choose their social environments, and to interact selectively with staff members. Because the elderly in work and medical settings have already lost some freedom of choice about their interpersonal experiences, they are most in need of protection against ageism.

But regardless of the setting, we must not forget that aging is a human process, and consequently that ageism is a human problem affecting us all. Combating ageism hurts no one, and helps everyone.

ACKNOWLEDGMENTS

We would like to acknowledge Margret Baltes, Traci Mann, and Alexandra Freund for helpful comments on earlier versions of this chapter. The writing of this chapter was supported in part by a National Science Foundation predoctoral fellowship to the first author, and grant AG08816 from the National Institute on Aging.

REFERENCES

Ajzen, I., & Fishbein, M. (1977). Attitude–behavior relations: A theoretical analysis and review of empirical research. *Psychological Bulletin, 84,* 888–918.

American Association of Homes for the Aging. (1991). *Fact sheet on nursing homes.*Washington, DC: Author.

Baltes, M. M., Burgess, R., & Stewart, R. (1980). Independence and dependence in self-care behaviors in nursing home residents: An operant-observational study. *International Journal of Behavioral Development, 3,* 489–500.

Baltes, M. M., & Reisenzein, R. (1986). The social world in long-term care institutions: Psychosocial control towards dependency? In M. Baltes & P. Baltes (Eds.), *The psychology of control and aging* (pp. 315–343). Hillsdale, NJ: Erlbaum.

Baltes, M. M., & Wahl, H. (1992). The dependency–support script in institutions: Generalization to community settings. *Psychology and Aging, 7,* 409–418.

Bandura, A. (1986). *Social foundations of thought and action.* Englewood Cliffs, NJ: Prentice-Hall.

Bandura, A. (1989). Regulation of cognitive processes through perceived self-efficacy. *Developmental Psychology, 25,* 729–735.

Brewer, M. B., Dull, V., & Lui, L. (1981). Perceptions of the elderly: Stereotypes as prototypes. *Journal of Personality and Social Psychology, 41,* 656–670.

Brewer, M. B., & Lui, L. N. (1989). The primacy of age and sex in the structure of person categories. *Social Cognition, 7,* 262–274.

Caporeal, L. R. (1981). The paralanguage of caregiving: Baby talk to the institutionalized aged. *Journal of Personality and Social Psychology, 40,* 876–884.

Caporeal, L. R., & Culbertson, G. (1983). Verbal response modes of baby talk and other speech at institutions for the aged. *Language and Communication, 6,* 99–112.

Caporael, L. R., Lukaszewski, M., & Culbertson, G. (1983). Secondary baby talk: Judgments by institiutionalized elderly and their caregivers. *Journal of Personality and Social Psychology, 44,* 746–754.

Carstensen, L. L. (1988). The emerging field of behavioral gerontology. *Behavior Therapy, 19,* 259–281.

Carstensen, L. L. (1993). Motivation for social contact across the life span: A theory of socio-emotional selectivity. In *Nebraska symposium on motivation: Developmental perspectives on motivation* (Vol. 40, pp. 209–254). Lincoln: University of Nebraska Press.

Carstensen, L. L., & Freund, A. (1994). The resilience of the aging self. *Developmental Review, 14,* 81–92.

Cartensen, L. L., Mason, S., & Caldwell, E. C. (1982). Children's attitudes toward the elderly: An intergenerational technique for change. *Educational Gerontology, 8,* 291–301.

Carstensen, L. L., & Pasupathi, M. (1993). Women of a certain age. In S. Matteo (Ed.), *American women in the nineties: Today's critical issues* (pp. 66–78). Boston: Northeastern University Press.

Chang, B., Chang, A., & Shen, Y. (1984). Attitudes toward aging in the United States and Taiwan. *Journal of Comparative Family Studies, 15,* 109–130.

Cheung, M. (1989). Elderly Chinese living in the United States: Assimilation or adjustment. *Social Work, 34,* 457–461.

Coupland, N., Coupland, J., Giles, H., Henwood, K., & Wiemann, J. (1988). Elderly self-disclosure: Interactional and intergroup issues. *Language and Communication, 8,* 109–133.

Crockett, W. H., & Hummert, M. L. (1987). Perceptions of aging and the elderly. In K. W. Schaie (Ed.), *Annual review of gerontology and geriatrics* (pp. 217–241). New York: Springer.

Dannefer, D., & Perlmutter, M. (1990). Development as a multidimensional process: Individual and social constraints. *Human Development, 33,* 108–137.

Deaux, K. (1984). From individual differences to social categories. *American Psychologist, 39,* 105–116.

DePaulo, B. M., & Coleman, L. M. (1986). Talking to children, foreigners, and retarded adults. *Journal of Personality and Social Psychology, 51,* 945–959.

Derby, S. E. (1991). Ageism in cancer care of the elderly. *Oncology Nursing Forum, 18,* 921–926.

Fernald, A., & Mazzie, C. (1991). Prosody and focus in speech to infants and adults. *Developmental Psychology, 27,* 209–221.

Gatz, M., & Pearson, C. (1988). Ageism revised and the provision of psychological services. *American Psychologist, 43,* 184–188.

Goodman, B. (1994). With end of mandatory retirement, U.S. schools face new challenges. *The Scientist, 8*(8), 1.

Greene, M., Adelman, R., Charon, R., & Friedmann, E. (1989). Concordance between physicians and their older and younger patients in the primary care medical encounter. *The Gerontologist, 29,* 808–813.

Greene, M., Adelman, R., Charon, R., & Hoffman, S. (1986). Ageism in the medical encounter: An exploratory study of the doctor–elderly patient relationship. *Language and Communication, 6,* 113–124.

Heckhausen, J., Dixon, R. A., & Baltes, P. B. (1989). Gains and losses in development throughout adulthood as perceived by different adult age groups. *Developmental Psychology, 25,* 109–121.

Hummert, M. L. (1990). Multiple stereotypes of elderly and young adults: A comparison of structure and evaluations. *Psychology and Aging, 5,* 182–193.

Isaacs, L. W., & Bearison, D. J. (1986). The development of children's prejudice against the aged. *International Journal of Aging and Human Development, 23,* 175–194.

Jorm, A. F. (1987). *A guide to the understanding of Alzheimer's disease and related disorders.* New York: New York University Press.

Kane, R. L., & Kane, R. A. (1990). Health care for older people: Organizational and policy issues. In R. H. Binstock & L. K. George (Eds.), *Handbook of aging and the social sciences* (pp. 415–437). San Diego, CA: Academic Press.

Kite, M. E., Deaux, K., & Miele, M. (1991). Stereotypes of young and old: Does age outweigh gender? *Psychology and Aging, 6,* 19–27.

Kite, M. E., & Johnson, B. T. (1988). Attitudes towards older and younger adults: A meta-analysis. *Psychology and Aging, 3,* 233–244.

Krauss, R. M., Garlock, C. M., Bricker, P. D., & McMahon, L. E. (1977). The role of audible and visible back-channel responses in interpersonal communication. *Journal of Personality and Social Psychology, 35,* 523–529.

Lee, J. (1986). Asian-American elderly: A neglected minority group. *Ethnicity and Gerontological Social Work, 4,* 103–116.

Levy, B., & Langer, E. (1994). Aging free from negative stereotypes: Successful memory in China and among the American deaf. *Journal of Personality and Social Psychology, 66,* 989–997.

Looft, W. R. (1971). Children's judgments of age. *Child Development, 42,* 1232–1284.

Lorge, I., Tuckman, J., & Abrams, A. (1954). *Attitudes of junior and senior high school students toward aging.* New York: Special Report of the New York State Joint Legislative Committee on the Problems of Aging.

MacDonald, B. (1991, July–August). Politics of aging: I'm not your mother. *Ms.*, pp. 56–58.

Mann, T. (1994). Informed consent for psychological research. *Psychological Science, 5*, 140–143.

Montepare, J., Steinberg, J., & Rosenberg, B. (1992). Characteristics of vocal communication between young adults and their parents and grandparents. *Communication Research, 19*, 479–492.

Myers, G. C. (1990). Demography of aging. In R. H. Binstock & L. K. George (Eds.), *Handbook of aging and the social sciences* (3rd ed., pp. 19–44). San Diego, CA: Academic Press.

National Academy on Aging. (1994). *Old age in the 21st century: A report to the Assistant Secretary for Aging, U.S. Department of Health and Human Services.* Syracuse, NY: Syracuse University.

Patterson, M. (1994, June 13). A woman's special dilemma. *U.S. News and World Report,* p. 93.

Perdue, C., & Gurtman, M. (1990). Evidence for the automaticity of ageism. *Journal of Experimental Social Psychology, 26*, 199–216.

Rodin, J. (1986). Aging and health: Effects of the sense of control. *Science, 233*, 1271–1276.

Rubin, K. H., & Brown, I. (1975). A life-span look at person perception and its relationship to communicative interaction. *Journal of Gerontology, 30*, 461–468.

Ryan, E. B., Giles, H., Bartolucci, G., & Henwood, K. (1986). Psycholinguistic and social psychological components of communication by and with the elderly. *Language and Communication, 6*, 1–24.

Schaie, W. K. (1993). Ageist language in psychological research. *American Psychologist, 48*, 49–51.

Siminoff, L. A. (1989). Cancer patient and physician communication: Progress and continuing problems. *Annals of Behavioral Medicine, 11*, 108–111.

Tsai, J. L., & Carstensen, L. L. (1991). *Social interaction with the elderly: A comparison of Chinese-American and Caucasian students.* Unpublished honors thesis, Stanford University.

Tuckman, J., & Lorge, I. (1952). The effects of institutionalization on attitudes toward old people. *Journal of Abnormal and Social Psychology, 47*, 337–344.

Tuckman, J., & Lorge, I. (1958). Attitudes toward aging of individuals with experience with the aged. *Journal of Genetic Psychology, 92*, 199–215.

Uddo, B. J. (1986). The withdrawal or refusal of food and hydration as age discrimination: Some possibilities. *Issues in Law and Medicine, 2*, 39–59.

Whitborne, S. (1987). Personality development in adulthood and old age: Relationships among identity style, health, and well-being. In K. Schaie & C. Eisdorfer (Eds.), *Annual review of gerontology and geriatrics* (pp. 189–216). New York: Springer Publishing

Zarit, J. M., & Zarit, S. H. (1987). Molar aging: The physiology and psychology of normal aging. In L. L. Carstensen & B. A. Edelstein (Eds.), *Handbook of clinical gerontology* (pp. 18–32). Elmsford, NY: Pergamon Press.

7

Multiple Variables in Discrimination

HOPE LANDRINE
ELIZABETH A. KLONOFF
ROXANNA ALCARAZ
JUDYTH SCOTT
PHYLLIS WILKINS

*I*n recent years, several multidimensional approaches to social stratification have emerged (e.g., Jeffries & Ransford, 1980). These models
recognize that U.S. society is stratified not only along the dimension
of social class, but also along several additional dimensions such as
age, gender, race/ethnicity, and other factors. Theoretically, stratification
along each of these dimensions is similar, because each is characterized by
these six features:

1. The ruling group (e.g., men, Whites, the upper class) possesses
greater power, privilege, and prestige than the subordinate (disadvantaged) group (e.g., women, racial/ethnic minorities, the poor).
2. The ruling group attempts to maintain its privileged status at the
expense of the subordinate group through a variety of means (e.g., self-
serving legislation and discrimination at the various levels detailed by Lott,
Chapter 2, this volume).

3. Those occupying similar positions share common experiences related to their status (Landrine, 1992a).

4. There is a supporting ideology (set of beliefs, norms, and values) that renders the unequal distribution of power, privilege, and prestige along that dimension legitimate and acceptable (Landrine, 1992a).

5. Prejudiced attitudes against and negative stereotypes of the subordinate group can be demonstrated to exist (Jeffries & Ransford, 1980).

6. There is the potential for status consciousness to emerge among the members of subordinate groups, and, with it, political action to improve the group's status (e.g., Ellemers, Wilke, & van Knippenberg, 1993; Lalonde & Silverman, 1994; Taylor, Moghaddam, Gamble, & Zellerer, 1987; Wright, Taylor, & Moghaddam, 1990).

From this multidimensional perspective, women, ethnic/cultural minorities, the poor, and children and the elderly occupy subordinate (low-status) positions, while men, Whites, the upper class, and those in the middle of the age continuum occupy ruling (high-status) positions. Members of each of the subordinate groups experience interpersonal discrimination based on their specific status (e.g., gender or race), and the previous chapters in this volume have demonstrated that this is indeed the case.

Although multidimensional theories have addressed social stratification and discrimination along each dimension separately, the question of the relationships among these status dimensions has received little theoretical attention (Gordon's [1964] theory of the "ethclass" is a notable exception). If age, gender, race/ethnicity, and social class are each related individually to power, privilege, prestige, and discrimination, then the effect of two or more of these dimensions must entail compounded deprivations ("multiple jeopardy") or advantages ("multiple advantage"). If men enjoy power, privilege, and prestige because of their gender, and Whites enjoy these because of their race, then do White men enjoy more power, privilege, and prestige than all other multiple-hierarchy groups (multiple advantage), and are White men least likely to be discriminated against in institutional and face-to-face interactions? If African-Americans face discrimination by race and women face discrimination by gender, then do African-American women face even more discrimination (multiple jeopardy)? If gays face discrimination because of their sexual orientation and women because of their gender, then do lesbians face more discrimination (multiple jeopardy) than gay men?

In this chapter we offer preliminary answers to such questions with respect to interpersonal discrimination (i.e., discrimination in face-to-face interactions). We present and examine the evidence for and against Ransford's (1980) "multiple jeopardy–advantage" (MJA) hypothesis, which argues the following: In multidimensional stratification systems, one's many status positions along a variety of status dimensions combine to create a "unique social space" (Ransford, 1980, p. 277) representing their intersection; these spaces are characterized by outcomes that cannot be accounted for by one status position alone, but can be explained by their intersection (i.e., by multiple advantage or multiple jeopardy in interpersonal discrimination).

First, we describe and clarify Ransford's (1980) MJA hypothesis, and present some national data on U.S. salaries as a preliminary, exploratory test of the hypothesis. We ask: Does the distribution of salaries by ethnicity × gender and by age × gender in the United States support the MJA hypothesis? Next, we review empirical investigations of discrimination in the social-psychological literature of 1980–1992 and ask: Do existing empirical investigations of interpersonal discrimination provide data relevant to the MJA hypothesis, and, if so, do those data support it? Finally, we present a preliminary empirical investigation that we conducted for this chapter as a partial test of the MJA hypothesis.

THE MULTIPLE JEOPARDY–ADVANTAGE HYPOTHESIS

MJA "refers only to a situation of extremes in a number of disadvantages (or advantages)" (Ransford, 1980, p. 279). For example, if we were to examine the intersection of the three status dimensions of race, gender, and social class, the MJA hypothesis

> would focus only on status combinations that result in disadvantaged positions on all three hierarchies (such as poor, black and female or low–low–low positions). [Likewise] the concept of multiple advantage is applied only to status combinations of combined advantage (e.g., upper-class white male or high–high–high positions). Multiple jeopardy does not apply to the mixed types of status combinations. When people face mixed status situations that place them high in one hierarchy [and] low in [another] (such as upper class black male) they do not encounter multiple jeopardy or advantage [but instead face "status inconsistency"]. (Ransford, 1980, p. 280)

Thus, to examine multiple jeopardy by gender and ethnicity, we would seek to ascertain whether women of color (low–low) face more discrimination than all other groups (men of color, White men, and White women). Likewise, to examine multiple advantage, we would seek to ascertain whether White men (high–high) have more advantages than all other groups. In both cases, data on the extremes test the hypothesis, whereas data on the mixed-status groups (White women and men of color, both high–low) do not. The MJA hypothesis predicts that (1) people who occupy a subordinate (low-status) position in more than one hierarchy will be found to be doubly disadvantaged, while (2) those who occupy a ruling (high-status) position in more than one hierarchy will be found to be doubly advantaged.

Additive versus Interactive MJA

Ransford (1980) suggested that multiple jeopardy can take two forms, which he termed "additive" and "interactive." In both cases, a low position along two or more status dimensions yields unique disadvantaged outcomes, but the pattern of disadvantage can vary considerably, depending upon the independent as well as the interactive effects of the status dimensions. Specifically, when an individual occupies a low-status position on two or more status dimensions, one or more dimension may exert an independent influence (or main effect, so to speak); others may exert no independent influence (no main effect where that specific outcome is concerned); and there is an interaction effect, which is synonymous with multiple jeopardy. The scenario in which some or all low-status positions have no main effects but contribute to two-, three-, and n-way interactions can be called "MJA, additive type" (Ransford, 1980). Alternatively, in some cases, all low-status positions entail disadvantages (each dimension has a main effect) and there is an interaction, which again is synonymous with multiple jeopardy. This scenario can be called "MJA, interactive type" (Ransford, 1980). Table 7.1 summarizes these possibilities and distinctions

TABLE 7.1. Interactive versus Additive MJA:
An Example Using Gender and Ethnicity

Additive MJA with two dimensions		
Possibility 1	Possibility 2	Possibility 3
Gender (G) = Significant	Gender (G) = Not significant	Gender (G) = Not significant
Ethnicity (E) = Not significant	Ethnicity (E) = Significant	Ethnicity (E) = Not significant
G × E = Significant	G × E = Significant	G × E = Significant

Interactive MJA with two dimensions
Gender (G) = Significant
Ethnicity (E) = Significant
G × E = Significant

for a hypothetical two-variable case involving gender and ethnicity. As indicated in Table 7.1, interactive MJA can take only one form, in that there must be main effects for every dimension (along with any number of interactions); by contrast, additive MJA can take several forms (i.e., some or no main effects may be present), and these increase in complexity as the number of status dimensions under consideration increases.

The distinction between the additive and interactive types of MJA is crucial to a full examination of the hypothesis for the following reasons. First, multiple jeopardy or advantage can be conceptualized as a statistical interaction effect—that is, a "unique space" or "unique outcome" that cannot be explained or predicted from knowledge of the main effects for status dimensions alone. Thus, multiple jeopardy or advantage can exist in the absence of main effects for some or all status dimensions; one need not demonstrate discrimination (main effects) along every or any dimension for multiple jeopardy to exist. For example, an academic department may demonstrate that there are no main effects for ethnicity or gender in tenure decisions: The percentage of minorities who are tenured equals the percentage of Whites who are tenured, and the percentage of women who are tenured equals the percentage of men. Yet there is a significant interaction effect in which women of color are least likely to be tenured (multiple jeopardy), with all other groups having equal probability of tenure. Let us imagine that the department contains just one (untenured) woman of color, many White women and men, and several men of color. If the untenured woman of color claims discrimination, the department is likely to counter that there is none because both minorities (men) and women (Whites) have been tenured. Such an argument rests on the erroneous assumption that for multiple jeopardy to exist, the main effects also must exist; this view equates multiple jeopardy with the interactive type and neglects the additive type. In addition, this view examines persons of mixed status (men of color, White women), who not only shed no light on MJA, but also shed little light on main effects.

Thus, in our examination of the social-psychological literature and of the videotape data from our research, we focus on statistical interaction effects as evidence of MJA whether main effects are present or not. The presence of such statistical interactions (interactive or additive types) supports the MJA hypothesis, whereas their absence does not.

Which Is "Worse," Interactive or Additive Multiple Jeopardy?

The question of which type of multiple jeopardy yields the greatest disadvantage has received little theoretical attention, and has not been empirically tested. Although some (e.g., Reid, 1988) have asserted that multiple jeopardy is necessarily interactive rather than additive, there appears to be little evidence or deductive argument to support that view. Conceptualizing this issue in terms of analysis of variance (ANOVA) may shed light on the answer.

As we have argued, MJA can be conceptualized as a statistical interaction effect. In interactive MJA this interaction occurs in the presence of main effects for all status dimensions, whereas in additive MJA this interaction occurs in the absence of main effects for one or more status dimensions. Some *a priori* statements can be made about the probability of ANOVA interactions in the presence versus absence of main effects. First, when significant main effects are present, first-order (two-variable) and particularly higher-order (three-, four-, and five-variable) interactions are more likely than not to be absent (Kerlinger, 1973, pp. 242–257). This is because so much of the variance is accounted for by the main effects that there is little remaining to be accounted for by interaction effects. Certainly, first-order interactions do occur (and sometimes are the outcomes of importance) in the presence of main effects, and higher-order interactions (although somewhat rare) also have been found. On the whole, however, the probability of finding a significant interaction effect decreases with the magnitude of effect size of the main effects; we therefore can predict that large main effects are likely to mean no interaction effect. Alternatively, when no main effects (or only one out of several main effects) are found, the presence and size of interactions cannot be predicted (Kerlinger, 1973).

These statistical factors suggest that interactive MJA is less likely to occur simply because it is a significant interaction effect found in the presence of significant main effects for *all* status dimensions. As the number of status dimensions increases (i.e., the number of significant main effects), the chances of significant higher-order interactions decreases. Thus, a Mexican-American lesbian, for example, may be discriminated against because of her ethnicity, because of her gender, *and* because of her sexual orientation (three main effects). The chances that she faces *unique* discrimination for being a Mexican-American lesbian, however (ethnicity × gender × sexual orientation interaction), are low. Although being discriminated against for three different reasons may be *experienced* by the Latina and perceived by others as an interaction effect, a higher-order interaction (a unique outcome *not* accounted for by the three main effects) nonetheless may be absent. Alternatively, additive MJA may be common simply because the interaction effects are not limited by main effects that consume a large proportion of the variance. If such interaction effects are present, they have the *potential* to be quite large. In light of this, we offer these counterintuitive hypotheses:

1. Additive multiple jeopardy is more common than interactive multiple jeopardy.
2. Additive multiple jeopardy entails greater disadvantaged outcomes

(is "worse") than the interactive type, in the sense that the magnitude of effect size of the interaction effect (if present) can be very large when main effects are absent.

3. Additive multiple jeopardy is also likely to be *experienced* as "worse" than the interactive type, for these two reasons: (a) Social support and the potential for group political action are necessarily absent, and (b) internal (victim-blaming) causal attributions are likely. Returning to our prior example of additive multiple jeopardy (i.e., a sole, untenured woman of color in a university department) may clarify this latter point.

In our prior example, there are no main effects for ethnicity or gender in tenure decisions in a university department composed of White women and men, several men of color, and one woman of color, but there is a significant ethnicity × gender interaction in which the sole woman of color is not tenured. In this situation, neither the men of color nor the White women are likely to believe that the woman of color has been discriminated against in the absence of main effects. Thus, the woman of color is unlikely to receive social support from either group; neither the White women nor the minority men are likely to join her in political action of any type; and her colleagues are likely to attribute the denial of tenure to something in or about ("wrong with") her rather than to external factors, because of the absence of main effects. Alternatively, if main effects for both ethnicity and gender are present (interactive MJA) such that men of color, White women, and the woman of color all have a low probability of tenure, social support from and political action with both groups should be available, and external causal attributions should be likely. Thus, disadvantaged outcomes may be statistically and phenomenologically greater in the additive than in the interactive scenario.

Finally, we suspect that the type of MJA discrimination effect (additive versus interactive) is likely to vary considerably with (1) the number of status dimensions under consideration, and (2) the type of behavior/outcome under investigation. These two factors may severely limit the hypotheses presented above. For example, the probability of interactive multiple jeopardy should decrease with increases in the number of status dimensions under investigation; the more independent variables (status dimensions) present, the higher the chances that at least one of these will have no significant main effect. Likewise, one type of MJA discrimination effect may occur in initial salary decisions or in treatment options offered to patients, whereas another type may operate in judgments of competence or in decisions to offer help. Indeed, it is reasonable to expect that the type of MJA discrimination effect is at least in part contingent upon the extent to which the behavior/outcome entails access to increased power (i.e., resources), because the function of discriminatory behavior is to maintain existing power relations. Thus, interactive multiple jeopardy may occur when the behavior/outcome threatens existing social relations (e.g., initial salary decisions, voting behavior), and additive multiple jeopardy may characterize discriminatory behavior in contexts/outcomes where the status quo remains relatively unaffected (e.g., decisions to help a stranger). Likewise, interactive type multiple jeopardy may be more common at the institutional level of discrimination, and the additive type at the cultural and interpersonal levels. However, because little is known about the behavioral and contextual parameters of MJA discrimination effects, these remarks are necessarily speculative.

We have presented Ransford's (1980) MJA hypothesis as it has been described in the sociological literature, and have elaborated its implications in order to clarify it. We can now turn to several types of empirical evidence to assess the extent to which the MJA hypothesis is supported by existing data.

SOME PRELIMINARY EVIDENCE FOR THE HYPOTHESIS: SALARIES

Before turning to an examination of the MJA hypothesis at the face-to-face level of discrimination, let us discuss it briefly at the institutional level. Specifically, we examined national data on the distribution of U.S. salaries by race/ethnicity × gender × age, with the assumption that if the MJA hypothesis is an adequate model for representing the intersections of status dimensions where discrimination is concerned, then evidence supporting the hypothesis should be seen at the institutional level. These data (taken from U.S. Bureau of the Census, 1991) are presented in Tables 7.2 and 7.3.

The MJA hypothesis predicts that African-American women and Latinas (low–low) will have lower salaries than all other groups, regardless of age (multiple jeopardy), and that White men (high–high) will have higher salaries than all other groups across age (multiple advantage). As indicated in Table 7.2, there is an obvious main effect for gender at each age (sixth row from the bottom), an obvious main effect for race (fifth row from the bottom), and an obvious main effect for ethnicity (fourth row from the bottom). Likewise, these variables intersect. White men's multiple advantage seems clear (Table 7.2, third row from the bottom), in that the salaries of all other groups were lower than those of White men at each age (numbers in the cells indicate how much lower at each age): On the average, the salaries of all other groups were $16,254 lower than those of White men. Similarly, evidence for Black women's race × gender multiple jeopardy seems clear (Table 7.2, bottom row), to the extent that all other groups combined had higher salaries than Black women at each age (each cell indicates how much higher at each age): On the average, the salaries of all others were $7,593 higher than those of Black women. Likewise, Latinas'

TABLE 7.2. Mean Income in the United States in 1989 by Age, Race/Ethnicity, and Gender

	15–24	25–29	30–34	35–39	40–44	45–49	50–54	55–59	60–64	65–69	70–74	75 & up
					Actual mean incomes							
Men												
White	9,108	22,483	28,062	33,576	37,672	39,992	38,710	35,617	31,205	23,228	19,421	16,032
Black	7,419	15,864	17,420	21,285	22,665	22,865	21,792	19,133	16,011	13,165	10,295	8,127
Latino	9,024	16,337	19,249	21,833	23,227	23,509	21,470	23,694	21,309	15,389	10,566	9,686
All men	8,875	21,650	26,803	32,199	36,387	38,174	36,942	34,005	29,716	22,288	18,737	15,284
Women												
White	7,060	14,362	14,926	16,101	17,355	17,255	15,522	13,976	12,895	12,179	11,567	10,950
Black	6,151	11,611	13,932	16,003	17,972	16,541	14,909	11,803	9,648	6,932	7,102	5,761
Latina	6,506	11,664	11,724	13,284	14,194	12,329	11,327	10,085	9,407	8,060	7,208	6,539
All women	6,947	14,008	14,848	16,108	17,442	17,370	15,495	13,892	12,544	10,640	11,204	10,491
					Effects for gender and race/ethnicity							
Men–women[a]	1,928	7,642	11,955	16,091	18,945	20,804	21,447	20,113	17,172	11,648	7,533	4,793
Whites–Blacks[b]	1,299	4,685	5,818	6,194	7,195	8,920	8,765	9,328	9,220	7,655	6,795	6,547
Whites–Latinos[c]	319	4,422	6,007	18,185	8,803	10,704	10,717	7,907	6,692	5,979	6,607	5,378
Others–White men[d]	−1,876	−8,515	−12,611	−20,237	−18,589	−21,492	−21,706	−19,878	−17,351	−12,083	−10,073	−7,819
Others–Latinas[e]	1,246	4,467	6,993	4,113	9,584	11,703	11,153	10,759	8,806	6,118	4,582	3,572
Others–Black women[f]	1,672	4,531	4,344	850	5,050	6,649	6,855	8,698	8,517	7,472	4,709	4,505

Note. The data are from the U.S. Bureau of the Census (1991).
[a]Main effect for gender: All men – all women. [b]Main effect for race: (White women + White men + Black women + Black men)/4 – (Latina women + Latino men)/2. [c]Main effect for ethnicity: (White women + White men + Black women + Black men)/4 – (Latina women + Latino men)/2. [d]Multiple advantage for White men: (Black women + Black men + Latino women + Latino men)/5 – White men. [e]Multiple jeopardy for Latinas: (White women + White men + Black men + Latino men)/5 – Latinas. [f]Multiple jeopardy for Black women: (White women + White men + Latino men + Latinas)/5 – Black women.

191

ethnicity × gender multiple jeopardy is also clear, in that Latinas had low salaries when compared to all other groups combined (Table 7.2, second row from the bottom): On the average, others' salaries were $9,443 higher than those of Latinas. If we ignore age for the moment, these data support the MJA hypothesis for gender × race/ethnicity, and indicate interactive MJA discrimination effects in salaries.

In Table 7.3, the three-way interaction data are summarized. For gender × race/ethnicity × age, the MJA hypothesis would predict a three-way interaction in which younger White men should have higher salaries than all others (multiple advantage), and older Black and Latina women should have lower salaries than all others. As predicted, younger White men had the highest salary ($39,992), and older Black ($6,932) and Latina ($8,060) women had the lowest salaries. As predicted by the MJA hypothesis, the largest multiple advantage for White men (difference between their salaries and those of everyone else) is at the younger age ($20,641 difference) rather than the older age ($11,868 difference).

TABLE 7.3. MJA Three-Way Interaction in Mean 1989 Salaries

| | Actual incomes | | | |
| | 45–49 years | | 65–69 years | |
	Men	Women	Men	Women
All	38,174	17,370	22,288	10,640
White	39,992	17,255	23,228	12,179
Black	22,856	16,541	13,165	6,932
Latino	27,772	12,329	16,464	8,060
Mean by age	27,772		16,464	

| | Differences | | |
	Overall	At 45–49	At 65–69
Men–women	16,226	20,804	11,648
White–Black	8,290	8,925	6,569
White–Latino	7,007	8,573	5,441
Others–White men	-16,254	-20,641	-11,868
Others–Latinas	9,443	12,554	6,333
Others–Black women	7,593	7,499	7,687
Age		11,308	

Note. The data are from U.S. Bureau of the Census (1991).

In summary, interactive MJA is clearly present in these salary data in a manner consistent with the hypothesis. There are clear main effects for gender (a $16,226 difference between men and women), age (an $11,308 difference), race (an $8,290 difference), and ethnicity (a $7,007 difference), as well as interactions among these factors.

Two comments about these data are needed. First, national salary data in and of themselves do not necessarily indicate institutional discrimination by race/ethnicity × age × gender, because it is possible that there are significant education differences among these status groups that are reflected in subsequent salary differences. However, other data presented in the same source (U.S. Bureau of the Census, 1991) indicate that salary differences by gender × race/ethnicity hold across levels of education, supporting a conclusion of (institutional) discrimination in salaries.

Second, national salary data are reported by the U.S. Bureau of the Census without tests for statistical significance and without the standard deviations that might permit us to conduct such tests post hoc. Thus, we have no evidence that the differences presented in Tables 7.2 and 7.3 are statistically significant. We strongly suspect, however, that differences of $9,443 per year (Latinas vs. all others), $16,226 per year (all women vs. all men), and $33,060 per year (young White men vs. older Black women) would be found to be highly significant. This suspicion is supported by studies of gender × ethnicity differences in salaries in which careful statistical analyses were conducted. For example, Idson and Price (1992) analyzed the salaries of Dade County, Florida, government employees by gender and race/ethnicity (Black and Latino). Even when level of education and job category/classification were controlled for, significant salary differences by gender, ethnicity/race, and gender × ethnicity/race were found: Idson and Price (1992) found that Black women's salaries were 61.5% those of White women, Latinas' salaries were 72.8% those of White women, and White women's salaries were 74.8% those of White men. White men had the highest salaries, and Black and Latina women had the lowest. Thus, Idson and Price's (1992) data indicate that MJA discrimination effects (interactive type) describe salary data well (i.e., describe discrimination at the institutional level), and suggest that some type of MJA discrimination effect also may be found at the interpersonal level.

EMPIRICAL INVESTIGATIONS OF INTERPERSONAL DISCRIMINATION, 1980–1992

To test the MJA hypothesis at the level of face-to-face (interpersonal) discrimination, we examined empirical investigations of such discrimination that were published between 1980 and 1992 in social- and feminist-psychological journals. Journals selected were the *Journal of Personality and Social Psychology*, the *Journal of Social Psychology*, the *Personality and Social Psychology Bulletin*, and *Psychology of Women Quarterly*. The first three journals were selected as representative of research in social psychology, and the fourth as representative of research in feminist psychology, with the assumption that empirical investigations of interpersonal discrimination were most likely to be published in these journals. The purpose of this study was to find empirical investigations of interpersonal discrimination that assessed more than one status variable simultaneously, and then to examine the extent to which interaction effects supportive of the MJA hypothesis were found.

Method

Selection of Articles

An article was defined as an empirical investigation of interpersonal discrimination if it met these three criteria:

1. Data were collected on and/or from research participants.

2. The investigator sought to ascertain the effects of one or more status dimensions (gender, race, ethnicity, social class, age, or sexual orientation) on discriminatory behavior of any type (i.e., the study examined the extent to which status affected ratings of attractiveness, amount of helping, or any social behavior, with a positive finding indicating discrimination along that status dimension with respect to the behavior in question).

3. These status dimensions were present as characteristics of the participants, and/or of stimulus persons (e.g., through photos or bogus *curricula vitae*), and/or of confederates (i.e., the characteristics were concretely present).

Using criterion 3, we excluded all studies of discrimination in which low or high status was manipulated (through the use of experimental minimal groups). For example, studies of discrimination in which White college students were assigned to experimental groups that were treated justly (like Whites and men) or unjustly (like minorities and women) (e.g., Ellemers et al., 1993; Lalonde & Silverman, 1994; Taylor et al., 1987) were excluded as less than appropriate investigations of discrimination along any status dimension. Likewise, using criterion 2, we excluded all studies in which participants were required to estimate how much they and/or their status group have been discriminated against (e.g., Crosby, 1984). Similarly, all studies of ethnic, gender, or other status differences (e.g., in helping, in conversational behavior, in aggression) that yielded data on group differences but not on discrimination per se were also excluded. Thus, for example, a study of the extent to which Blacks versus Whites helped a White confederate would be excluded as a study of group differences, whereas a study of the extent to which Whites helped a Black versus a White confederate would be included as a study of interpersonal discrimination in helping based on race.

Thus, studies selected for inclusion according to these criteria tended to be experimental investigations of discrimination in which the effect of a status dimension on some behavior was measured, and status was typically a characteristic of either stimulus persons (photographs, bogus *curricula vitae*, television characters) or confederates, rather than of participants.

Procedure

All abstracts and methods sections of all articles published in the four above-named journals from 1980 to 1992 were read by one of us (the first reader), and selected to be included (or not) as a study of interpersonal discrimination according to the criteria detailed above. If the first reader was less than sure about including the article, the article was sent to another of us (the second reader) for a decision. The second reader examined the article and made a decision; this procedure erred in the direction of including rather than excluding studies. Of the more than 5,500 articles read initially, only three were sent to the second reader for a decision; all three were excluded by the second reader. Next, the second reader examined all articles that had been selected for inclusion by the first reader and reassessed the extent to which these articles met the criteria. Only two articles selected by the first reader were rejected by the second.

Results

The results of this review are presented in Table 7.4. As indicated in this table, only 271 articles on interpersonal discrimination were found out of the 5,538 articles published in these journals from 1980 to 1992. Empirical investigations of interpersonal discrimination accounted for a mere 4.89% of the published studies. Of the total articles published in these four journals during this 12-year period, 3.12% examined gender discrimination, 1.10% focused on racial/ethnic discrimination, and less than 1% focused on discrimination along some other status dimension (age discrimination, 0.14%; social class discrimination, 0.18%; discrimination based on sexual orientation, 0.29%). Studies of interpersonal discrimination that examined the effects of multiple statuses were nearly nonexistent. Of the 271 discrimination studies, only 3 examined more than one status dimension, so that only these 3 articles can shed light on the MJA hypothesis.

TABLE 7.4. Articles Published on Interpersonal Discrimination in Selected Journals, 1980–1992, by Type of Discrimination and Interaction of Status Categories

Journal	Years	Total issues	Total articles	Number of articles on discrimination based upon:						Σ	% of total
				Gender	Age	Race	Sex or.[a]	Social class	Interaction		
Psychology of Women Quarterly	1980–1992	49	433	40	0	1	0	0	0	41	9.47%
Journal of Social Psychology	1980–1992	39	1,518	37	5	20	5	5	2	74	4.78%
Journal of Personality and Social Psychology	1981–1992	144	2,679	65	2	24	4	3	0	98	3.66%
Personality and Social Psychology Bulletin	1980–1992	56	908	31	1	16	7	2	1	58	6.39%
Σ	12 years	288 issues	5,538 articles	173	8	61	16	10	3	271	4.89%

Note. Percentage of total articles (n = 5,538) on: gender discrimination, 3.12%; ethnic discrimination, 1.10%; discrimination against gays, 0.29%; social class discrimination, 0.18%; interaction of statuses, 0.05%.
[a]Sexual orientation.

196

Finally, as shown in Table 7.4, 173 of the 271 articles on interpersonal discrimination (63.84%) focused on discrimination based on gender, with other status variables receiving little attention; sexism received more attention than racism, classism, ageism, and heterosexism combined. These data suggest the following:

1. Interpersonal discrimination has received little recent empirical attention from social and feminist psychologists. Consequently, definitive conclusions about discrimination are difficult to draw. More studies of discriminatory behavior in which status is concretely present are needed.

2. Conclusions about gender discrimination (173 studies) and perhaps about race discrimination (61 studies) might be drawn in light of the wealth of studies available. However, because most studies of gender discrimination examined the behavior of Whites, and many studies of race discrimination examined the behavior of men, race and gender remain inextricably confounded. Conclusions about race discrimination from studies of men, or about gender discrimination from studies of Whites, might obscure many issues and might yield premature and erroneous generalizations.

3. Conclusions about discrimination based on age (8 studies), social class (10 studies), and sexual orientation (16 studies) must remain tentative in light of the scant empirical evidence found in this review, as well as the tendency for these studies to include Whites and/or men only as participants.

4. Only extremely tentative conclusions can be drawn about discrimination based on the intersections of status categories from the mere three empirical investigations uncovered in this review. We can at best examine these studies to ascertain (a) whether interaction effects appeared, and (b) whether those effects were in the direction predicted by the MJA hypothesis.

THREE STUDIES OF THE INTERSECTION OF STATUS CATEGORIES

Study 1: Shutter (1982)

In a study of interpersonal interaction in intra- and interracial dyads, Shutter (1982) examined initial conversations among (an equal number of) Black and White women and men who were assigned to dyads of the same or different gender, race, and gender × race. Each dyad was placed together in a waiting room, where the partners' behavior was unobtrusively observed. Dependent variables included asking the other person personal questions, asking the other person other types of questions, the amount of time the partner was spoken to, and the total number of questions of any type asked.

Shutter found no main effects for gender or for race, but he did find several significant, complex race × gender interactions: How Blacks and Whites behaved was contingent upon their own gender and race, as well as on the gender and race of the partner. For example, among the many interaction effects found were these:

1. Blacks asked women more questions than men, while Whites asked men more questions than women.
2. Women asked Black women the most questions, while men asked Black men the most questions.
3. Whites talked longer to men than to women, whereas Blacks talked longer to women than to men.
4. Women asked more questions of same-race partners, but men asked more questions of other-race partners.
5. When Blacks interacted with Blacks, the other gender was asked more questions than the same gender.
6. When Blacks interacted with Whites, Black men asked both genders an equal number of questions, whereas Black women asked questions only of White women, and did not ask White men *any* questions.

If we define "discrimination" in this study as ignoring/avoiding (not talking to or barely talking to) a person with whom one is sitting in a small waiting room, then these data suggest that Black women and men discriminated against men, whereas White women and men discriminated against women. No main effects were found, and the many complex interaction effects were not in the direction predicted by the MJA hypothesis because Blacks and Whites tended to discriminate in opposite directions, as did women and men. However, the MJA hypothesis focuses on the discriminatory behavior of Whites (or perhaps of White men), and predicts that they will afford White men double advantages and Black women double disadvantages. The hypothesis does not mention the behavior of minorities. Thus, to evaluate the extent to which this study supports the MJA hypothesis, only the behavior of White women and men toward Black versus White women and men should be examined. Unfortunately, the data were not presented in a manner that would permit such an analysis.

Thus, we can conclude two things from Shutter's study: (1) Evidence for additive MJA was found in this study, in that there were no main effects but several interaction effects for each dependent variable; and (2) the extent to which the specifics of the data demonstrate both multiple jeopardy and multiple advantage cannot be ascertained, because the data (however interesting) were not presented in a manner that would permit such an analysis.

Study 2: Yarkin, Town, and Wallston (1982)

The second study investigated causal attributions for success made by White women and men about the performance of a White versus Black × man versus woman stimulus person. In a between-subjects design, each participant read one description of a highly successful banking officer who was requesting a promotion. The gender of the stimulus person was varied by first name, and race was varied by undergraduate school (Howard vs. American University) and community service (NAACP vs. Chamber of Commerce). On scales ranging from 0 ("not at all important") to 9 ("extremely important"), participants rated the extent to which ability, motivation, task difficulty, and luck played a role in the stimulus person's success. Analyses indicated that the gender of participants did not contribute to the results, and thus the data from women and men were combined for all other analyses.

A main effect for the gender of the stimulus person was found for attributions of ability, motivation, and luck: When the stimulus was presented as a woman (regardless of race), her success was attributed more to luck and motivation than to ability. Likewise, a main effect for the race of the stimulus person was found on ability and motivation: When the stimulus was presented as Black (regardless of gender), participants attributed success more to motivation than to ability. Finally, a significant gender × race interaction effect emerged for ability, motivation, and luck. Post hoc comparisons revealed that White men's success was attributed more to ability and less to luck and motivation than was the case for the remaining three groups, none of which differed significantly from one another.

If we define "discrimination" in this study as attributing a stimulus person's success to factors other than ability, both race and gender discrimination (main effects) were found. Interaction effects revealed multiple advantage for White men (i.e., White men had the highest attributions to ability), but no multiple jeopardy for Black women (i.e., Black women did not have the lowest attributions to ability or the highest to other factors). In summary, Yarkin et al. (1982) tested the MJA hypothesis explicitly, and found multiple advantage of the interactive type, but no multiple jeopardy. These data thus provide partial support for the MJA hypothesis.

Study 3: Mathnes, Brennan, Haugen, and Rice (1985)

In the third study, White women and men from eight age groups (ranging from 10 to 70 and above) rated the physical attractiveness of models (photographs) who differed by gender and age. A multivariate analysis of variance (MANOVA) revealed main effects for the gender and for the age of the model, as well as a significant age × gender interaction. The follow-up ANOVA data on the main effects and the interaction were presented only in graphs that could not be interpreted (with no means, standard deviations, or post hoc comparisons). The nature and direction of the main effects and interaction were unclear. In light of these ambiguities, we exclude this paper from our conclusions.

Again, these were the *only* studies (out of 271 articles on interpersonal discrimination published in selected journals from 1980 to 1992) that investigated discrimination along more than one status dimension. Our review found no studies involving intersections of sexual orientation or social class with status variables such as gender or race/ethnicity. Although such studies might have been uncovered if we had included other journals in our literature search (and, as indicated in Chapter 3, a few other studies do exist), the absence of such studies in this representative sample of journals speaks to the general tendency of the discipline to ignore intersections among status variables.

SUMMARY OF FINDINGS THUS FAR

Thus far we have found the following with respect to the MJA hypothesis:

1. There is convincing evidence for interactive MJA discrimination effects in salaries (institutional level of discrimination).
2. At the interpersonal (face-to-face) level of discrimination, there is some evidence of possible additive MJA discrimination effects in conversational behavior.
3. There is some evidence for possible interactive multiple-advantage (but not multiple-jeopardy) discrimination effects in causal attributions for success.

These findings are consistent with our hypothesis that interactive discrimination effects may occur for behaviors with implications for power (e.g., salaries, attributions for success), and that additive MJA effects may occur for behaviors largely unrelated to access to rewards and resources (e.g., conversational behavior). These few studies, however, are less than adequate tests of the hypothesis; consequently, no definitive conclusions can be drawn from them. Thus, we conducted a simple pilot study with the hope of shedding some light on the empirical viability of the MJA hypothesis.

INTERACTIONS IN TWO AFRICAN-AMERICAN
FAMILY SITUATION COMEDIES

Lott (1989) examined interactions among prime-time television (TV) characters (on primarily White shows) to investigate sexist discrimination in face-to-face situations. Undergraduate student raters watched TV characters and tallied the frequency of three types of behaviors: (1) neutral or positive approach (nonaggressive head or body movement toward another); (2) aggressive approach (aggressive verbal behaviors and threatening movements); and (3) distancing (head or body movements away from another; movements that increased the distance between characters). The third behavior (distancing) was defined as discriminatory because prior research demonstrated that people (i.e., White people) turn away from and/or increase the distance between themselves and people they dislike or wish to exclude as a result of race, familiarity, and other factors.[1]

Lott (1989) found that men TV characters distanced themselves from women characters significantly more often than they did from other men characters, whereas women characters distanced themselves from men and from other women about equally. This creative, naturalistic-observation methodology is an unobtrusive measure of nonverbal discriminatory behavior that has the potential to elucidate the validity of the MJA hypothesis. Examining the behaviors of TV characters who differ by race, age, social class, and status (e.g., parents and children, butlers and their employers) may clarify the intersections of a diversity of status variables in interpersonal discrimination. Likewise, the extent to which sexist discrimination occurs among Blacks also can be explored by analyzing characters in African-American situation comedies (sit-coms).

We chose two African-American TV sit-coms to investigate with Lott's (1989) methodology and coding categories. First, we taped all current (first-run) African-American sit-coms that were televised during the second week of November 1993. Shows were *The Fresh Prince of Bel Air, Roc, The Sinbad Show, Where I Live, Family Matters, Martin, Living Single,* and *In Living Color.* Then, two of us (Landrine and Klonoff) watched all eight shows, and selected the two shows in which the greatest number of status variables (gender, race, social class, age) were represented. *Roc, Where I Live,* and *Family Matters* were rejected because of the relative absence of women and/or girls as main characters. Although *Martin, Living Single,* and *In Living Color* have many women characters (75% of the characters in *Living Single* are women), these three shows were rejected because all of the characters are of approximately the same age and social class. Thus, the two shows selected for analysis were *The Fresh Prince of Bel Air* and *The Sinbad Show,* in which several different status variables are represented. By accident rather than design, these two shows are family sit-coms in which the majority of the characters are related to each other as mother, child, father, grandfather, cousin and the like.

Method

Participants

Undergraduate students in a health psychology class in a California university were offered extra credit for participating in a study called "Interactions of Television Characters." Fifty-four of the 76 students volunteered to participate. These 54 participants included 43 women and 11 men, who represented 28 Whites (51.9%) and 26 people of color (48.1%). Their ages ranged from 20 to 45 years (mean = 25.81, σ = 6.83).

Procedure

Students signed up to come to the lab for 1½ hours to watch a videotape of TV shows; they were unaware of which TV shows they would see, as well as of the purpose of the study. All students were scheduled within the same 4-day period in order to reduce their opportunities to discuss the task with one another. The videotape contained one episode of *The Fresh Prince of Bel Air*, followed by one episode of *The Sinbad Show*; all students saw the shows in that order. Four to eight students watched the shows together. Target main characters to be observed by students were randomly assigned to control for experimenter bias, as well as for students' expectations, implicit demands to code women and men differently (i.e., implicit compare/contrast demands), and other participant effects. Thus, each student was assigned one main character to watch on each show, and the names of assigned characters were written on coding sheets randomly distributed to students after they entered the lab. None of the students, assistants, or researchers knew which character which student was to watch; students also were unaware of which characters their peers were watching. Any given student might have watched two women, two men, or a man from one show and a woman from the other; and on any viewing occasion, all, some, or none of the students might have watched the same character. Discussion among students during the shows was not permitted, and coding sheets were handed in before students left the lab.

As students entered the lab, they were handed instruction pages and were asked to take a seat and read their handouts. The instructions were the same as Lott's (1989, discussed in Chapter 2, this volume), with one exception. Our participants were instructed to code every interaction their target character had, regardless of the number of characters (standing in the foreground or background) on the screen. In the Lott study, participants coded interactions only when there were only two characters on the screen. By expanding the method to include the presence of others, we have the potential to find greater variance in behavior, should behavior in part be a function of such contextual features. Although we did not analyze the data for such contextual variance, all interactions were included, regardless of context; this alone may lead our findings to differ from Lott's (1989). Finally, Lott (1989) analyzed only for differences in distancing behavior, whereas we analyzed for differences in positive, aggressive, and distancing behaviors; we defined "discrimination" as treating characters differently along any of these three behavioral dimensions as a function of the character's status.

Materials

Students received handouts instructing them to observe one character from each show and to code that character's behavior as "neutral or positive approach" (target character makes head or body movements toward the other person on the screen, and these movements are not threatening or insulting); "aggressive approach" (target character says something aggressive, or moves toward the other person with the obvious intent of threatening or doing damage to that person); or "distancing" (target character makes a head or body movement away from the other person, and increases the distance between himself or herself and the other person).

On the next page was a description of each of the characters on *The Fresh Prince of Bel Air*, the first show to be watched; that description is reproduced in Table 7.5. This was provided because characters' names often are not used until late in the show, yet students were to code interactions using the characters' names. After carefully studying this description of the characters on *The Fresh Prince of Bel Air*, students asked the assistant for coding sheets that would indicate which character they were to watch. At this point, the assistant reiterated the instructions and answered questions; while reiterating the instructions, she also demonstrated (on the blackboard) how to enter the tally marks until all students understood their task. The assistant then handed out the coding sheets, and the students watched *The Fresh Prince of Bel Air*, a half-hour show.

When coding of *The Fresh Prince of Bel Air* was completed, students handed in their coding sheets to the assistant and were instructed to study the description of the characters on the next show, *The Sinbad Show*. When this was done, they were randomly given coding sheets informing them of the character they were to observe. The description of characters on *The*

TABLE 7.5. Description Given to Study Participants of Characters on *The Fresh Prince of Bel Air*

Show #1: *The Fresh Prince of Bel Air*

In this show, there are these main characters:

Hillary Banks: A Black woman in a yellow pantsuit at the beginning of the show, the older daughter in this family.

Carlton Banks: A young Black man in a white V-neck sweater at the beginning of the show, the son in this family.

Will Smith: A young Black man in a red sweatshirt and vest at the beginning of the show, the nephew in this family.

Philip Banks: A tall, overweight, balding, older Black man with a beard, the father in this family.

Ashley Banks: A young Black girl dressed in jeans and a flowered tank top at the beginning of the show, the younger daughter in this family.

Vivian Banks: A somewhat older Black woman dressed in black slacks and a multicolored blouse at the beginning of the show, the mother in this family.

Jackie: A young Black woman wearing a weird, feathered hat and blue jeans, who is first seen in the bookstore.

Geoffry ("G"): A short, balding Black man in a tie and apron, the butler for the Banks family.

TABLE 7.6. Description Given to Study Participants of Characters on *The Sinbad Show*

Show #2: *The Sinbad Show*

In this show, there are these main characters:

David Sinbad: A large Black man in blue jeans and a blue jean vest, and standing on a chair at the beginning of the show, the father in this family.

Grandpa: An older, bearded Black man with grey hair, in a blue plaid shirt, standing in the kitchen at the beginning of the show, David Sinbad's father in this show.

Zana ("Z girl"): A small Black female child, David Sinbad's adopted daughter in this show.

L. J.: A small Black male child, David Sinbad's adopted son in this show.

Clarence: A Black man in a ski outfit and sunglasses who comes to the door at the beginning of the show, David Sinbad's neighbor and friend.

Eddie Belk: This character appears later at the ski lodge. He is a Black man, first seen wearing a purple ski outfit.

Sinbad Show is reproduced in Table 7.6. Students then watched *The Sinbad Show*. When this was complete, they turned in their anonymous coding sheets and left the lab. Data on the gender, age, and ethnicity of the student raters were collected on the coding sheets as well.

Results

Data were analyzed by main target character. For example, all students who observed the Will Smith character were treated as a group ($n = 6$). Then, how Will treated other characters (recipients of Will's behavior) was examined in terms of the recipient's gender, social class, age, and other factors. All characters were observed about equally often, by approximately seven students. Each target character, however, interacted with three to seven other characters; thus, each target character had three to seven "case observations," which constituted the sample size (n) for analysis. Thus, for example, if the Will Smith target character interacted with Hillary, Carlton, Jackie, Philip, and Vivian (five recipient characters), there would be five case observations for the Will Smith target character *per participant*, regardless of how many times Will interacted with each of these recipients (multiple interactions with a single recipient were added as a total for that recipient). The n available for this analysis was 30 observations (5 recipients × 6 subjects).

Gender of Target × Gender of Recipient

We selected four characters from *The Fresh Prince of Bel Air* who are equal in age and represent all social classes: Will Smith (man, lower class), Carlton Banks (man, upper class), Hillary Banks (woman, upper class), and Jackie (woman, lower class). Within the show, all four characters are unmarried young adults of the same age. Carlton and Hillary are siblings who live together in (upper-class) Bel Air, California, with their parents. Will Smith is a lower-class young man from a Philadelphia slum who has been sent to live with his rich relatives, the Banks family. Jackie is a lower-class young woman from Will's old neighborhood who now attends "ULA" on a scholarship; Will, Carlton, and Jackie are all freshmen at "ULA." To examine how men and women treated men and women characters on the show, scores assigned to Will were added to those assigned to Carlton to represent men targets, and Hillary's and Jackie's scores were added to represent women targets. These results are shown in Table 7.7.

As indicated in Table 7.7, the MANOVA (119 observations) for gender of target (main effect) was significant, $T^2 = .113$, $F (3, 113) = 4.28$, $p = .007$; Carlton and Will treated characters in a manner that differed from Hillary's and Jackie's treatment of others. The follow-up ANOVAs for this main

TABLE 7.7. Gender of Target with Ages Equal: Will and Carlton versus Jackie and Hillary

MANOVA[a]			
	Hotelling's T^2	F	p
Gender of target (GT)	.113	4.28	.007
Gender of recipient (GR)	.090	3.48	.018
GT × GR	.091	3.44	.019

ANOVA for gender of target[b]				
	Women	Men	SS	F	p
Positive behavior	2.65	3.10	16.07	2.36	.127
Aggressive behavior	1.40	0.94	0.00019	0.00006	.994
Distancing behavior	2.35	0.66	26.70	6.07	.015

ANOVA for gender of recipient[b]				
	Women	Men	SS	F	p
Positive behavior	3.31	2.70	0.23	0.03	.854
Aggressive behavior	0.60	1.42	26.32	7.80	.006
Distancing behavior	0.65	1.62	29.59	6.73	.010

ANOVA for interaction: Gender of target × gender of recipient[c]		
	SS	F	p
Positive behavior	44.43	6.52	.012
Aggressive behavior	12.76	3.78	.054
Distancing behavior	29.57	6.72	.011

Interaction effect: Cell means					
	Gender of recipient				
	Positive behavior		Aggressive behavior		Distancing behavior	
Gender of target	Women	Men	Women	Men	Women	Men
Women	1.5	3.03	0.0	1.87	0.60	2.93
Men	3.79	2.46	0.76	1.09	0.66	0.66

[a] $df = 3, 113$ for each F.
[b] $df = 1, 113$ for each F.
[c] $df = 1, 115$ for each F.

effect are shown in Table 7.7, where it is clear that women target characters engaged in more distancing of other (recipient) characters than did men target characters. Likewise, the main effect of the gender of the recipient character was also significant, $T^2 = .09$, F (3, 113) = 3.48, $p = .018$, and indicated that men characters were the recipients of both more aggressive behavior and more distancing behavior than women characters. Finally, the interaction between gender of the target × gender of the recipient character was significant, $T^2 = .091$, F (3, 113) = 3.44, $p = .019$. The follow-up ANOVAs (shown in Table 7.7) and post hoc (joint univariate, Scheffe) tests at $\alpha = .05$ revealed the following: (1) On positive behaviors, women and men target characters treated the other gender more positively than they did the same gender; (2) on aggressive behaviors, both women and men target characters subjected men recipient characters to more aggression than they did women recipients, with no aggression at all ever shown to a woman recipient by a woman target; and (3) on distancing behaviors, women target characters distanced from men recipient characters significantly more often than they did from women recipients or than men targets distanced from recipients of either gender; the other groups did not differ significantly from one another.

Gender of Target × Gender of Recipient: Upper-Class Characters Only

We repeated the analysis above for upper-class characters only. We selected Carlton and Hillary as the representatives of upper-class men and women, and examined their treatment of women and men recipients (with 57 observations); these results are presented in Table 7.8. As indicated, the main effect for the gender of the target was not significant, $T^2 = .11$, F (3, 51) = 1.88, $p = .145$, indicating that Hillary did not differ from Carlton in treatment of other characters. However, the main effect for the gender of the recipient was significant (Table 7.8), and indicated that both Hillary and Carlton subjected men recipients to more positive behaviors and to more distancing behaviors than women recipients. The interaction of gender of target × gender of recipient was not significant.

In Table 7.9, we present the results for an analysis of Hillary's behavior alone; we were interested in the extent to which this main character, a Black, upper-class woman, treated men and women differently. The MANOVA (with 32 cases) for the gender of the recipient of Hillary's behavior was significant, $T^2 = .419$, F (3, 28) = 3.91, $p = .019$, indicating that Hillary treated women and men characters differently. The follow-up ANOVAs shown in Table 7.9 indicated that Hillary was more aggressive toward men than toward women characters; no other effects on any other behavioral (dependent) variable emerged.

TABLE 7.8. Gender of Target × Gender of Recipient: Carlton versus Hillary

MANOVA[a]			
	Hotelling's T^2	F	p
Gender of target (GT)	.1104	1.876	.145
Gender of recipient (GR)	0.1809	3.08	0.036
GT × GR	.034	0.576	.633

ANOVA for gender of recipient[b]					
	Women	Men	SS	F	p
Positive behavior	1.21	2.69	26.72	7.04	.011
Aggressive behavior	0.68	1.289	5.99	2.70	.106
Distancing behavior	0.63	1.34	6.23	5.08	.028

[a]$df = 3, 51$ for each F.
[b]$df = 1, 53$ for each F.

A Lower-Class Man's Behavior toward Men versus Women

A similar analysis for Will Smith's behavior is shown in Table 7.10. Here, we were interested in the extent to which this lower-class Black man, another main character—indeed, the one after whom the show is named—treated women and men characters differently. The MANOVA (with 54 cases) for the gender of the recipient of Will's behavior was significant, $T^2 = .256, F (3, 50) = 4.267, p = .0009$, and indicated that Will treated men versus women characters differently. The follow-up ANOVAs shown in Table 7.10 revealed that women characters received more positive behaviors from Will than did men characters; no other effects were found.

TABLE 7.9. Gender of Recipient: Hillary as Target

ANOVA for gender of recipient[a]					
	Women	Men	SS	F	p
Positive behavior	1.56	2.65	7.78	1.69	.202
Aggressive behavior	0.00	1.09	7.64	11.56	.002
Distancing behavior	0.67	1.35	3.00	1.91	.178

[a]$df = 1, 30$ for each F.

TABLE 7.10. Gender of Recipient: Will as Target

| | ANOVA for gender of recipient[a] | | | | |
	Women	Men	SS	F	p
Positive behavior	4.82	2.31	85.19	10.36	.002
Aggressive behavior	0.57	0.81	0.75	0.298	.51
Distancing behavior	0.68	0.27	2.26	3.54	.07

[a]$df = 1, 52$ for each F.

Social Class of Target × Gender of Recipient

As shown in Table 7.11, we further explored the issue of the possible gender × social class interaction. We compared the behavior of Will and Carlton—characters differing only in their social class—to explore the extent to which upper- and lower-class Black men treated men and women differently. As indicated in Table 7.11, the MANOVA for the social class of the target was significant, indicating that Will treated other characters in a manner that differed from how Carlton treated them. Will showed more positive behaviors than did Carlton toward all characters, whereas Carlton engaged in more distancing from all characters than did Will. The MANOVA for the gender of the recipient of Will and Carlton's behavior was not significant, however, indicating that Will and Carlton treated men and women similarly. A significant interaction effect for social class of target × gender of recipient also emerged. ANOVAs and post hoc (joint univariate Scheffe) tests at $\alpha = .05$ revealed the following: Will treated women more positively than men (while Carlton's positive behaviors were not affected by the gender of the person he interacted with), and Carlton engaged in significantly more distancing behavior with men than with women.

Social Class of Men Recipients

To examine social class effects alone, we analyzed how all target characters (summed together) treated Philip Banks (a Black upper-class adult, father in the Banks household) and Geoffry (the butler and housekeeper for the Banks family, a Black man approximately the same age as Philip). The MANOVA for the social class of the recipient (Philip vs. Geoffry) was not significant, $T^2 = .119$, $F (3, 3) = 1.19$, $p = .329$. Thus, regardless of their social class, Black, adult men were treated similarly by the other characters on the show.

TABLE 7.11. Social Class × Gender of Recipient: Will versus Carlton

MANOVA[a]

	Hotelling's T^2	F	p
Social class of target (SC)	.362	8.806	.0005
Gender of recipient (GR)	.027	0.654	.583
SC × GR	.224	5.45	.002

ANOVA for social class of target[b]

	Will	Carlton	SS	F
Positive behavior	3.61	2.00	50.74	7.74
Aggressive behavior	0.69	1.48	9.60	3.15
Distancing behavior	0.48	1.04	4.03	5.93

ANOVA for interaction: Social class of target × gender of recipient[b]

	SS	F	p
Positive behavior	78.46	11.970	.001
Aggressive behavior	0.17	0.005	.941
Distancing behavior	5.42	7.980	.006

Interaction effect: Cell Means

	Positive behavior		Distancing behavior	
	Gender of Recipient			
Social class of target	Women	Men	Women	Men
Will (lower)	4.82	0.90	0.68	0.60
Carlton (upper)	2.31	2.73	0.269	1.33

[a] $df = 1, 73$ for each F.
[b] $df = 1, 75$ for each F.

Age and Gender

Finally, we examined the role of age by turning to *The Sinbad Show* and exploring how Sinbad (a Black middle-class adult) treated his adopted son (L.J.) and his adopted daughter (Zana); these results are shown in Table 7.12. The MANOVA for the gender of the recipient (L. J. vs. Zana) of Sinbad's behavior was significant, $T^2 = 1.21$, $F (3, 20) = 8.04$, $p = .001$. Follow-up ANOVAs revealed that Sinbad exhibited more positive behav-

TABLE 7.12. Adult Treatment of Children × Gender of Recipient: Sinbad Interacting with Zana versus L.J.

	ANOVA for gender of recipient[a]				
	Girl	Boy	SS	F	p
Positive behavior	5.18	2.69	36.93	5.47	.029
Aggressive behavior	0.82	3.23	34.68	5.696	.026
Distancing behavior	1.27	1.00	0.443	0.303	.588

$^a df = 1, 22$ for each F.

iors toward the girl child and more aggressive behaviors toward the boy child; no effects for distancing emerged.

We also examined the extent to which children on *The Fresh Prince of Bel Air* (Hillary and Carlton targets) treated their parents (Philip and Vivian recipients) differently as a function of the parents' gender. The MANOVA (with 44 observations) for gender of the recipient parent was not significant, $T^2 = .109$, $F (3, 40) = 1.46$, $p = .239$. Hillary and Carlton treated their parents similarly, regardless of the parents' gender.

Discussion of Pilot Study

This pilot study found that (1) women target characters engaged in significantly more distancing behavior than did men target characters; (2) women target characters distanced from men recipient characters significantly more often than from women recipient characters; (3) men recipient characters were subjected to significantly more aggression and distancing than women recipient characters by both men and women targets, but particularly by women targets; (4) women target characters displayed zero aggressive behavior toward women recipients; and (5) women recipients were treated significantly more positively than men recipients. In summary, women characters discriminated against men and in favor of women, in positive, aggressive, and distancing behaviors. These preliminary results with Black TV characters are the opposite of those found by Lott (1989) for primarily White TV characters. Thus, we tentatively suggest that gender-related interpersonal discrimination probably differs significantly by race/ethnicity, and that such a finding highlights the need to include race/ethnicity in studies of gender discrimination. Our data also imply that significant race × gender interaction effects in interpersonal, discriminatory behavior may be found in studies where both of these status dimensions are included and examined systematically.

We had hoped to examine race of target × gender of target behavior toward race of recipient × gender of recipient characters, because such an analysis would constitute a test of the MJA hypothesis. Unfortunately, we could not do this because, even though White men and women recipient characters did appear on the shows, very few of the target characters interacted with them and the number of interactions with White recipients was quite small. Likewise, on these Black sit-coms, there were *no* White main (target) characters. Thus, TV shows remain essentially segregated by race/ethnicity, and this segregation severely curtails analyses of the intersections of status variables.

Three concerns about this study can be raised. First, we did not attempt to analyze for the reliability of participants' ratings of the characters, simply because assessing reliabilities for so many target characters interacting with a plethora of recipients would have been difficult at best. However, given that this was a pilot study whose purpose was to begin to explore unexamined issues, and whose results thereby were tentative, we believe that this issue is less pressing than it would have been in a study of another sort. A second concern is that we did not assess for the role of the gender or the ethnicity of the participants in ratings attributed to the characters. Consequently, we do not know what role participants' status variables played in the study, and this again highlights the tentative nature of our findings.

The final and most serious concern raised by this pilot study is the appropriate interpretation of Black characters' nonverbal behavior. We suspect that movements defined as aggressive behaviors and as positive behaviors vary cross-culturally, but do not vary so significantly that threats and smiles from Black characters cannot be interpreted as aggressive and positive behaviors (respectively); our interpretation of these two behaviors is justifiable and nonproblematic. Movements defined and interpreted as distancing (excluding) behaviors, however, are quite a different and a difficult issue. Lott (1989) was perfectly justified in interpreting White characters' head and body movements away from another as distancing, because research (e.g., Word et al., 1974) suggests that excluding (discrimination) is what this behavior means when exhibited by Whites. What movements away from another mean when exhibited by Blacks is questionable for a number of reasons.

First, studies of distancing as discrimination have by and large involved Whites only; thus, we do not know that moving/turning away from another is how Blacks also would indicate discrimination. Second, a wealth of evidence on ethnic differences in nonverbal behavior indicates that (1) Blacks maintain a larger distance between themselves and those they interact with (including other Blacks) than do members of any other ethnic group (e.g., Argyle & Dean, 1965; Baxter, 1970; Hanna, 1984; Rozelle &

Baxter, 1975); and (2) Blacks tend to look away ("gaze aversion," usually a sign of distancing) and to stand with their bodies slightly turned away (turning away is also usually a sign of distancing) from those they interact with, regardless of the others' ethnicity (e.g., Argyle & Cook, 1976; Hanna, 1984; Garratt, Baxter, & Rozelle, 1981). Thus, we must ask: What does it mean when a Black character turns his or her body away from another in an interaction? Is this "distancing" (discrimination) or normal nonverbal behavior within the culture? What does the behavior turning/moving away *mean* when engaged in by Blacks, and how do we determine that?

Elsewhere (Landrine, 1992b, 1993; Landrine, Klonoff, & Brown-Collins, 1992), we have argued that movements engaged in by persons of different cultures are not necessarily the same behaviors; that is, they do not necessarily have the same label and meaning. This is because labels and meanings are not inherent in movements, but rather are attributed to movements by cultures, and these attributions can vary significantly across cultures. For example, for the Japanese, looking/turning/standing away from others is typically a sign of respect (Argyle & Cook, 1976). Likewise, for Blacks, facing someone directly and standing within the distance Whites consider "normal" is often interpreted as "superior, disrespectful, threatening or insulting" (Argyle & Cook, 1976, p. 29). Blacks prefer that others stand at an angle (turn away from them) when interacting; doing so is interpreted as friendly, and failing to do so is interpreted as hostile (Garratt et al, 1981).

Thus, looking/turning/moving away from others is not in itself a meaningful behavior, but instead is a meaningless movement engaged in by people of all cultures. Looking/turning/moving away only becomes a type of behavior—with a label and a meaning (e.g., exclusion versus respect)—when a culture attributes these to it. What the movement means and what it should be called, as well as its antecedents and consequences, depend on its cultural context (Landrine, 1992b; Landrine et al., 1992).[2]

In light of these cultural differences in the meaning attached and attributed to moving/turning away, there are two possibilities. The first is that moving/turning away for Blacks means what it means for Whites—namely, excluding. Therefore, Black men and women characters (women particularly) distanced and excluded (discriminated against) Black men characters—a result that is the opposite of that found previously for Whites. The second possibility is that moving/turning away for Blacks means respect or friendliness. Therefore, Black men and women characters (women in particular) included Black men (discriminated in their favor)—a result similar to that found previously for Whites *if and only if* the behavior in question is interpreted in the opposite manner. The question here is not whether Black women characters treated Black women and men characters differently, because they did. The question is whether that treatment constituted distancing/excluding or something else. We do not know which of these interpretations is more culturally appropriate and accurate.

The difficulties inherent in interpreting nonverbal behavior cross-culturally highlight the need to examine the intersections of status categories in interpersonal discrimination using a different methodology. Below, we discuss two excellent methods that have been used to study racial discrimination in face-to-face situations, and discuss how they might be applied to test the MJA hypothesis.

RESEARCH NEEDED TO EXPLORE THE MULTIPLE JEOPARDY–ADVANTAGE HYPOTHESIS

Most unobtrusive studies of racial discrimination (see Crosby, Bromley, & Saxe, 1980, for a comprehensive review) entail sophisticated experimental designs of two types: (1) those involving aggressive behavior and (2) those focusing on helping behavior. These two general types of experimental designs have become two alternative paradigms for investigating interpersonal discrimination, and they have yielded clear, empirical evidence for racial discrimination in face-to-face situations, as well as data on a few of the many contextual parameters (mediators) of that discrimination. These experimental approaches to investigating interpersonal discrimination are widely accepted and well researched, and can be expanded to include additional status variables in order to investigate the MJA hypothesis systematically.

Discrimination in Aggressive Behavior

The Methodology

One strategy for unobtrusively studying discrimination was developed by the Donnersteins (e.g., Donnerstein & Donnerstein, 1972, 1973, 1976; see Crosby et al., 1980, for a full review) and focuses on aggressive behavior. In this design, White men come to the lab under the guise of participating in a study of learning. A rigged drawing assures that the White men are assigned the role of teachers and that the other participants (White and Black men who are actually confederates of the experimenter) are assigned the role of learners. Participants acting as teachers are seated at a shock machine, where they administer bogus shocks to a White or a Black learner each time the learner makes a mistake. The pattern of mistakes is preprogrammed and consistent across race of confederate learner. Participant teachers are free to choose the intensity level of the shocks (direct aggression) as well as the duration of the shocks (indirect aggression) that they deliver to the learner; the pattern of direct versus indirect aggression displayed toward White versus Black learners is then analyzed as evidence of discrimination. In many of these studies, other independent (contextual) variables are included, such as the potential for the learner to retaliate (half of the participants are told that teacher and learner will change places for the second part of the study) and censure/anonymity (half of the participants are told that their behavior will be recorded).

This methodology can be expanded readily to include other status variables. In addition, because delivering shocks to others is likely to be considered aggressive across several cultures, this methodology allows us to examine discrimination in aggressive behavior among many U.S. ethnic groups.

Adding Status Variables

Age. Age can be investigated via the Donnersteins' methodology by adding children and older adults to the group of young adult confederate learners. If we investigate gender × three levels of age (child, young adult, older adult) and hold race constant (White only), what would we find? The MJA hypothesis predicts that young White girls and old White women (both low–low) would receive the most intense/longest shocks. Is that what we would find? We suspect not.

Gender. Gender clearly can be added to race in this methodology, and both direct and indirect (more subtle) aggression on the part of women versus men and Blacks versus Whites toward members of gender, race, and gender × race groups can be examined. The MJA hypothesis predicts that White men (high–high) would receive the least intense/shortest shocks, and that Black women (low–low) would receive the most intense/longest shocks. Is this what we would find, or would Black men receive the most intense/longest shocks and White women the least intense/shortest? We strongly suspect that the latter would be the case.

Sexual Orientation. Sexual orientation × gender (holding race constant as White only) can also be studied via this methodology. Sexual orientation can be manipulated by having some confederates wear gay-related stimuli, such as T-shirts proclaiming "Gay and Proud" or pink triangle buttons. The MJA hypothesis predicts that White heterosexual men (the sexual orientation of the confederates would need to be assessed and controlled) would deliver the most intense/longest shocks to lesbians (low–low) and the least intense/shortest shocks to heterosexual men (high–high). Would the data support this hypothesis? Or would gay men receive the most intense/longest shocks and heterosexual women the least intense/shortest? We suspect the latter.

Multiple Variables. Let us suppose that we use this methodology to investigate race × gender × age and aggression. The MJA hypothesis predicts that young Black girls and old Black women (low–low–low) would receive the most intense/longest shocks. Is that what we would find? Or would young Black boys and Black men receive the most shocks?

Discussion

These four examples suggest that the MJA hypothesis may not be an accurate account of the manner in which dimensions of status interact in interpersonal discrimination. The MJA hypothesis assumes a simple, linear interaction among status dimensions, in which (1) all low status positions are equivalent to one another and (2) all high-status positions are equivalent to one another, such that (3) the combination of *any* high statuses yields multiple advantage, and (4) the combination of *any* low statuses yields multiple jeopardy. Our examples suggest, however, that *all low positions on status dimensions are not equivalent social stimuli, and consequently that the nature of interpersonal discrimination effects is in part contingent upon the specific low-status variables under investigation.* Although "woman," "child," "Black," and "gay" are similar in that they are all low positions on the status dimension in question, they are nonetheless significantly different statuses socially, historically, and politically (i.e., they have different sociocultural contexts and contingencies). For example, whereas "gay" and "Black" are low statuses construed to be evil, "child" is a low status construed as innocent and good. Thus, aggression against Blacks and gays may be tolerated, but aggression against children may be responded to with moral outrage, because the social context condones the former and punishes the latter. Likewise, White middle-class college students in a laboratory Donnerstein paradigm may indeed shock a Black confederate, but are highly unlikely to shock a White girl child.

Status positions also differ in the social roles and behavioral prescriptions associated with them. For example, as part of their gender role, most men have learned that they should protect women and children and that it is wrong to attack them physically; this differs from what they have learned about gays. Although men in the world do hit women and children, we suspect that men college students are unlikely to deliver intense/long shocks to them in the lab, and are more likely to deliver such shocks to gays. Finally, some statuses may have such a strong valence that combining them with other statuses may have little effect. For example, "homeless" may be such a negative social stimulus that combining it with "Black" or "gay" does not increase discrimination.

Because the social stimulus value of low-status positions is not equivalent, the interactions of status dimensions in interpersonal discrimination are not linear, but are instead chaotic.[3] The interaction of "child" and "girl" may yield one result, that of "Black" and "woman" a different result, and that of "gay" and "woman" yet another result, despite the fact that each of these is a low–low interaction. The MJA hypothesis predicts that each of these combinations will be treated similarly (e.g., will receive the most intense/longest shocks), but this prediction is probably incorrect. Likewise, even though "woman" and "Black" are low statuses that are independently discriminated against (such that the low–low combination should be discriminated against most), the intersection of "man" and "Black" may elicit greater aggression. This is because "Black man" is a unique, powerful social stimulus that means far more than the sum of "Black" and "man" in the U.S. sociocultural context. In the American consciousness, "Black man" means drive-by shootings, gang violence, drug abuse, and a plethora of social ills—in short, a hostile stimulus to be feared and treated with hostility.

Thus, the sociocultural/historical context shapes the meaning of low-status positions, and thereby dictates the nature of interpersonal discrimination against persons who occupy specific, different low-status positions. The pattern of interpersonal discrimination seen against persons occupying specific positions along multiple dimensions cannot be predicted from the status (high vs. low) of the positions alone, but can be predicted from a contextualistic-behavioral analysis. As its name implies, the "contextualistic-behavioral" approach analyzes behavior-in-context as a single unit. This approach *does not* examine the manner in which the context changes the perception of a stimulus or the frequency and intensity of a response (behavior), with these viewed as separate from and occurring in a context. Rather, this approach assumes that behaviors and stimuli differ (are not the same) across different contexts because the context is an integral part of them. For example, "reading a newspaper on the subway on the way to work" and "reading a newspaper while your significant other is trying to talk to you about a serious issue" would ordinarily be considered "the same" behavior (viz., "reading the newspaper"). From a contextualistic perspective, however, these are very different behaviors. The first is "killing time on the subway" or "avoiding contact with strangers on the subway." The second is "displaying hostility" or "communicating lack of interest in the conversation." Whatever the second behavior is, it clearly *is not* "reading the newspaper," any more than "reading the newspaper in the middle of having sex" is mere "reading the newspaper." Thus, "the same" movement (e.g., moving or turning away from another person, reading a newspaper, avoiding eye contact) in one context has different antecedents and contingencies, and so is given a different label and meaning (viz., is a different behavior) in another. For discussions of contextualistic behaviorism, see Biglan, Glasgow, and Singer (1990); Rosnow and Georgoudi (1986); Hayes, Hayes, Reese, and Sarbin (1993); and Landrine (1993).

Discrimination in Helping Behavior

The Methodology

A second strategy for unobtrusively studying interpersonal discrimination involves investigations of helping (see Crosby et al., 1980, for a comprehensive review). In all of these studies, participants are given the opportunity to help a Black or White man who is usually a confederate of the experimenter, and the dependent variable is the amount of help given. Some of these studies involve face-to-face helping (e.g., the White or Black confederate asks for change for a quarter, or drops his groceries and waits for help). In other studies, the helping situation is more remote (not face-to-face). One example is the "last-dime technique": Black or White confederates (using racially specific speech inflections) pretend to have dialed the wrong telephone number and to have used their last dime, and so ask the person they have called to place the call for them. Making the call for Whites and not making it for Blacks is evidence of racial discrimination. Another common approach is the "lost-letter technique": An application for graduate school is left in an airport telephone booth. The "applicant" is depicted as a Black or White man in a photograph attached to the bogus application. Also attached are a stamped, addressed envelope and a note asking "Dad" to mail the application. Mailing the application for Whites and not mailing it for Blacks is a measure of racial discrimination. In both cases, the helping behavior utilized is likely to be understood as helping across cultures.

Adding Status Variables

Sexual Orientation. Suppose that confederates (in the last-dime technique) request that the people they have called by error call their lover/spouse for some emergency, with half of the confederates referring to the person as "my lover" and giving a same-sex first name, and half referring to the person as "my husband/wife" and giving an opposite-sex name. The MJA hypothesis predicts that the lovers of lesbians (low–low) would be least likely to be telephoned, and that the wives of heterosexual men (high–high) would be most likely to be called. Is this what we would find? Or would we find that no calls whatsoever are made to the partners of gays, regardless of the gays' gender, but that many calls are made to the spouses of heterosexuals, regardless of the heterosexuals' gender? We strongly suspect that the latter would be the case.

Gender. Gender can be added to race/ethnicity in the dropped-groceries, last dime and lost-letter approaches, and gender × ethnicity/race discrimination can thus be explored. The MJA hypothesis predicts that minority women (low–low) would be helped the least in each case (i.e., participants would not help them pick up their groceries, participants would not make the call for them, and their applications would be least likely to be mailed). Is this what we would find? Or would results reveal that minority men are most discriminated against (viz., no one helps a Black or Mexican-American man pick up his groceries, no one makes the phone call for him, and no one mails his application)? We suspect that the latter would be found.

Age. Age, too, can be readily investigated by adding children and older people to the confederates in the dropped-groceries technique. The MJA hypothesis would predict (holding race constant as all Whites) that young White girls and old White women would be least likely to be helped. Is that what we would find? Or would we find that young White girls and old White women are most likely to receive help in picking up their groceries, with young adult White men receiving the least help—results that are the opposite of what the hypothesis would predict?

Discussion

These three examples, in the context of those given for the Donnersteins' paradigm, also suggest that the MJA hypothesis may be too simple to account for the complexities involved in interpersonal discrimination in response to multiple status dimensions. These examples suggest that *all behaviors are not equivalent social acts, and consequently that interpersonal discrimination effects vary with the type of behavior under investigation.* Behaviors differ in their likelihood of being punished (contingencies), in their sociocultural evaluation and appraisal, and in the extent to which they are prescribed or prohibited. Hitting differs from helping, and so results for aggressive behavior may not hold for helping. People may help an old woman (low–low) pick up her groceries and may also refuse to shock her. Thus, the sociocultural/historical context shapes the meaning of types of behaviors, and so dictates the nature of interpersonal discrimination within and between specific types of behavioral arenas.

Finally, if interpersonal discrimination in response to multiple status dimensions varies with the specific status groups and behavior under investigation, then such discrimination is also likely to vary with the interaction between type of behavior × specific status variables. People may help an old woman (low–low) pick up her dropped groceries and may refuse to shock her; yet the same people may fail to help a Black woman (also low–low) pick up her groceries and may deliver intense shocks to her. Thus, the historical and current sociocultural contexts shape the meaning of types of behaviors and of low-status positions, and so dictate the type of interpersonal discriminatory behavior that can be exhibited against different, specific low-status persons. In contextualistic-behavioral terms, we are suggesting that the interaction of specific status stimulus × specific behavioral response changes the nature of the behavior under investigation and so the results. When the stimulus is "girl child" (low–low) and the behavior is "deliver shocks," the combination is "child abuse" and so is likely to be rejected by college student participants. When the stimulus is "Black woman" or "lesbian" (both also low–low) and the behavior is "deliver shocks," the combination is not "child abuse" (even though the behavior is ostensibly "the same"), and participants in laboratory experiments may be more inclined to do so.

CONCLUSIONS

Most contemporary approaches to interpersonal discrimination along any single status dimension appear to construe discriminatory behavior as a knee-jerk reflex response to any status as (1) an isolated stimulus and (2) an equivalent stimulus. Where the first of these is concerned, it is clear that status attributes are never isolated. The "women" and "men" in studies of gender discrimination also possess an ethnicity and age, just as the "Blacks" and "Whites" in studies of racial discrimination necessarily possess a gender; both groups also present additional status variables, such as social class (inferred from speech or clothing), attractiveness, weight, and sexual orientation. Several additional implicit dimensions of status are always present, along with the explicit status dimension under investigation. Although these additional implicit dimensions of status may not be of interest to the investigator, they nonetheless may influence the behavior of the participants, and indeed may account for more of the variance in participants' behavior than the explicit variable may. This has already been demonstrated to be the case: Studies have shown that the negative stereotype of "Blacks" and positive stereotype of "Whites" are not based on explicit race, but rather on the implicit social class (Whites are middle-class, Blacks are poor) presumed to be correlated with race. When both race and class are made explicit, the negative stereotype of Blacks disappears (see Landrine, 1985, for a review of these studies).

Because status attributes are never isolated, but instead appear in coherent packages or gestalts, all studies of discrimination along a single (explicit) status dimension are necessarily studies of the intersections of status dimensions and in this sense are partial tests of the MJA hypothesis. Thus, for example, the studies of the Donnersteins do not demonstrate racial discrimination per se; rather, they demonstrate that White men are more likely to be aggressive toward Black men than toward White men (race × gender discrimination). Are the Donnersteins' results a function of race, or of an implicit gender × explicit race interaction in which aggression is shown toward the unique social stimulus "Black man"? Likewise, the Donnersteins demonstrated that White men are more aggressive toward *presumably heterosexual* Black men than toward *presumably heterosexual* White men. If this implicit sexual orientation had been made explicit, and both Black and White men had been presented as gays, would different results have appeared? Wouldn't White men show more aggression toward White gay men than toward Black gay men because the sexual orientation of the former is more threatening and offensive? How much of the variance would be accounted for by implicit status dimensions such as gender, social class, and sexual orientation?

Similarly, where the equivalent-stimulus assumption is concerned, it seems clear that all low-status positions are *not* socially equivalent stimuli and thus may not interact in a simple, linear, deterministic manner. All behaviors also are not socially equivalent, and they may interact with the interactions of statuses in complex, chaotic ways.

Thus, the simple assumptions that any status is isolated and is equivalent to any other status do not facilitate careful examination of the intersections of status categories in interpersonal discrimination; they deny the importance of additional but implicit status dimensions; and thereby they obscure more than they elucidate with respect to discrimination along a single explicit status dimension as well as along multiple such dimensions. A more contextualistic-behavioral analysis is needed, in which (1) the contextual features and parameters of different types of status categories (the stimulus values of different statuses) are analyzed, in conjunction with (2) a similar analysis of the nonlinear, chaotic manner in which these can combine, in the context of (3) an analysis of the different appraisals and contingencies (probability of punishment) of engaging in different discriminatory behaviors (distancing vs. hitting vs. helping).

The MJA hypothesis is too broad as stated, and requires major revision to be amenable to the type of analysis we suggest. The hypothesis must be more specific regarding the nature of the interaction among specific status positions with respect to specific discriminatory behaviors. Studies of discrimination along a single status dimension could benefit similarly from such contextualism by attending to and analyzing the variety of implicit status dimensions entailed. When the MJA hypothesis is revised in a manner that entails specific, contextualized empirical predictions, many tests of it will be needed. Our analysis suggests that the hypothesis can be systematically evaluated by means of the paradigmatic aggression and helping methodologies that have been employed previously to investigate racial discrimination. Additional tests of the predictions of the additive versus interactive types of MJA will also be required to elucidate the empirical viability of this important distinction. Finally, our analysis suggests that the findings of such future studies are likely to highlight the limitations of the findings of previous studies on interpersonal discrimination along a single status dimension, while simultaneously illuminating the need for contexualistic models of discriminatory behavior in face-to-face situations.

NOTES

1. For example, in a study of nonverbal, face-to-face, racial discrimination, Word, Zanna, and Cooper (1974, Study 1) asked undergraduate White men to interview either a White or a Black "high school student"; these "students" were confederates of the experimenter. Results revealed that White men placed their chairs significantly farther away from the Black than from the White confederates. Other studies have found similar evidence for distancing as an unobtrusive measure of discrimination. The difficulty here, however, is that almost all of these studies involved White participants. Thus, we do not know whether discrimination on the part of Blacks would also take the form of distancing. We return to this point later in the chapter.

2. In this sense, cultures are not patterns of behavior or patterns of movements, but rather, are different patterns of meanings/labels attributed to the same, inherently meaningless movements. Because different cultures attribute different meanings/labels to the same movements, errors in intercultural communication are common (Landrine, 1992b). For example, Whites stand near Blacks, facing them directly and looking them in the eye as a sign of friendliness and attention, but Blacks interpret these movements as hostile attempts at intimidation. Blacks turn away and move away from Whites and do not look at them as a sign of friendliness, but Whites interpret this as inattention and distancing.

3. "Chaotic" here refers to the theory of chaos, which argues that minor changes in one variable can result in large, bizarre, unpredicted changes in another, revealing a hidden complexity in simple models, such as a simple linear race × gender MJA model. We are suggesting that when the stimulus is "Black," changing gender from "woman" to "man" can elicit a change in beliefs about and behavior toward the stimulus that is synergistic and unpredictable, and that far exceeds the outcome obtained when the same is done with the stimulus "White." For discus-

sion of this relatively new mathematical theory, see Gleick (1987) and Peterson (1988).

REFERENCES

Argyle, M., & Cook, M. (1976). *Gaze and mutual gaze*. Cambridge, England: Cambridge University Press.

Argyle, M., & Dean, J. (1965). Eye-contact, distance and affiliation. *Sociometry, 28,* 289–304.

Baxter, J. C. (1970). Interpersonal spacing in natural settings. *Sociometry, 33,* 444–456.

Biglan, A., Glasgow, R. E., & Singer, G. (1990). The need for a science of larger social units: A contextual approach. *Behavior Therapy, 21,* 195–215.

Crosby, F. (1984). The denial of personal discrimination. *American Behavioral Scientist, 27*(3), 371–386.

Crosby, F., Bromley, S., & Saxe, L. (1980). Recent unobtrusive studies of black and white discrimination. *Psychological Bulletin, 87*(3), 546–563.

Donnerstein, E., & Donnerstein, M. (1972). White rewarding behavior as a function of the potential for black retaliation. *Journal of Personality and Social Psychology, 24,* 327–333.

Donnerstein, E., & Donnerstein, M. (1973). Variables in interracial aggression: Potential in-group censure. *Journal of Personality and Social Psychology, 27,* 143–150.

Donnerstein, E., & Donnerstein, M. (1976). Variables in interracial aggression: Exposure to aggressive interracial interactions. *Journal of Social Psychology, 100,* 111–121.

Ellemers, N., Wilke, H., & van Knippenberg, A. (1993). Effects of the legitimacy of low group or individual status on individual and collective status-enhancement strategies. *Journal of Personality and Social Psychology, 64*(5), 766–778.

Garratt, G. A., Baxter, J. C., & Rozelle, R. M. (1981). Training university police in black-American nonverbal behaviors. *Journal of Social Psychology, 113,* 217–229.

Gleick, J. (1987). *Chaos: Making a new science*. New York: Penguin Books.

Gordon, M. (1964). *Assimilation in American life*. New York: Oxford University Press.

Hanna, J. L. (1984). Black/White nonverbal differences. In A. Wolfgang (Ed.), *Nonverbal behavior: Perspectives, applications, intercultural insights* (pp. 373–409). New York: C. J. Hogrefe.

Hayes, S. C., Hayes, L. J., Reese, H. W., & Sarbin, T. R. (1993). *Varieties of scientific contextualism*. Reno, NV: Context Press.

Idson, T. L., & Price, H. F. (1992). An analysis of wage differentials by gender and ethnicity in the public sector. *The Review of Black Political Economy, 20,* 75–97.

Jeffries, V., & Ransford, H. E. (Eds.). (1980). *Social stratification: A multiple hierarchy approach*. Boston: Allyn & Bacon.

Kerlinger, F. N. (1973). *Foundations of behavioral research* (2nd ed.). New York: Holt, Rinehart & Winston.

Lalonde, R. N., & Silverman, R. A. (1994). Behavioral preferences in response to social injustice: The effects of group permeability and social identity salience. *Journal of Personality and Social Psychology, 66*(1), 78–85.

Landrine, H. (1985). Race × class stereotypes of women. *Sex Roles, 13,* 65–75.

Landrine, H. (1992a). *The politics of madness.* New York: Peter Lang.

Landrine, H. (1992b). Clinical implications of cultural differences. *Clinical Psychology Review, 12,* 401–415.

Landrine, H. (1993, April 23). *Contextualism as a framework for analyzing ethnic differences.* Invited address delivered at the joint convention of the Western and Rocky Mountain Psychological Associations, Phoenix, AZ.

Landrine, H., Klonoff, E. A., & Brown-Collins, A. (1992). Cultural diversity and methodology in feminist psychology: Critique, proposal, empirical example. *Psychology of Women Quarterly, 16*(2), 145–163.

Lott, B. L. (1989). Sexist discrimination as distancing behavior: II. Primetime television. *Psychology of Women Quarterly, 13,* 341–355.

Mathnes, E. W., Brennan, S. M., Haugen, P. M., & Rice, H. B. (1985). Ratings of physical attractiveness as a function of age. *Journal of Social Psychology, 125*(2), 157–168.

Peterson, I. (1988). The dragons of chaos. In I. Peterson, *The mathematical tourist: Snapshots of modern mathematics* (pp. 143–174). New York: W. H. Freeman.

Ransford, H. E. (1980). The prediction of social behavior and attitudes. In V. Jeffries & H. Ransford (Eds.), *Social stratification: A multiple hierarchy approach* (pp. 265–295). Boston: Allyn & Bacon.

Reid, P. T. (1988). Racism and sexism: Comparisons and conflicts. In P. A. Katz & D. A. Taylor (Eds.), *Eliminating racism: Profiles in controversy* (pp. 203–221). New York: Plenum.

Rosnow, R. L., & Georgoudi, M. (1986). *Contextualism and understanding in behavioral science.* New York: Praeger.

Rozelle, R. M., & Baxter, J. C. (1975). Impression formation and danger recognition in experienced police officers. *Journal of Social Psychology, 96,* 53–63.

Shutter, R. (1982). Initial interaction of American Blacks and Whites in interracial and intraracial dyads. *Journal of Social Psychology, 117,* 45–52.

Taylor, D. M., Moghaddam, F. M., Gamble, I., & Zellerer, E. (1987). Disadvantaged group responses to perceived inequality: From passive acceptance to collective action. *Journal of Social Psychology, 127*(3), 259–272.

U.S. Bureau of the Census. (1991). *Money income of households, families and persons in the United States, 1988 and 1989* (Current Population Reports, Series P-60, No. 172). Washington, DC: U.S. Government Printing Office.

Word, C. O., Zanna, M. P., & Cooper, J. (1974). The nonverbal mediation of self-fulfilling prophecies in interracial interaction. *Journal of Experimental Social Psychology, 10,* 109–120.

Wright, S. C., Taylor, D. M., & Moghaddam, F. M. (1990). Responding to membership in a disadvantaged group: From acceptance to collective protest. *Journal of Personality and Social Psychology, 58*(6), 994–1003.

Yarkin, K. L., Town, J. P., & Wallston, B. S. (1982). Blacks and women must try harder: Stimulus persons' race and sex attributions of causality. *Personality and Social Psychology Bulletin, 8*(1), 21–24.

Index